Imagination & AUTHORITY

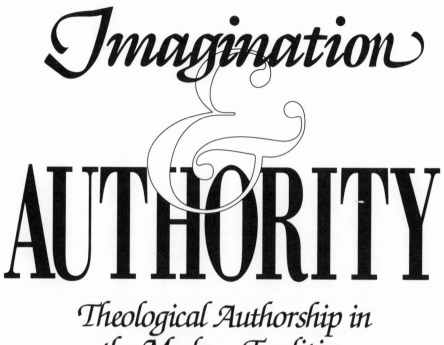

Imagination & AUTHORITY

Theological Authorship in the Modern Tradition

JOHN E. THIEL

FORTRESS PRESS   **MINNEAPOLIS**

IMAGINATION AND AUTHORITY
Theological Authorship in the Modern Tradition

All Scripture quotations are from the New Revised Standard Version Bible, copyright © 1989 by the Division of Christian Education of the National Council of the Churches of Christ in the United States.

Excerpts adapted from *Theological Studies* 47 (December 1986): 573-98, are reprinted by permission. Excerpts adapted from *The Heythrop Journal* XXV, XXVII, XXX (April 1984, July 1986, January 1989) are reprinted by permission.

Cover design: Brian Preuss

Library of Congress Cataloging-in-Publication Data

Thiel, John E.
    Imagination and authority : theological authorship in the modern tradition / John E. Thiel.
        p.   cm.
    Includes bibliographical references and index.
    ISBN 0-8006-2516-1 (alk. paper)
    1. Theology—Authorship.   2. Theology—Methodology.   3. Catholic Church—Doctrines.   4. Postmodernism—Religious aspects—Christianity.   5. Creative ability—Religious aspects—Christianity.   I. Title.
    BR118.T484   1991
    230'.01—dc20   91-35270
                                                                           CIP

The paper used in this publication meets the minimum requirements of American National Standard for Information Sciences—Permanence of Paper for Printed Library Materials, ANSI Z329.48-1984.   ∞™

Manufactured in the U.S.A.   AF 1-2516
95   94   93   92   91   1   2   3   4   5   6   7   8   9   10

For my parents
Louise Alagia Thiel
and
Arthur Edwin Thiel

Contents

Contents

Preface

THIS BOOK examines the nature, exercise, and limitations of creativity in the theological enterprise. Although the issue of creativity in Catholic theology remains the focus of this study, the concerns of the Protestant tradition are thoroughly represented. It is not uncommon for studies of theological theory or practice to address the theme of creativity generally, as a methodological desideratum or as an explanation for the originality that has come to be expected of serious work in any modern discipline. The approach taken here is more specific. The theme of theological responsibility guides an examination of the role of creativity in the theologian's vocational self-understanding.

This book offers a way of appreciating how the theologian has come to be configured as a modern practitioner of his or her craft. Since the early nineteenth century, I argue, modern theologians can be distinguished from their premodern precursors by their commitment to the vocational ideal of authorship. By *theological authorship* I mean the assumption that the theologian is a creative agent whose talent is essential to the performance and the results of the theological task. The talent of authorship can be exercised in any number of ways, and this variety accounts for the diversity of theological methods, styles, and conclusions that have appeared in the nearly two hundred years that the assumption of creative authorship has governed theological reflection. However it is practiced, though, creative authorship is by now axiomatic to the modern understanding of theological responsibility and expresses a view of the theological vocation that is shared by all nonfundamentalistic theologians, whether they are liberal or conservative in their commitments.

Making such a close connection between modernity and theological authorship may initially strike some readers as problematic. It may suggest that premodern theologians were neither authors nor creative, which I would hardly maintain. It may suggest that a single theme has been endowed with explanatory powers that can only prove insufficient to account for a most complex period in the history of theology. Instead, I only defend the more modest position that the theme of authorship illuminates the character of modern theology. It does not offer an exhaustive explanation of the theologian's self-understanding or work.

The close connection between modernity and theological authorship also may suggest that this work has its basis in the apparently jejune observation that modern theologians find a need to be creative. In some respects, this study begins with this most simple observation. But as this project has developed in the course of the past seven years, I have been impressed by the degree to which this simple observation has remained unexamined, in spite of the fact that it has figured so prominently in the history of theology from the age of Romanticism to the present. I hope that the following chapters can remedy this situation to some degree by their attention to the prevalence of the theme of authorship in the history of modern theology and in the most pressing theological debates of our time.

To give a brief overview, the Introduction provides a theoretical framework for the study by exploring the shift from premodern to modern understandings of the theologian's vocational responsibility. Chapters 1 and 2 examine the first efforts of Protestant and Catholic theologians of the early nineteenth century, specifically Friedrich Schleiermacher and Johann Sebastian Drey, to articulate the vocational ideal of theological authorship. As Schleiermacher and Drey struggled to formulate a theological method in step with the critical spirit of the Enlightenment, they turned their attention to the role of the practitioner, the subject of method, and sought to understand theological talent in the setting of romantic notions of creativity. Chapter 3 begins by tracing the intellectual history of creative agency from the seventeenth century through the early nineteenth century and the manner in which this history provided a resource for a modern conceptualization of the theologian. The chapter continues by exploring the relations between theological imagination and ecclesiastical authority in the last 150 years of Catholic tradition. Chapter 4 considers possible alternatives to the modern period's decidedly romantic conception of authorship in Mark Taylor's deconstructive criticism and George Lindbeck's postliberal theological agenda. Theological method is highlighted in chapter 5, particularly the way in which recent theological debates about the issue of "foundations" for theology indirectly take stands on the viability of different conceptions of authorship. Here, as in chapter 4, postliberalism is used to clarify by way of contrast what is distinctive about a Catholic understanding of authorship. Chapter 6 concludes the study by analyzing further what is distinctive to a Catholic understanding of theological authorship and by offering an *apologia* for the place of creativity in a confessional tradition that is unused to the happy juxtaposition of novelty and orthodoxy.

As I completed this book early in the summer of 1990, the Congregation for the Doctrine of the Faith published a teaching entitled *Instruction on the Ecclesial Vocation of the Theologian* (May 24, 1990). Since the place of the *Instruction* in the ambivalent history of relations between the magisterium and theologians was (and remains) unclear, I thought better of treating it in the thematic analysis of this history offered in chapter 3. Two observations, however, are worthy of note here. The *Instruction* confirms that chapter's claim that the magisterium has by now accepted the indispensability of the theologian's creativity to the success of the theological task. Unfortunately, the *Instruction*'s suspicious regard for that creativity, articulated in its denial of the legitimacy of public theological dissent, seems to be a throwback to a time when creative theology was judged to be an oxymoron. I must confess that the tone and commendations of the *Instruction* dampen my hope for the rapprochement of authority and imagination for which this study argues. Yet hope abides as one of the theological virtues on which the future of the church depends.

I would like to express my gratitude to the National Endowment for the Humanities for a fellowship that allowed me to devote my energies to research and writing for a full academic year, to Fairfield University for a sabbatical leave during that same time, and to the Department of Religious Studies, Yale University, for receiving me as a fellow during the 1989–1990 academic year. I am especially grateful to David H. Kelsey, my host at Yale, for his generous hospitality during my time there.

So many people helped me to bring this project to fruition that they cannot all be mentioned here. The late Hans W. Frei encouraged and guided this work in its earlier stages. Although I know he would not have been comfortable with some of the theological conclusions presented here, I will ever remain grateful for our many conversations that enabled me to arrive where I did. David W. Tracy and Brian A. Gerrish, University of Chicago Divinity School, and Francis Schüssler Fiorenza, Harvard Divinity School, offered support and encouragement without which this project would have been much longer in the making. Even before the publication of his important work *Theologia*, Edward Farley, Vanderbilt University, graciously shared with me much of his ground-breaking research on the theological encyclopedia, a favor that takes literary shape in the discussion of encyclopedia in what follows. Timothy G. Staveteig, Academic Editor, Fortress Press, has been a most helpful and accommodating editor.

I am grateful to my colleagues in the Department of Religious Studies at Fairfield for their continued support. Those who read and criticized earlier versions of this project with much care were Vincent M. Burns, S.J., G. Simon Harak, S.J., Paul F. Lakeland, Christopher F. Mooney, S.J., and Sally B. Purvis. James J. Buckley, Loyola College, and David H. Kelsey and Cyril J. O'Regan, Yale University, were equally generous in giving their time and energy to the same task. However the final results presented here be judged, I know very well that this book is much better for all their efforts than it otherwise would have been.

My wife, Dorothea, and my sons, David and Benjamin, showed much patience to an author reflexively preoccupied with the theme of authorship. Finally, I would like to thank my parents for all the encouragement they have given to me through the years. Being able to dedicate this book to them is a small thing by comparison, but nevertheless something that I am pleased to have the opportunity to do.

John E. Thiel

Theological Authorship in the Modern Tradition

*D*EFINING the temperament of modern theology and passing judgment on its various traits have been the ardent and self-conscious endeavors of theologians in the last two hundred years. Modern theology may be indistinguishable from its premodern counterparts if measured in traditional Augustinian fashion as the task of faith seeking understanding. But one important way in which modern theology differs from the theology of earlier times lies in its efforts to define and evaluate its character as the theology of a particular period. At their best, the exercises of definition and evaluation have been searches for modern theology's legitimate identity and attempts to situate that identity within a long tradition of theological reflection in which faith has sought understanding. When conducted well, these exercises have also been self-critical, intent on exposing the weaknesses inherent both in the assumptions of modern theology and in its specific styles of execution.

More often than not, however, the definition and evaluation of modern theology's character have been conducted as exercises in polemics between rival theological camps. In its most familiar and by now tiresome scenario, the stereotypically conservative theologian accuses the stereotypically liberal theologian of betraying the substance of the tradition for the sake of the most fleeting and ephemeral relevance, while the stereotypically liberal castigates the stereotypically conservative theologian for an uncritical, fundamentalistic appropriation of the past that forsakes the needs of the present. An unfortunate result of this polarization is a tendency to identify the modern character of more recent theology with the liberal position alone, perhaps because its rightful concern for timeliness in the expression of traditional faith is so easily caricatured as a celebration of the present at the expense of the past. The false identification of *liberal* and *modern* wrongly assumes that the adjectives *conservative* and *modern* are mutually exclusive, as though the call for theological relevance were voiced by only some contemporary theologians or as though theologians who understand themselves as conservative necessarily promulgate a premodern theological agenda. By wrapping liberal sensibilities in the mantle of the modern, liberal theologians fail to appreciate the full range of the contemporary theological pluralism they heartily applaud, and conservative theologians distance their rightful concern for the time-honored past from its proper relationship to the present.

This study eschews the identification of modern and liberal theology. It assumes that the term *modern theology* comprises the legitimate, but not the stereotypical, concerns of both liberal and conservative theological styles. Regardless of the stance one takes on the appropriate emphases and balances to be struck in an authentic modern theology, I believe that there is sound agreement within the theological community that the task of defining and evaluating the character of modern theology is crucial both for the vocational self-understanding of theologians and, through their work, for the self-understanding of the church. This examination of the theme of theological authorship is an exercise in such vocational and ecclesial self-understanding. In the following chapters this goal will be pursued by tracing the historical emergence of this seminal, though often overlooked, assumption of modern theology, by considering how perceptions of theological authorship have shaped recent relations between theologians and the magisterium in the Roman Catholic tradition, and by suggesting ways in which attention to the issue of authorship can clarify the appropriate role of imagination in Catholic approaches to theological method.

TRAITS OF MODERN THEOLOGY

Our conception of what constitutes the modern dimension of theology has been formed in a variety of ways, none of which completely captures all that the adjective suggests. The term *modern theology* began to appear with some frequency in book titles of the late nineteenth century.[1] But the notion of modern theology did not flourish until the twentieth century, when it gained currency both as a historical rubric invoked to periodize theology in a manner similar to the arts and literature and, more importantly, as a value judgment about the state of theology in its most recent period.

Were self-designation the surest determination of a theological position as modern, the clearest candidate for the rubric would be the Ockhamist school of the fourteenth century, which described itself as the *via moderna*.[2] Rarely, though, have theologians of any age, including ours, portrayed their own work as modern. In the twentieth century the term has been employed most commonly not to identify one's own theological style or commitments but in order to label the style and commitments of others. This finds neutral expression, for example, in the titles chosen by editors for theological series or anthologies whose groupings of issues or theologians reflects some (often tacit) assumption that a family resemblance—whether historical or thematic but in any case modern—is shared by those serialized or anthologized. Far more influential, however, has been the twentieth-century use of the term by neoorthodox critics of modernity for whom the brand "modern" served as a stinging appraisal of the work of their theological opponents.

The most consequential example of such negative appraisal from the Catholic tradition is the use of the term *modernist* in the encyclical *Pascendi dominici gregis* (1907). In the judgment of *Pascendi*, the modernist masquerades as a theologian in order to betray the true cause of theology. The worst of heretics, the modernist subverts the Tridentine understanding of theological science promulgated by Vatican I. The modernist abandons the age-old verities enshrined in the Catholic theological tradition, professing adherence instead to the critical perspective of recent times. That the latter-day virtues of historicism, relativism, and skepticism can now be welcomed at the threshold of theology is, in *Pascendi*'s view, clearly symptomatic of the modernist malady.

1. For example, Carl Schwarz, *Zur Geschichte der neuesten Theologie*, 1856; Franz Reinhold von Frank, *Geschichte und Kritik der neueren Theologie*, 1894. Both cited in Horst Stephan and Martin Schmidt, *Geschichte der evangelischen Theologie in Deutschland seit dem Idealismus*, 3d ed. (New York: Walter de Gruyter, 1973), xiii.

2. Steven Ozment, *The Age of Reform 1250–1550: An Intellectual and Religious History of Late Medieval and Reformation Europe* (New Haven, Conn.: Yale Univ. Press, 1980), 61.

This pejorative use of the term does much to explain the avoidance of its use even as a rubric of historical periodization in Catholic encyclopedias, dictionaries, and lexicons. Karl Rahner's entry on "Theology" in *Sacramentum Mundi*, for example, discusses the orientations commended by the Second Vatican Council under the proleptic rubric of the "Theology of the Future" after pointing out that the "baroque scholasticism" of the seventeenth, eighteenth, and early nineteenth centuries "failed for the most part to enter into frank dialogue with the modern era, as the age of a transcendental philosophy and the beginnings of the 'exact' sciences."[3] Much like Rahner, P. de Letter avoids the periodization of recent theology as "modern" in his article on theology in the *New Catholic Encyclopedia*, speaking instead of the "revival of theology" in the nineteenth and twentieth centuries after a period of decline in the seventeenth and eighteenth centuries.[4] Yves Congar's well-known article on theology in the *Dictionnaire de théologie catholique* groups post-Tridentine theologies under the heading of "new forms" of theology born of modern needs, a generic rubric that stands in vague contrast to his earlier, more focused analyses of patristic and medieval theologies.[5] Johannes Baptist Metz's article on theology in *Lexikon für Theologie und Kirche* offers only a passing conceptualization of theology's character in the modern period (*Neuzeit*) by suggesting that the post-Enlightenment distinction between systematic and historical theology casts light on a redefinition of theology's problematic in this period: "the relationship between faith and history."[6] As we shall see in chapter 3, it was precisely the acceptance of this relationship as theology's problematic that *Pascendi* defined as the error of modernism. As the entries just cited

3. Karl Rahner, "Theology," in *Sacramentum Mundi: An Encyclopedia of Theology*, vol. 6, ed. K. Rahner et al. (New York: Herder & Herder, 1970), 244.

4. P. de Letter, "Theology," in *New Catholic Encyclopedia*, vol. 14 (New York: McGraw-Hill, 1967), 55–58.

5. Yves M.-J. Congar, "Théologie," in *Dictionnaire de théologie catholique*, vol. 15, ed. A. Vacant et al. (Paris: Librairie Letouzey et Ané, 1946), 346–47. Later in the entry Congar includes a rubric entitled "La Théologie née des tendances modernes," under which he treats the efforts of seventeenth-century theology to defend the Council of Trent by coming to grips with the "modern" movement of the Renaissance (432). In both instances the adjective *modern* describes historical currents in which theology must swim, but not a quality of theology itself. The English presentation of this seminal article appears as M.-J. Congar, *A History of Theology*, trans. H. Guthrie (New York: Doubleday & Co., 1968).

6. J. B. Metz, "Theologie," in *Lexikon für Theologie und Kirche*, vol. 10, ed. J. Höfer and K. Rahner (Freiburg: Herder, 1965), 64.

attest, *Pascendi*'s powerful influence in the twentieth century has hampered Catholic efforts to come to grips with the character of modern theology as such.

No theologian has shaped the notion of modern theology more, and with a negative force as powerful in its own way as that of *Pascendi*, than the Protestant Karl Barth. His theological call to arms in the *Epistle to the Romans* (1922) castigated the nineteenth-century liberal tradition from Schleiermacher to his teacher Harnack as a celebration of cultural achievement and vainglorious aspiration under the guise of religion, for Barth an all-too-human manifestation of original sin. Barth frequently employed the term *modern* not merely as a historical referent but as a label of opprobrium for the liberal tradition that reigned in Europe until the First World War. This was especially true of the early Barth, whose dialectical approach to the categories of God and humanity, grace and nature were predicated on an oppositional understanding of his own relationship to the liberal tradition from which he broke. In a famous 1926 essay, Barth excoriated Schleiermacher for substituting "the modern pagan feeling for life"[7] for Christian revelation in his theology, a judgment he took to be generally true of "the history of modern Protestant theology" about which he wrote in his later, more balanced *Protestant Theology in the Nineteenth Century* (1947).[8] Even in that work Barth could speak of Lessing as "one of the first quite obvious heralds of the programme of Protestant modernism,"[9] a sentiment that differs little from the pejorative characterization expressed in his view that the "theologians of the modern age" were exposed as arrogant advocates of self-apotheosis best of all by the left-wing Hegelian Feuerbach.[10]

Although "modern theology" immediately suggests the intellectual endeavor of theologians in recent times, these brief observations should put us on guard against the more parochial concerns that have colored the meaning of the term in the common parlance

7. Karl Barth, "Schleiermacher" (1926), in *Theology and the Church: Shorter Writings, 1920–1928*, trans. L. P. Smith (London: SCM Press, 1962), 191. See John E. Thiel, "Barth's Early Interpretation of Schleiermacher," in *Barth and Schleiermacher: Beyond the Impasse?* ed. J. O. Duke and R. F. Streetman (Philadelphia: Fortress Press, 1988), 17f.

8. Karl Barth, *Protestant Theology in the Nineteenth Century: Its Background and History*, trans. J. Bowden (London: SCM Press, 1972), 15.

9. Ibid., 263.

10. Karl Barth, "Feuerbach" (1926), in *Theology and the Church: Shorter Writings, 1920–1928*, 229.

of the academy and the churches. If defining and evaluating the character of modern theology are in the interests of theologians and the churches they serve, then the effective accomplishment of these tasks requires an ongoing analysis that transcends the biases of particular theological agendas. I would like to make some small contribution to that large project by identifying a number of traits that I believe are essential to modern theology and with which all non-fundamentalist theological camps will agree. This discussion will provide an opportunity for introducing the theme of our study.

Even though some may quibble about the historical antecedents of the modern temperament, theologians largely agree that the crisis produced by the Enlightenment's intellectual and political devastation of the authority of the feudal world marks a watershed in the history of theology and supplies a point of historical reference for the beginnings of its modern era. The attack on the traditional authority of king and priest that attended the rise of political liberalism in the eighteenth century entailed a radical questioning of the social and ecclesial assumptions on which the practice of theology had previously been based. The work of Enlightenment philosophers like Lessing and Kant to establish rationalistic epistemologies that could justify the predictability expected in the application of scientific theory undermined the traditional theological expectation that truth claims could be at once historical and necessary. Traditional theological appeals to the truth of scriptural revelation, the object of theological reflection, no longer held currency in the world of the educated public.

The Enlightenment intellectual heritage, then, which continues to the present day, thwarts the medieval assumption that the discipline of theology is an exercise in the intellectual common sense of culture. Modern theology is post-Enlightenment theology and so must face the challenge posed by the Enlightenment to the very possibility of theological reflection. This does not suggest that modern theology must accept the assumptions of the Enlightenment completely nor that theology must embrace a brand of apologetics in the style of Enlightenment criticism if it is to be judged modern. The Frankfurt School has exposed enough of the Enlightenment's own intellectual shortcomings, prejudices, and even naïveté[11] to render suspect any

11. Max Horkheimer and Theodor W. Adorno, *Dialectic of Enlightenment*, trans. J. Cumming (New York: Herder & Herder, 1972).

claim that the Enlightenment has pronounced the final word on theology or that its criticism has established only a certain range of legitimate theological responses. Yet any modern theology must possess the trait of disciplinary self-awareness, an understanding of its assumptions, claims, and limitations formed in dialogue with Enlightenment criticism. This trait is expected of all systematic, intellectual endeavor in the post-Enlightenment era, but it is an especially important one for theology. No other discipline was so shaken by the Enlightenment critique of knowledge. Consequently no other discipline has had to reckon to the same degree as theology with the differences between its premodern and modern practice. Modern theology, then, must come to grips with its own historical, epistemic, and sociocultural settings, and it must be prepared to articulate how its assumptions, methods, and practices differ from those at work in premodern, that is, pre-Enlightenment, theology.

A second trait of modern theology is the historical orientation of its many methods and approaches. Although one can speak of pluralism in premodern theology, modern theology is distinguished by the acceptance of methods and approaches that attempt to reckon both with the limitations placed by the conditions of historical existence on epistemic claims, theological or otherwise, and with the ebb and flow of contingent events that make up the ever-shifting narratives of our personal and cultural histories. In other words, modern theologies recognize the legitimacy of the historicocritical method, even if they disagree about how it should be applied. They also accept the need to give theological account of historical variability, whether that variability is seen as a sign of hope or despair. This commitment to theology's historicity is nowhere more evident than in the division of theological labor that the academy today takes for granted or in the many approaches to theology, all of them expressions of historical concern or perspective, currently devoted to the service of the Christian churches. In this respect the very pluralism of theological subfields such as scriptural studies, systematics, and ethics, and approaches such as hermeneutical, feminist, and narrative theologies, might be understood as expressions of the historical orientation of modern theology.

A third trait of modern theology is its attention to the individualism championed by the Enlightenment, however appropriate or problematic that individualism is judged to be. Enlightenment thinkers gave their project of political reform little chance of success if individual aspirations and actions continued to be constrained by the Christian doctrine of human nature's fallenness. A rationally formulated social contract called for the rebuilding of the political world on the foundation of a new anthropology that asserted the ideal of human perfectibility, the power of autonomous moral reasoning, and the inestimable value of political virtues rooted in human nature itself. The Enlightenment celebration of human autonomy, exemplified in the quest to cast off the political and ecclesiastical shackles of feudal tradition, was voiced most succinctly in Kant's well-known definition of the reform movement: "Enlightenment is man's release from his self-incurred tutelage. Tutelage is man's inability to make use of his understanding without direction from another. Self-incurred is this tutelage when its cause lies not in lack of reason but in lack of resolution and courage to use it without direction from another."[12]

In the post-Enlightenment period, these strong claims on behalf of individualism and the dignity of human nature have been moderated at the hands of successive intellectual movements and at times have even been accused of promulgating the very tyranny that they sought to overthrow. Yet the intellectual, political, and economic movements that may be considered progeny of the Enlightenment— liberalism, romanticism, capitalism, Marxism, existentialism, and feminism, to name a few—all take their point of departure from the so-called turn to be subject that became the hallmark of the Enlightenment reform. Modern theology is no exception. By claiming that modern theology owes some dimension of its identity to Enlightenment individualism, I do not mean to suggest that theology must embrace some form of an idealistic anthropology in order to be modern. Although many theological approaches have done so, I would not consider the positive regard for a subjectivist standpoint as definitive of modern theology. I would suggest, however, that all types of modern theology must grapple with the Enlightenment challenge to traditional authority expressed in its anthropology and would claim that a modern theology is one that faces rather than retreats from the subjectivist orientation engendered by the Enlightenment.

12. Immanuel Kant, "What Is Enlightenment?" in *On History*, trans. L. W. Beck et al. (Indianapolis: Bobbs-Merrill Co., 1963), 3.

These first three traits sketch the character of modern theology by focusing on the reconceptualization of its body of knowledge, its method, and its principal themes in the post–Enlightenment era. The fourth trait of modern theology shifts its attention from theology as a subject matter with particular concerns to theology as a discipline constructed by a practitioner. Modern theology emerged as theologians embraced an understanding of their discipline that took account of the critical sensibilities of the Enlightenment. But theologians also adopted a new understanding of their own role in the theological enterprise. In the early nineteenth century, theologians began to assume that their own individual talent contributed to the integrity of theology, even to the most fundamental respects in which theology could be considered meaningful for both the church and society at large. Theologians appealed to theories of the imagination current in intellectual circles of the time to explain the creativity they now claimed on behalf of their own work. In a manner analogous to understandings of the practitioner in artistic and literary endeavor, theologians conceived of themselves as authors and measured the authority of their work, its value for the church, not only in terms of its faithfulness to ecclesial tradition but also in terms of its creativity, its resourcefulness in explicating the contemporary meaning of ancient religious truths.

Theological authorship, the fourth trait of modern theology, is often overlooked as one of the characteristics definitive of post-Enlightenment theology. Perhaps this is because our own cultural myopia as moderns leads us to assume too quickly that theological practitioners of every age conceived of their labor, authority, and vocational responsibility in much the same way. As we shall see, this inattention to the modern assumption of theological authorship has not mitigated its influence upon the history of modern theology but only has made discussion of that influence less direct and articulate than it should be. We will be in a much better position to appreciate theological authorship as a distinctly modern theme if we understand it and the other three traits of modern theology as a matrix of theological assumptions that is by now nearly two centuries old. The uniqueness of this matrix, and the place of theological authorship within it, can be grasped more fully if we compare its assumptions with those of premodern theology. The important work of the philosopher of science Thomas S. Kuhn can be helpful in this respect.

PARADIGMS AND DISCIPLINARY
ASSUMPTIONS

Kuhn's classic study *The Structure of Scientific Revolutions* has engaged the intellectual community since its publication in 1962.[13] At least part of the book's ability to stir strong response, both positive and negative, on the part of its readers may be attributed to its willingness to consider the roles played by insight and prejudice on the part of practitioners of a discipline whose search for truth is often thought to be completely rational and value-free. Kuhn's work has highlighted the degree to which changes in fundamental scientific understandings occur not only as careful steps in the inexorable march of disciplinary logic but also as a slowly won allegiance to a different way of conceiving the fundamental principles of science. Kuhn, then, emphasizes the authority of overarching perspectives in the history of science and considers the workings of that authority in times of stability and in times of upheaval. The principal and most controversial category Kuhn employs to account for shifts in epistemic authority in the history of science is that of the paradigm.

In Kuhn's view, science at any given time functions in accordance with, and as an expression of, a framework of assumptions, rules, and methods that Kuhn describes as a paradigm, a structure of meaning that establishes legitimate scientific practice for succeeding generations of practitioners. Paradigms gain authoritative stature by accounting for natural phenomena through a theoretical construct that "is sufficiently unprecedented to attract an enduring group of adherents away from competing modes of scientific activity" and that is "sufficiently open-ended to leave all sorts of problems for the redefined group of practitioners to resolve."[14] Among Kuhn's examples are Ptolemaic and Copernican astronomies, Aristotelian and Newtonian dynamics, and corpuscular and wave optics. Normal science is theorizing, experimentation, and validation that take place under the auspices of these paradigmatic assumptions. Normal science does not question the assumptions of the paradigm but engages in "fact-gathering,"[15] which brings greater evidential breadth and theoretical refinement to the paradigm. Even though it embodies the

13. Thomas S. Kuhn, *The Structure of Scientific Revolutions*, 2d ed. (Chicago: Univ. of Chicago Press, 1970).
14. Ibid., 10.
15. Ibid., 25.

day-to-day exercise of scientific investigation, normal science does not give free rein to the creative impulse. Fully committed to the routinization of the paradigm as a particular worldview, the practitioners of normal science conduct their business by unconsciously respecting a set of rigid strictures on admissible innovation. In a striking image, though one that does not carry pejorative connotations, Kuhn describes much of normal science as "mop-up work,"[16] problem solving in the service of the paradigm's general assumptions that shuns the rupture that "*unexpected* novelty"[17] would bring to the paradigm.

Ironically, paradigms are threatened as their limits are stretched by the work of normal science that purports to serve their interests. As experimentation yields results beyond the explanatory grasp of established theory, the assumptions of the reigning paradigm come under scrutiny. Their questionability, however, is not pressed by the mainstream of scientific inquiry. In Kuhn's account of scientific change, a new paradigm is born as the old construct of meaning is challenged by the insights of an individual or small group that celebrates rather than represses fissures in its established theory. Through its commitment to the validity of novel experimental evidence and a competing paradigmatic vision, the minority party of practitioners at least adjusts, and at most undermines, the authority of the established paradigm, thus threatening the more staid workings of normal science. It is hardly surprising, then, that the insights of the emerging paradigm are not welcomed by the established scientific community, since the life work of its practitioners is jeopardized by the new theory.

Kuhn's work is an interesting contribution to the sociology of knowledge and is particularly valuable for explaining how knowledge functions in a community of tightly defined and strongly held assumptions. Kuhn's attention to the rupture of unexpected novelty and its accompanying crisis in accepted fact and theory does much to explain the revolutionary moment in the history of science. Equally important, however, is that insight's corollary—namely, that nearly all of the history of science takes place within "ordinary time" in which innovation is strictly moderated by the paradigm's conceptual limits.

There are several ways in which normal science under any paradigm safeguards its assumptions. Kuhn notes that the routinization

16. Ibid., 24.
17. Ibid., 35.

of paradigms has been fostered by the appearance of scientific text-books in the early nineteenth century. By virtue of their authoritative content and their compact style of presentation, textbooks discourage the reinvestigation of the paradigm's basic assumptions and validating experimentation and seal the student's commitment to a scientific tradition that, from within, is no longer recognized as a particular paradigmatic model. In addition to textual canonization, there are also personal lines of defense against the prospect of a shift in par-adigms. The authority of a paradigm is often associated with an individual renowned for the paradigm's seminal insight or for ex-emplary commitment to the task of its normal science. Such au-thorities often provide powerful vocal opposition to the theoretically or factually avant garde. Lord Kelvin's confident dismissal of X rays as an elaborate hoax and Einstein's intellectual disdain for quantum mechanical probabilism are among Kuhn's illustrations of the dogged resistance of scientific authorities to change.[18] The persistence of this defensive posture in the spirit of inquiry is perhaps best attested in Kuhn's observation that the iconoclastic impetus of the new paradigm quickly produces its own version of the previous authority structure with its own complements of authorities, textbooks, and intellectual common sense.

Clearly, many parallels can be drawn between Kuhn's description of the workings of knowledge in the discipline of science and the workings of knowledge in the discipline of theology, as Kuhn himself points out.[19] The value of Kuhn's theoretical reflections for theology is witnessed in several recent theological works that employ his ideas to periodize the history of theology, to explain the distinctiveness of its presuppositions in particular eras, or to serve as a basis for con-structive methodological reflections.[20] This study shares these same applicative goals, although it will use Kuhn selectively in attempting to achieve them. I would like to apply Kuhn's central category of

18. Ibid., 59, 163.
19. Ibid., 136.
20. The work that most extensively considers Kuhn's theory as a resource for theology is a collection of papers presented at a 1983 International Ecumenical Symposium at Tübingen on the theme "A New Paradigm for Theology": *Paradigm Change in Theology*, ed. H. Küng and D. Tracy, trans. M. Köhl (New York: Cross-road, 1989). See also Hans Küng, *Theology for the Third Millenium: An Ecumenical View*, trans. P. Heinegg (New York: Doubleday & Co., 1988); Garrett Green, *Imagining God: Theology and the Religious Imagination* (New York: Harper & Row, 1989).

the paradigm to the history of theology as an academic discipline in order to elucidate the distinctiveness of modern theology, particularly its assumption that theologians are authors whose creativity is essential to their enterprise.

In spite of its centrality to his argument, Kuhn's notion of the paradigm is employed equivocally in the pages of *The Structure of Scientific Revolutions*.[21] Kuhn addressed the objections of his critics to this and other ambiguities in a lengthy postscript to the second edition of the book. In that essay Kuhn acknowledges the imprecisions in the first edition's conception of the paradigm and attempts to distinguish between two uses of the term. In its first and more general use, the term "stands for the entire constellation of beliefs, values, techniques, and so on shared by the members of a given community." In a second and more particular use, the term "denotes one sort of element in that constellation, the concrete puzzle-solutions which, employed as models or examples, can replace explicit rules as a basis for the solution of the remaining puzzles of normal science."[22] Kuhn regards this second, particular use of the term *paradigm* as the "central element"[23] of his thesis, presumably because this function of paradigms as experimental exemplars determines the routine of normal science.[24] Here, however, I would prefer to focus more directly on the broader understanding of paradigm. Although much of this book will examine specific features of theological authorship, features analogous to Kuhn's more restricted understanding of paradigms as exemplars, the elucidation of theological authorship will be better served by the use of Kuhn's general category.

Kuhn's general use of the term *paradigm* describes a "constellation of group commitments," a broad set of presuppositions that constitute the identity of a particular approach to scientific inquiry.[25] Kuhn concedes to his critics that the conception of a "disciplinary matrix"

21. Margaret Masterman distinguishes twenty-one different uses of the term in the first edition of the book. Margaret Masterman, "The Nature of a Paradigm," in *Criticism and the Growth of Knowledge*, ed. I. Lakatos and A. Musgrave (New York: Cambridge Univ. Press, 1970), 61–65.

22. Kuhn, *The Structure of Scientific Revolutions*, 175.

23. Ibid., 187.

24. See Ian G. Barbour, *Myths, Models and Paradigms: A Comparative Study in Science and Religion* (New York: Harper & Row, 1974), 108–09.

25. Kuhn, *The Structure of Scientific Revolutions*, 181.

more aptly renders the meaning of this wider use of the conception of paradigm:

> For present purposes I suggest "disciplinary matrix" [as a terminological substitute for "paradigm"]: "disciplinary" because it refers to the common possession of the practitioners of a particular discipline; "matrix" because it is composed of ordered elements of various sorts, each requiring further specification. All or most of the objects of group commitment that my original text makes paradigms, parts of paradigms, or paradigmatic are constituents of the disciplinary matrix, and as such they form a whole and function together.[26]

The paradigm understood as a disciplinary matrix describes a configuration of shared assumptions that fix the integrity of a particular mode of knowledge and the means by which it is sought and refined. Any disciplinary matrix is characterized by expressive and emotional denominators common to practitioners who share its assumptions. Kuhn's examples of "symbolic generalizations," "metaphysical" beliefs, and "values"[27] as such common stock evince the degree to which he conceives of the general use of paradigm as a worldview whose definitive characteristics are molded by human sentiment as much as by technical formulation. This wider conception of the paradigm as a disciplinary matrix provides a framework for understanding the history of academic theology in terms of the notion of theological authorship.

PARADIGMS OF THEOLOGICAL RESPONSIBILITY

The conception of theological authorship emerged in the post-Enlightenment period concurrently with a shift from what I label the classical to the romantic paradigm of theological responsibility. By *theological responsibility* I refer to the vocational norms to which the theologian is accountable in his or her intellectual efforts to clarify the truth of an ecclesial tradition. Theological responsibility concerns the issue of authority as it relates to the theological vocation. By what authority does the theologian speak and judge? To whom or what is the theologian answerable? By what criteria is the legitimacy

26. Ibid., 182.
27. Ibid., 182–85.

of the theologian's speaking and judging measurable? The answers one gives to these questions will reflect a particular understanding of the role of the theologian in the church and thus of the nature of theological responsibility. Although versions of what constitutes authoritative responsibility are as nuanced as the theological positions they reflect, I would like to suggest that two broad judgments about the theologian's proper vocational responsibility have been at work in the Christian tradition since the birth of theology as an academic discipline. Recalling Kuhn's emphasis on the vocational interests at stake in the workings of any disciplinary matrix, and his view that a "paradigm governs, in the first instance, not a subject matter but rather a group of practitioners,"[28] we may consider the respective assumptions about theological responsibility associated with the classical and romantic paradigms.

It is difficult to speak of theology as a discrete discipline prior to the twelfth century. At that time schoolmen began to apply the distinct methods of the classical disciplines of grammar, rhetoric, and especially dialectic to the study of the biblical text that had commonly been known as *sacra pagina*. The result was a new academic discipline, gradually identified as *theologia*, preoccupied with the definition of its own theory and content and elaborated by its students in textbooks and commentaries.[29] The notion of responsibility that emerged in this classical understanding of the theological task was shaped largely by the previous history of biblical interpretation. The study of *sacra pagina* involved the exposition of the meaning of the Bible by regular appeal to the established tradition of ecclesial authorities. With few exceptions[30] it was assumed throughout the Middle Ages that these

28. Ibid., 180.
29. Cf. Congar, *A History of Theology*, 50–84; G. R. Evans, *Old Arts and New Theology: The Beginnings of Theology as an Academic Discipline* (Oxford: Clarendon Press, 1980), 19–46. More generally, see Frank Whaling, "The Development of the Word 'Theology,'" *Scottish Journal of Theology* 34 (1981): 289–312.
30. The most striking exception is Peter Abelard (1079–1142), whose *Sic et Non* illustrated the diversity of patristic opinion on a variety of doctrinal matters. The suspicions against Abelard throughout his career, acted on in his condemnation at the councils of Soissons and Sens, indicate how challenges to the unity of the tradition, especially by an individual who appealed to personal talent as a theological resource, were received during the period in which theology emerged as an academic discipline. In his *Historia Calamitatum* Abelard recounts the way his early theological lectures, which rivaled those of his master Anselm of Laon, departed from the commentarial approach of *sacra pagina*. Peter Abelard, *The Story of Abelard's Adversities*, trans. J. T. Muckle (Toronto: Pontifical Institute of Mediaeval Studies, 1964), 21–24.

authorities, whether Augustine, Boethius, or John Damascene, spoke with a single voice on doctrinal matters and that the expression of this univocal authority constituted the tradition of orthodox teaching. The tradition's recognition of the authority's status was not founded principally on the originality of his interpretations but on the consistency of his insights with those offered by his predecessors and with the received doctrinal tradition.[31] This harmonization of the biblical text and the tradition of its interpretation reflected the Catholic assumption that God's revelation was presented in both scripture and tradition.

As theology came to be defined as an academic enterprise in the twelfth and thirteenth centuries, its assumptions about the responsibility incumbent on its practitioners took shape along the lines of this classical notion of authority. The biblical text remained the primary authority to which the academic theologians considered themselves responsible, though, as in the tradition of *sacra pagina*, the individual interpreter sought the truth of the text in the wisdom of the recognized authorities of the past. This is illustrated most clearly in the development of the *Quaestio* method in the twelfth and thirteenth centuries, which eventually required that not only biblical interpretation but also metaphysical speculation be legitimated by reference to the tradition of authorities. As was the case in the study of *sacra pagina*, the authority of revelation as interpreted by tradition tended to eclipse the value of individual insight and thus of individual theological judgment.

It is difficult to speak of there being any conception of individual authority in this high-medieval notion of theological responsibility. This is obviously not to say that the work of theologians like Lombard, Aquinas, and Bonaventura possessed no distinctiveness or originality capable of being identified with the intellectual style and creativity of these individuals. In the classical paradigm, however, distinctiveness and originality were not valued traits to be celebrated by a theologian's contemporaries. Soundness, or "orthodoxy" in ecclesial terms, was the true mark of theological achievement, and that quality could be earned only through the passing of time and the favorable judgment of the ages. Ironically, at least in terms of

31. See Beryl Smalley, "Ecclesiastical Attitudes to Novelty c. 1100–c. 1250," in *Studies in Medieval Thought and Learning: From Abelard to Wyclif* (London: Hambleton Press, 1981), 97–115.

modern sensibilities, theological achievement in the context of the classical paradigm entailed the identification of the individual's theological labors with the tradition of authorities and thus the forsaking of any claim to originality or individual authority. In other words, consummate theological achievement in the High Middle Ages demanded the blending of individual theological voice into the harmonious chorus of the past authorities, the standard of theological responsibility from which individual authorship was finally indistinguishable.[32]

The classical paradigm is not limited to the Catholic tradition of the Middle Ages. It is also characteristic of classical Protestantism, albeit in a somewhat altered form. In many respects the denominational splintering of Christianity in the sixteenth century can be understood in terms of the issue of theological responsibility. The rise of the doctrine of papal infallibility in the late Middle Ages[33] altered the high-medieval notion of theological authority and yielded a conception of theological responsibility against which the reformers rebelled. By the early sixteenth century, Catholicism understood theologians to be responsible to the tradition of authorities, finally epitomized in the authority of the present Roman pontiff as the most authentic interpreter of God's revelation in scripture and tradition. Classical Protestantism rejected this conception of theological responsibility and understood theological speaking and judging to be responsible to the Word of God alone. Both Luther and Calvin judged the magisterial commitment of Roman Catholic theology to be a false allegiance worthy only of rejection. When the reformers did appeal to the authority of the tradition, they tended to be selective, refusing to accept the medieval assumption that the authorities of the

32. In response to his own rhetorical question, "Could theologians individually or at least corporately, be acknowledged as possessing true doctrinal or magisterial authority?" Avery Dulles asserts that the "notion that theologians have authority is well-founded in the tradition" ("The Magisterium in History: A Theological Reflection," *Chicago Studies* 17 [1978]: 273). His examples, however, lend credence to my view that in the classical paradigm theologians have no *individual* authority. The Council of Vienne (1312), he notes, "invoked the testimonies of the Fathers and the opinions of 'the modern doctors of theology' as grounds for endorsing certain positions. . . . To contradict the unanimous opinion of theologians on a question of faith or morals, [contends the sixteenth-century theologian Melchior Cano], is heresy or close to heresy" (273).

33. See Brian Tierney, *Origins of Papal Infallibility 1150–1350* (Leiden: E. J. Brill, 1972).

tradition spoke univocally on doctrinal matters. Like medieval theologians before them, they considered Augustine to be the preeminent traditional authority, although principally because he expounded a doctrine of sin and grace biblically supportable in Paul and amenable to Reformation spirituality.[34] For the reformers, individual acts of theological thinking and judging gained their legitimacy through their faithful exposition of the scriptural text, whose proper author was God.[35]

Even though these sixteenth-century conceptions of theological responsibility differ significantly, they do share a common presupposition that is noteworthy and justifies their being ranked under a single rubric. First, both assume that legitimate theology is responsible to God through the objective authority of God's revelation, whether through scripture traditionally expounded in the case of Roman Catholicism or through scripture alone in the case of Protestantism. Second, both assume that the exercise of this responsibility is incompatible with the theologian's individual creativity or originality. In the context of medieval and Tridentine Catholicism, the authorities of the tradition, as expounders of a single divine truth available to the church through their writings, were understood to be speaking with a single voice from which the theologian could dissent only at the risk of heresy. Although the Reformers rejected the theological normativeness of Catholic tradition, they affirmed the tradition's presupposition that truth was not to be found in the novelty of individual or collective acts of theologizing. If Luther's hermeneutical principle of *scriptura sui interpres*, and its expectation that the shared faith of a plurality of interpreters will produce a single interpretation, appears naive to the modern inheritor of Christian pluralism, it is because its noetic and authoritative presuppositions are entirely medieval.

34. See Jaroslav Pelikan, *The Christian Tradition 4: Reformation of Church and Dogma (1300–1700)* (Chicago: Univ. of Chicago Press, 1984), 138–41.
35. See B. A. Gerrish, "Doctor Martin Luther: Subjectivity and Doctrine in the Lutheran Reformation," in *Seven-Headed Luther: Essays in Commemoration of a Quincentenary 1483–1983*, ed. P. N. Brooks (Oxford: Clarendon Press, 1983), 1–24; B. A. Gerrish, "The Word of God and the Words of Scripture: Luther and Calvin on Biblical Authority," in *The Old Protestantism and the New: Essays on the Reformation Heritage* (Chicago: Univ. of Chicago Press, 1982), 51–68. More specifically, cf. Scott H. Hendrix, "Luther against the Background of the History of Biblical Interpretation," *Interpretation* 37 (1983): 229.

In the postscript to the second edition of *The Structure of Scientific Revolutions*, Kuhn defines the attitudinal boundaries of a scientific community's paradigm as "what . . . its members share that accounts for the relative fulness of their professional communication and the relative unanimity of their professional judgments."[36] If the preceding, and admittedly sweeping, analysis is defensible, then it suggests that theological practitioners throughout the medieval period, as well as in the sixteenth and seventeenth centuries, found this fullness and unanimity in the shared assumption that God is the sole author of the truth of salvation in scripture or tradition or both.

The negative expression of this classical assumption is also enlightening, especially as an anticipation of its paradigmatic successor. In the classical paradigm, there was no conception of *individual* theological authorship. Theologians were not seen to be functioning as authors in the modern sense that their vocation entailed the creative presentation of divine truth through individual experience or original insight. Because theologians were not authors, they did not possess authority. Theological responsibility in the classical paradigm was seen as the theologian's *representative* faithfulness to divine revelation. In the classical Roman Catholic tradition, theological representation took the form of speculative commentary on scripture or commentary-based speculation; in the classical Protestant tradition, theological representation took the form of exegesis. This essentially singular assumption about the nature of theological responsibility remained undisturbed until challenged by the Enlightenment's attack on its authoritative foundations.

Although the reformers generally accepted the medieval understanding of authority, the tenor of their theologies did much to supplant the classical paradigm of theological responsibility. The reformers had, after all, focused on the centrality of the individual's experience of faith,[37] maintained the individual believer's access to the literal sense of scripture,[38] and fostered a view of the church as

36. Kuhn, *The Structure of Scientific Revolutions*, 182.
37. B. A. Gerrish agrees with Ernst Troeltsch's judgment that Luther's emphasis on the subjectivity of faith provides "the crucial link between the old Protestantism and the new" ("From 'Dogmatik' to 'Glaubenslehre': A Paradigm Change in Modern Theology?" in *Paradigm Change in Theology*, 168).
38. Brevard Childs has argued that the reformers' achievement was "to offer an interpretation of the literal sense which . . . held together the historical and theological meaning [of scripture]" ("The Sensus Literalis of Scripture: An Ancient

a community within which the individual could find relationship to God apart from the mediating offices of the priest. In addition to the subjective emphases in these theological themes, the manner in which remarkable historical change occurred in the sixteenth century contributed to the later formation of a different understanding of the theological vocation. The virtual transformation of late-medieval European society by the personal efforts, criticism, and courage of the great reformers—Luther, Zwingli, and Calvin—did much to cultivate the modern identification of authority and autonomy and its assumption that meaning is established through the committed work of individuals. The fact that the reformers were first and foremost theologians encouraged the application of this modern notion of authority to the sphere of theological reflection.

This notion of individual authority blossomed fully in the eighteenth and nineteenth centuries in the intellectual movements of the Enlightenment and Romanticism. The Enlightenment understanding of autonomy entailed only impatient disdain for what were considered to be the heteronomous truth claims of Christian scripture and tradition. This disdain manifested itself in a rigorous attack on these revelational mainstays of classical theology and provided the impetus for a paradigm shift in conceptions of the theological task. In the early nineteenth century the Christian churches sought a means to defend the integrity of their theological vision against the criticism of Enlightenment rationalism and found their most valuable resource in the growing movement of Romanticism.

It would be impossible in the limits of the present study to give account of the various types and theories of Romanticism. For the sake of brevity we can say that the romantic movement, especially as it was theologically appropriated, was generally concerned with the subjective reconciliation of meaning and history. Meaning, the romantics claimed, was not accessible in an objective metaphysical referent. It could be found only in its historical development, especially as focused in the experience of individuals or communities. However this experience was described—as feeling, fancy, wit, imagination, or sympathy—its veridical force was seen as a repudiation

---

and Modern Problem," in *Beiträge zur alttestamentlichen Theologie: Festschrift für Walther Zimmerli zur 70. Geburtstag*, ed. H. Donner et al. [Göttingen: Vandenhoeck & Ruprecht, 1977], 87). This achievement, however, as short-lived as it was, served the principally theological concern of the Reformation watchword *sola scriptura* and its claims about the individual's relationship to God.

of the Enlightenment's neoclassical formalism, mechanistic episte-mologies, and confidence in the absolute moral value of practical reason. According to James Engell, the romantics invested the imag-ination with the power of "resolving and unifying . . . all antitheses and contradictions," of relating "the static to the dynamic, passive to active, ideal to real, and universal to particular." In the writings of the romantics, "imagination becomes the process to understand and to view both the world and the self,"[39] a perspective on the historicity of experience that stands in contrast to the Enlightenment search for truth in the atemporal workings of universal reason.

The appropriation of this romantic understanding of history enabled theologians to argue that Enlightenment criticism, with its static understanding of truth, appreciated neither the depth nor the dynamism of divine revelation, now conceived as an ever-growing historical continuum. From the assumption that the truth of tradition is a developing truth, there follows the need for a means of probing meaningful but often subtle modifications in the communal expe-rience of faith—a means the romantics located not in the classical foundations of theology but in the theologian's talent. The romantic conception of theological authorship was born in this ascription of authorial ability, and thus authority, to the individual theologian. At least in the founding assumptions of the romantic paradigm, the theologian possesses a sort of ecclesial genius—a talent exercised in the sensitive discernment, the felicitous expression, and the careful guidance of ecclesial truth in history. Since this development was primarily accessible in and through experience, the importance ac-corded to individual creativity in theological reflection was remark-ably enhanced. The theologian's task was no longer seen as the mi-metic *representation* of an objective revelation but as the imaginative *construction* of the historical experience of salvation. This shift in conceptions about the very nature of the theological enterprise was one that highlighted the theologian's creativity and gave rise to the romantic paradigm of theological responsibility.

This conception of theological responsibility took shape in the first theologies of tradition formulated in the early decades of the nineteenth century by Friedrich Schleiermacher (1768–1834) and Jo-hann Sebastian Drey (1777–1853). In their apologetical efforts to

39. James Engell, *The Creative Imagination: Enlightenment to Romanticism* (Cam-bridge: Harvard Univ. Press, 1981), 8. Engell is quick to point out, however, that the Enlightenment, and not Romanticism, "created the idea of the imagination" (3).

address the Enlightenment, these romantic theologians resisted the more traditional notion of theological responsibility as faithfulness only to the scriptural text, the normative creeds of the Christian past, or the present judgments of an ecclesiastical hierarchy. They promulgated an alternative conception of responsibility that presumed a historical understanding of religious meaning, one that was not as easily susceptible to rationalistic criticism as the classical understanding of theological responsibility proved to be. Both Schleiermacher and Drey understood Christian tradition as a fluid movement in which the established doctrine of the past was enlivened by its encounter with the contemporary moment in the development of Christian faith. In their shared theory of doctrinal development, Schleiermacher and Drey believed it was incumbent on the theologian to discern and express the present form that the faith experience had assumed in the community of Christian believers. They understood this present faith as the latest manifestation of Christian truth in history and so as the humble contribution of the contemporary generation of believers to the development of Christian tradition.

To whom or to what, though, is the theologian responsible in discerning and expressing the present and ever-transient moment in the development of Christian tradition? On whom or on what does the theologian rely to assure the legitimacy of the theological construction of belief? Like classical theologians, Schleiermacher and Drey believed the theologian to be responsible to God and the constancy of God's salvational promise revealed in scripture and tradition. Schleiermacher and Drey, however, assumed that this responsibility encountered its historical object in the developing experience of the theologian's ecclesial community. They believed that the authority of tradition lies not only in its past creeds but also in the living faith of contemporary believers. This understanding of tradition, shaped by the historical sensibilities of Romanticism, might be likened to an ongoing conversation between the ecclesial past and the ecclesial present in which a remarkable array of voices, both new and old, can be heard and a wide range of perspectives, both new and old, can be distinguished.

Theological authorship plays an important role in this historical understanding of tradition and its corresponding conception of theological responsibility. It is the theologian's talent that apprehends and articulates the most significant and representative among the church's recent voices and perspectives. Unlike the classical paradigm, the romantic paradigm values theological originality; indeed it is an indispensable quality of theological construction attuned to the tradition's latest development. The theologian's creativity is at the service of the ecclesially novel as it discerns and expresses the contemporary state of faith in the community of believers. Practitioners in the romantic paradigm follow the lead set by Schleiermacher and Drey in refusing to equate theological novelty with theological aberration, and by recognizing that the theological innovation of today could very well be the time-honored belief of the future.

The creativity of theological authorship, however, is not exhausted in the theologian's service to the ecclesial present. In the romantic paradigm, the theologian's talent does much to establish the coherence of the conversation of tradition by formulating meaningful relationships between the ecclesial past and present, by suggesting worthy topics for an ecclesial dialogue across the ages, and by offering insights into the continuity between ancient and modern belief. To accomplish these tasks, theological talent may turn for assistance to the many auxiliary methods and technical tools that have proliferated in the growing sophistication of its discipline in the post-Enlightenment period. But the talent of authorship primarily involves an act of the imagination and as such cannot be accounted for in terms of definable rules, method, or disciplinary technique.

I do not intend to suggest that the theological imagination in the romantic paradigm "authors" tradition as a sheer act of creativity comparable to the power and authority of God in the classical paradigm. Like the classical paradigm, its romantic successor judges God to be the author of scripture and tradition and theological responsibility a matter of faithfulness to the truth of the divine creativity in the Bible and in history. The romantic paradigm's developmental understanding of these products of divine authorship, however, opened the way for an appreciation of the authorial contributions of the individual theologian as an interpreter of the meaning of scripture and tradition for a particular community and in a specific time. The romantic paradigm assumed that the theologian exercised vocational responsibility as an author whose individual talent contributed something valuable, and even indispensable, to the normativeness of the Christian tradition. As such, the paradigm licensed the theologian's partial or relative authority as the author of theological constructions essential to a developing tradition's self-understanding, coherence, and integrity. This conception of theological authorship stands in sharp contrast to the classical paradigm's suspicion of all nonsupernatural authority and sanctions an understanding of theological responsibility that the classical paradigm would have judged ecclesially anomic.

The reader may raise the objection at this point that the paradigmatic division of the history of theology suggested here is conceptualized in an anachronistic fashion. If the focus of our study is modern theology's endorsement of the ability and practice of theological authorship, then it may be prejudicial to describe premodern theology in terms of what it lacks rather than in terms of what it possesses. Why not, for example, characterize premodern theology in terms of its subject matter or in terms of its homogeneity or in terms of its assumption that its right practice requires a proper theological *habitus*[40] or in terms of its untroubled acceptance of biblical and traditional authority? To say that premodern theology lacks a conception of theological authorship might only be offering the jejune observation that premodern theology is not modern. This observation would be a legitimate objection were it being suggested here that premodern theology is deficient because it lacks a conception of theological authorship, as though modern theology were in this respect privileged in relation to its premodern forebear. Such is not the case. I pass no negative judgment on the classical paradigm as it flourished prior to the Enlightenment, although I do think that any theology committed to the assumptions of the classical paradigm during the post-Enlightenment period is anachronistic. The comparison of premodern and modern theology in terms of the paradigms suggested here intends only to present a contrast in assumptions that helps us to understand the character of modern theology better.

THE ROMANTIC PARADIGM'S RANGE

Kuhn's paradigmatic analysis of shifts in disciplinary matrices in the history of science elucidates the fundamental changes in theology's methodological assumptions since the twelfth century. The High Middle Ages witnessed the development of a scientific theology elaborate in method, rich in technical vocabulary, and varied in possible applications. The textbooks, commentaries, and disputed questions of high- and late-medieval, as well as Tridentine, Catholicism served

---

40. Edward Farley, *Theologia: The Fragmentation and Unity of Theological Education* (Philadelphia: Fortress Press, 1983), 31f.

as exemplars, to use Kuhn's term, for the conduct of normal (theological) science within this Roman version of the classical paradigm. Luther's rebellion against the scholastic textbooks and his ad hoc theological style were of no avail in establishing a new presentational form for Protestant theology. Melanchthon's *Loci Communes* and Calvin's *Institutes* provided early exemplars for an extended tradition of textbook-normal science in the Protestant, exegetical version of the classical paradigm.

The confluence of several intellectual and political agendas in the eighteenth century—the rise of modern science, the ascendancy of empirical or critical epistemologies, the redefinition of societal programs through revolutions on both sides of the Atlantic—provided anomalies significant enough to challenge the very viability of the shared paradigm and to shake the assumptions of the traditional textbooks. It is a matter of historical fact that Roman Catholicism resisted the challenge posed by these anomalies longer than Protestantism did. But the Enlightenment did not present a crisis only to one confession, nor did it single out one or the other version of the classical paradigm as the object of its assault. Christianity itself or, theologically speaking, the classical paradigm of theological responsibility was the target of Enlightenment criticism because the Christian tradition's notion of authority, whether embedded in its doctrines or in its expectations for legitimate theological representation, presented the greatest obstacle to the success of the Enlightenment's intellectual and political agendas.

The romantic paradigm of theological responsibility was a response to the crisis provoked by the Enlightenment, and true to the expectations of Kuhn's theory, this creative initiative emerged "first in the mind of one or a few individuals" who learned "to see [theological] science and the world differently."[41] As an alternative disciplinary matrix for theology began to take shape in the early nineteenth century, theological authorship emerged as an important assumption within the new paradigm. Attention to the role of the theologian's creativity, insight, and talent within the process of theological reflection has done much to justify the integrity of theology as a modern discipline in the eyes of the academy, for the assumption of theological authorship ranks the theological practitioner within the same spectrum of personal possibilities and limitations encountered by practitioners in all interpretive disciplines. As this study will show, the

41. Kuhn, *The Structure of Scientific Revolutions*, 144.

assumption of theological authorship often has not been so favorably judged by those still committed to, or at least nostalgic for, a premodern conception of theological authority. This has been especially true in the Roman Catholic Church, in which the assumption of theological authorship has had a particularly troubled history.

In spite of suspicions about theological authorship in both the Catholic and Protestant traditions, this assumption now constitutes a central exemplar for normal science in the discipline of theology and, as I have argued, is a definitive trait of all forms of modern theology, whether conservative or liberal in orientation. The commitment of modern theology to certain assumptions does not mean that theologies need be singular in style in order to be judged modern, as though the ascription of traits—or even a single trait—to modern theology entails a monolithic understanding of its nature or practice. Indeed, modern theology is so characterized by methodological and stylistic pluralism that the attempt to procrusteanize its range to a particular method or style would vitiate the rich diversity in its actual history. This holds true even for a specific assumption of the romantic paradigm like theological authorship. In the modern period the exercise of authorship through theological construction[42] has taken three

42. This term gained popularity through the work of Gordon Kaufman, though I would like to distinguish sharply between Kaufman's use of the term and my own. In Kaufman's view, theology "is (and always has been) essentially a constructive work of the human imagination, an expression of the imagination's activity helping to provide orientation for human life through developing a symbolical 'picture' of the world roundabout and of the human place within that world" (*The Theological Imagination: Constructing the Concept of God* [Philadelphia: Westminster Press, 1981], 11). Yet Kaufman seems to regard this constructive enterprise as utterly imaginative and without any responsibility to the ecclesial authority of the Bible or tradition. Indeed, in his understanding theological responsibility appears to be completely vested in the free play of the imagination and its theological constructions (15–16; 274).

My use of the term *construction* describes forms of theological inquiry and procedure that are postclassical or modern—that is, committed to the broad, theological assumptions of the romantic paradigm. In this sense "theological construction" stands in contrast to the classical paradigm's mimetic approach to theologizing as "representation." In its use here, the term intends to convey the romantic paradigm's assumption that individual creativity plays some role, however small, in acts of theological conception and expression and that this imaginative dimension of the theological enterprise necessarily entails its historicity and susceptibility to criticism and revision. I assume, however, that acts of theological construction derive any legitimacy they might possess from the theologian's exercise of imagination in a manner faithful to scripture and tradition.

principal forms, of which there are many variations or hybridic combinations: description, speculation, and criticism.

Description is best represented in the work of the two most influential Protestant theologians of the modern period, Friedrich Schleiermacher and Karl Barth.[43] Barth's hostility to Schleiermacher's *Bewusstseinstheologie* should not disguise the degree to which he and Schleiermacher follow the exegetical course of theological interpretation set by the reformers. Barth excoriates Schleiermacher for his inattention to biblical revelation and his willingness to structure Christian dogmatics on the basis of human experience. But Barth, like Schleiermacher, understands the enterprise of dogmatics to entail the description of the faith of the church. Their expository approach to dogmatics exhibits a common antipathy toward philosophical speculation as a dimension of theological reflection, perhaps because both Schleiermacher and Barth assume that the description of ecclesial faith is self-referential. Theological description, in their view, looks principally to the belief of the church for the meaning it seeks to expound. While Schleiermacher sees the task of *Glaubenslehre* as the exposition of immediate, pious consciousness and Barth the task of *Dogmatik* as the exposition of the biblically revealed Word of God, both regard the meaning of theology's historical object to be so simple and compelling that its close description by the theologian readily yields the recognition and edification of the ecclesial community.

The more recent work of Hans Frei, George Lindbeck, Ronald Thiemann, and Stanley Hauerwas that has come to be known as postliberal theology bears a family resemblance to Barth's descriptive theology.[44] These postliberal theologians argue that scripture's own narrative framework renders the meaning of the gospel message for theological reflection. Theological interpretation must resist the temptation to translate the meaning of the scriptural narrative into extrascriptural categories, as though the meaning of scripture could be separated from its narrative form. For the postliberals, theology is a descriptive endeavor whose insights must be shaped by scripture's own grammar of faith. Faithful acts of theological description align

43. The insight into the similarity between Schleiermacher and Barth in their approaches to the theological task is Hans Frei's and is developed in his unpublished Shaffer Lectures delivered at Yale in 1983.

44. See William C. Placher, "Postliberal Theology," in *The Modern Theologians: An Introduction to Christian Theology in the Twentieth Century*, vol. 2, ed. D. F. Ford (Oxford: Basil Blackwell, 1989), 115–28.

themselves closely with the contours of the biblical story and regard its narrative as the authoritative measure of the many secular stories that vie for the believer's commitment.

The speculative approach to theological construction has been pursued by those who have appropriated the main philosophical currents of this period—idealism, existentialism, hermeneutics, and process thought, to name a few—as methodological bases for the theological task. In the modern period, a speculative approach to theological construction entails the acceptance of a critical or post-critical stance on the limitations of knowledge. It implicitly involves the theological adoption of at least anthropological, and often even metaphysical, themes judged by the speculative theologian to clarify the meaning of the gospel in its contemporary setting. While many Protestant theologians have embraced the speculative style—Rudolf Bultmann, Paul Tillich, Eberhard Jüngel, and John Cobb may serve as examples—the Catholic tradition has found this approach to be most in keeping with its classical understanding of the theological enterprise as an attempt to bring the intelligibility of reason to bear on the tradition of faith. It can be illustrated in the work of the Catholic Tübingen school, the transcendental theologies of Karl Rahner and Bernard Lonergan, Hans Urs von Balthasar's theological aesthetics, and the hermeneutical theology of David Tracy.

Criticism as a modern form of theological construction is the most recent of the three and can be dated from the beginnings of political theology in the late 1960s. Criticism takes its point of departure from a hermeneutics of suspicion directed both toward the myths of progress that have shaped the modern world and the distorting and exclusionary power latent in classical and modern expressions of Christian doctrine. This approach to theological construction sometimes minimizes or eschews the importance of grounding theology in a universal theory, focusing instead on the "regional" or "local" implications of the gospel for existential particularities such as culture, race, gender, or socioeconomic circumstance. It is represented by different forms of liberation theology that articulate the perspectives on the tradition offered by Third World Christians and minority groups and has taken concrete shape in black, Hispanic, Asian, Latin American, Native American, African, and feminist theologies.

These three forms of theological construction may seem to be more different than alike. In many respects they are. Even within each of the three forms, the differences between particular illustrations of description or speculation or criticism are occasionally more striking than their similarities. Their commonality, however, lies in the assumption they share about the role played by the theological practitioner in theological description, speculation, or criticism. All three forms of theological construction are ways of exercising theological authorship. All are ways in which modern theologians have applied their imaginative talent in order to bring clarity to the gospel message, coherence to the Christian tradition, and the strength of the theological virtues of faith, hope, and love to the church. All are ways in which the theologian's creativity may serve the church authoritatively by providing insight into ecclesial meaning that otherwise could easily pass unnoticed.[45] All are ways in which the modern theologian functions as an author and so illustrate conceptions of the theological task that depart markedly from classical assumptions about the proper role of the theological practitioner.

Since the appearance of Kuhn's *The Structure of Scientific Revolutions*, it has become fashionable for interpreters of the history of ideas to regard every twist and turn in the movement of thought and every intellectual novelty no matter how inconsequential as a paradigm shift. This is not the approach we will take in this study. Our paradigmatic division of the eight-hundred-year history of theology as an academic discipline has identified only one consequential shift in theological assumptions. For some readers, no doubt, this restrictive use of the idea of the paradigm will be judged to misrepresent the very pluralism of modern theology. Even if it be granted that the three modern exercises of authorship subscribe to the notion of the theologian's creative responsibility, the diversity among them in their regard for that creativity's power and application may seem too great to warrant their inclusion under a single paradigm. Perhaps this is because we have become enamored of Kuhn's category only as a means of explaining historical variability. The notion of the paradigm, however, is just as valuable for characterizing the unity of a discipline's assumptions, a unity that in the case of modern theology already has demonstrated a capacity to endure for centuries. If we define the romantic paradigm minimalistically in terms of the

45. On this last point, see Theodore W. Jennings, Jr., "Theology as the Construction of Doctrine," in *The Vocation of the Theologian*, ed. T. M. Jennings, Jr. (Philadelphia: Fortress Press, 1985), 67–86.

assumption of the theologian's individual authorship, then its range is wide indeed. It extends to all forms of post-Enlightenment theology committed to the authorial status of the theologian, regardless of the way the power of the theologian's creative talent is conceived or the way the ability of authorship is applied.

The following two chapters will detail the birth of the romantic paradigm in the work of Friedrich Schleiermacher and Johann Sebastian Drey. Their conceptions of theological authorship laid the groundwork for the modern self-understanding of the theological practitioner. Their contribution to the formulation of this conception brought definitive precision to the romantic paradigm in a new wave of theological textbooks that began to appear in the late eighteenth and early nineteenth centuries. The romantic categories in which they naturally and inescapably expressed the emerging paradigm proved to be especially problematic for the Catholic tradition's reception of the theologian's new status.

Part One

Imagination and Doctrinal Development

Chapter One

Authorship in Romantic Protestant Theology

*T*O UNDERSTAND modern theology under the rubric of the romantic paradigm is not unlike a host of attempts on the part of the older disciplines to outline the differences between their pre-modern and modern expressions. Practitioners of disciplines whose histories traverse these periods—literature, philosophy, history, and theology among them—have tried to give account of the variances in method, style, execution, and content that have differentiated their newer from their older forms. This undertaking, however, nearly always addresses the discipline's method or content alone and ignores differences in the way a discipline's practitioner is conceived in one time or another. This inattention poses particular difficulties for a discipline like theology, in which the practitioner's self-understanding reflects the broader structures of biblical, traditional, and ecclesial authority to which the discipline is committed. To some degree, ignorance of vocational practice entails ignorance of the complex ways in which authority is at work in the theological enterprise.

Modern theology may assume that the theologian is an author, but attention to this conception of theological authorship has largely been eclipsed by the work that authorship entails. Perhaps it is not surprising that the actual business of theology, in Kuhn's terms its normal science, has occupied theological practitioners far more than self-conscious reflection on their vocational assumptions. Such may be the fate of any discipline as its workaday routine diverts attention from its abiding assumptions. This inattention to theological authorship has had negative consequences for the church's self-understanding in general but especially for its appreciation of the different and often subtle ways in which authority is conceived and exercised by an influential segment of its members. In the Roman Catholic tradition, this lack of attention to the assumption of theological authorship frequently has hampered the effective settlement of authority disputes between theologians and the magisterium.

This chapter and the next show that the modern assumption of theological authorship has been closely associated with another assumption of the romantic paradigm, that of the development of doctrine. Like theological authorship, the development of doctrine is a mainstay of modern theology. Indeed, its prevalence as a category in post-Enlightenment theology too readily invites its use as a description of the entire doctrinal tradition. This rubric can be employed legitimately to account for order amid the temporal flux of the Christian doctrinal tradition, as it is in Jaroslav Pelikan's magisterial work *The Christian Tradition: A History of the Development of Doctrine.*[1] But its application to the premodern period as a noetic category ascribed to theological practitioners within the classical paradigm is anachronistic. Under the classical paradigm of theological responsibility the *idea* of the development of doctrine was unknown. This fact is frequently overlooked by theological practitioners within the romantic paradigm who fail to recognize that conceptions like "progressive development," "historical teleology," and even "historicity" are products of the post-Enlightenment era.[2] Consequently they do not distinguish properly between the assumptions of their own disciplinary matrix and those of another.[3]

1. Jaroslav Pelikan, *The Christian Tradition: A History of the Development of Doctrine,* 5 vols. (Chicago: Univ. of Chicago Press, 1971–89).

2. See, for example, Hayden White, *Metahistory: The Historical Imagination in Nineteenth-Century Europe* (Baltimore: Johns Hopkins Univ. Press, 1973).

3. Following the lead of John Henry Newman, modern theologians and church historians frequently interpret the entire history of doctrine in terms of the category of development. In this approach, which is perfectly legitimate, a particular doctrine is examined with reference to its successive formulations in the past. To the degree that the history of those formulations is judged to be meaningfully coherent, it is cited as evidence of the doctrine's development. Cf. Jaroslav Pelikan, *Development of Christian Doctrine: Some Historical Prolegomena* (New Haven, Conn.: Yale Univ. Press, 1969). Jan Walgrave is incorrect in stating that the "idea of doctrinal development was present from the beginning in Christian self-understanding and was

Since its appearance in the nineteenth century, the principle of doctrinal development has contributed significantly to the interpretation of the continuity of Christian tradition. The development of doctrine has a become a central presupposition of theological hermeneutics and a fixture in modern approaches to theological method. Although we associate this principle with John Henry Newman's *Essay on the Development of Doctrine* (1845), an earlier, original theory of development can be found in the work of Friedrich D. E. Schleiermacher (1768–1834). It was Schleiermacher's theory that introduced the conception of theological authorship to the Christian tradition.

Schleiermacher was the most influential theologian of early nineteenth-century Germany, though his earlier reflections on doctrinal development seem to have had no influence on Newman.[4] Often regarded as the "father of modern theology," he is most remembered for the passionate style of his *On Religion* (1799) and the professorial thoroughness of his dogmatics, *The Christian Faith* (1821–22; 1830–31), summarily referred to as the *Glaubenslehre*.[5] It is in Schleiermacher's *Brief Outline on the Study of Theology* (1811; 1830), however, that one discovers the first consideration of doctrinal development as a methodological principle of Christian theology.[6] This theological

---

never entirely obscured in the course of its history" (*Unfolding Revelation: The Nature of Doctrinal Development* [Philadelphia: Westminster Press, 1972], 3). Walgrave explains the modern distinctiveness of this idea by claiming that "in recent times . . . the problem arose of how to reconcile the historical facts of development with the claim of substantial immutability" (46). This position fails to take into account that the realist and nominalist epistemologies of premodern theologies could only describe what Walgrave calls development as a newly recognized or discovered noetic correspondence. The idea of historical development—whether organically or teleologically described—cannot be entertained within classical epistemologies.

4. Owen Chadwick notes that Newman could not read German and concludes that Newman did not even have direct knowledge of the theological work of the Catholic Tübingen school on doctrinal development, which was closer in style to his own theory. (*From Bossuet to Newman: The Idea of Doctrinal Development* [Cambridge: Cambridge Univ. Press, 1957], 111).

5. Friedrich D. E. Schleiermacher, *Der christliche Glaube nach den Grundsätzen der evangelischen Kirche im Zusammenhange dargestellt*, 2 vols., 7th ed., ed. M. Redeker (Berlin: Walter de Gruyter, 1960). All references are to the first volume. English edition, *The Christian Faith*, ed. H. R. Mackintosh and J. S. Stewart (Edinburgh: T. & T. Clark, 1968). A complete listing of Schleiermacher's works can be found in Terrence N. Tice, *Schleiermacher Bibliography 1784–1984*, Princeton Pamphlets no. 101 (Princeton, N.J.: Princeton Theological Seminary, 1985).

6. Friedrich Schleiermacher, *Kurze Darstellung des theologischen Studiums zum Behuf einleitender Vorlesungen*, ed. H. Scholz (1910; reprint, Darmstadt: Wissenschaf-

encyclopedia, which blends the explicitly romantic thought-world of Schleiermacher's earliest writings with his, by 1804, growing theological commitments, advances a conception of doctrinal development that envisages the theologian's personal talent as an ecclesial resource. This chapter will consider in turn the methodological matrix of Schleiermacher's theory of doctrinal development in the literary genre of theological encyclopedia, the particular features of Schleiermacher's theory itself, and the important role played in that theory by theological authorship.

FRIEDRICH SCHLEIERMACHER'S ENCYCLOPEDIA

Schleiermacher delivered his first lectures on theological encyclopedia at Halle in the winter semester of 1804–5. Originally appearing in the university register under the title "Enzyklopädie und Methodologie," the lectures were repeated twelve times over a period of almost thirty years, being last read at Berlin in the winter semester of 1831–32.[7] The *Brief Outline* appeared relatively early in this history in the year 1811. The revised version of the text, published in 1830, essentially presented the content of the first edition in a form that aimed at greater clarity.

Schleiermacher's theological encyclopedia was not the first work of its kind but a contribution to a literary genre that by 1811 had at least a forty-seven-year history in German academia.[8] The theological

---

tliche Buchgesellschaft, 1973). English edition, *Brief Outline on the Study of Theology*, trans. Terrence N. Tice (Richmond: John Knox Press, 1970). Scholz's critical edition is based on the second edition of 1830 but incorporates the propositions of the first edition of 1811 as footnotes to the text.

7. For a history of the *Kurze Darstellung* from conception to publication in critical edition, see Heinrich Scholz, "Einleitung," in Schleiermacher, *Kurze Darstellung*, xii–xxxvii.

8. The first work on theological method to include the word *encyclopedia* in its title is Samuel Mursinna, *Primae lineae encyclopediae theologicae in usum praelectionum ductae* (Halae Magdeburgicae, 1764). A brief and general overview of the history of the theological encyclopedia is found in G. Henrici, "Encyclopedia: Theological," *New Schaff-Herzog Encyclopedia of Religious Knowledge*, vol. 4, ed. S. M. Jackson (New York: Funk & Wagnalls Co., 1908–14), 125–28. For a more thorough treatment of the history of the theological encyclopedia, which leads to a constructive position on that history's consequences for modern theological education, see Edward Farley, *Theologia: The Fragmentation and Unity of Theological Education* (Philadelphia: Fortress Press, 1983). Cf. Edward Farley, "The Reform of Theological Education as a Theological Task," *Theological Education* 17 (1981): 93–117.

encyclopedias of the late eighteenth and early nineteenth centuries were not reference collections of learned entries alphabetically arranged to provide an overview of a particular body of knowledge. These works were methodological in orientation and encyclopedic to the degree that they defined the nature of theology, schematized the interrelations of its various subdisciplines, and considered theological theory's practical applications for the life of the church. The early contributions to the genre originated in the eighteenth century's renewed quest for logical rigor and the unity of knowledge. But a more seminal reason for their appearance was the increasing awareness on the part of academic disciplines in general of the need to reconceive their fundamental principles and procedures in light of the new spirit of criticism. In this regard the theological encyclopedia issues from the conviction that theology deserves to be ranked among disciplines responsive to the expectations of legitimate *Wissenschaft*.[9]

The explanation that theologians of the time willingly and happily kept theological pace with the normative criteria of secular sciences cannot account entirely for their particular attention to methodology. The developments in those sciences, especially the natural and philosophical, often entailed the criticism of the Christian tradition and, by extension, the tradition's theological expression. Since Enlightenment thinkers judged the proper constitution of knowledge in ahistorical terms, the historical foundation of Christian truth claims persistently became the target of its rationalistic assault. Enlightenment thinkers vented their usually hostile regard for theology by applying historical criticism to the Christian churches' authoritative mainstays—whether scripture, tradition, or both. The blossoming interest in method that we find in the early encyclopedias attests to

9. The emergence of the genre of theological encyclopedia could be viewed as the first widespread application of historical criticism to the discipline of theology itself. This is not to suggest that the historicocritical method functioned in the eighteenth century as it has in the nineteenth and twentieth. Walter Kasper has observed that the contemporary understanding of historical criticism has been determined by the birth of the positive sciences in the previous century, which has differentiated our very conception of knowledge and its scope. Walter Kasper, "Verständnis der Theologie damals und heute," in *Glaube und Geschichte* (Mainz: Matthias Grünewald, 1970), 18. Enlightenment criticism may have led to the differentiation of disciplinary knowledge, but its practitioners fully expected that its application would distinguish between spurious and authentic epistemic claims and thereby establish the *unity* of knowledge. The theological encyclopedists made this goal their own.

their authors' felt need to justify the theological enterprise in the face of the Enlightenment challenge. In this important regard, the genre of theological encyclopedia increasingly became an exercise in apologetics.

The very structure of the theological encyclopedias provides further and clearer evidence of their authors' apologetic concerns. In some of the earlier encyclopedias, theology comprised the disciplines of exegesis, church history, and dogmatics, a threefold pattern that articulated both Protestant and Roman Catholic assumptions about the proper content of theology current since the seventeenth century. Gradually, and definitively with Karl R. Hagenbach's *Encyklopädie und Methodologie der theologischen Wissenschaften* (1833), practical theology was introduced to this scheme to form a fourfold pattern that endured throughout the subsequent history of the genre. What the three- and fourfold patterns have in common that departs from more classical conceptions of theology is a distinctly modern awareness of the historical dimensions of Christian faith and its theological expression. As we shall see, it was this encyclopedic matrix, with its apologetical concern for the historical integrity of the Christian faith, that gave rise to the development of doctrine as a methodological principle of theology.

Schleiermacher's *Brief Outline on the Study of Theology* is an extremely compact presentation of the whole of theological science. In its final edition, the text comprises 338 propositions to which are appended short, discursive explanations. In Scholz's critical edition the text fills only 131 pages, surprising brevity not only for the author of the painstakingly detailed and lengthy *Glaubenslehre* but also for a contribution to a literary genre in which works at times spanned several volumes. Yet, despite its brevity and formal tone, Schleiermacher's *Brief Outline* proposed an original theological program, though one whose influence on subsequent contributions to the encyclopedic genre has been spotty at best.

As noted earlier, the theological encyclopedias of the late eighteenth and early nineteenth centuries tended to structure their subject matter in terms of the increasingly common fourfold pattern of theological study: exegesis, church history, dogmatics, and practical theology. Schleiermacher did not depart from the theological content presented in the fourfold pattern but rearranged its subject matter into a novel threefold schema that designated the areas of theological study as philosophical, historical, and practical. The result was a new understanding of the very nature of the discipline, which Schleiermacher sketched in the encyclopedia's definition of theology: "Theology, in the sense in which the word is here always taken, is a positive science whose parts are bound into a whole only through their common relation to a certain mode of faith, that is, a certain form of the God-consciousness. Consequently, the parts of Christian theology are bound into a whole through their relation to Christianity."[10] One familiar with Schleiermacher's later work might find his innovation in what one would assume to be his first technical use of the word *God-consciousness* (*Gottesbewusstsein*), the term Schleiermacher employs throughout his *Glaubenslehre* to designate the experiential basis of Christian doctrine. In fact, Schleiermacher did not use this term in the first edition of the encyclopedia but added it to the augmented edition of 1830 in order to bring the theological vocabulary of the encyclopedia in line with his later work.[11] The most significant term in the definition—one that Schleiermacher included in both editions and that conveys something of the innovation he ventured in the encyclopedia—is the adjective *positive*.

Theology, for Schleiermacher, is a positive science, a branch of *Wissenschaft* whose particular content is directed to "the completion of a practical task."[12] The practical goal of theology lies in the preparation of candidates for the ministry and the cultivation of their abilities for roles of leadership in the church. As Schleiermacher notes in his *Occasional Thoughts on Universities in a German Setting* (1808), this sort of training can take place in a university setting only if theology can demonstrate its right to stand with disciplines like jurisprudence and medicine in the curriculum of higher learning. Unlike speculative philosophy, these disciplines are not "pure" but applied forms of science. Whether they complete their tasks in the health, legal order, or piety of the state, the positive sciences, in Schleiermacher's view, render a practical service to culture.[13] In order

10. Schleiermacher, *Kurze Darstellung*, § 1, 1.

11. The first edition of the *Kurze Darstellung* gives a more abbreviated, though similar, definition of theology: "Die Theologie ist eine positive Wissenschaft, deren verschiedene Teile zu einem Ganzen nur verbunden sind durch die gemeinsame Beziehung auf eine bestimmte Religion: die der christlichen also auf das Christentum" (*Kurze Darstellung*, 1).

12. Schleiermacher, *Kurze Darstellung*, § 1, 1.

13. Friedrich Schleiermacher, *Gelegentliche Gedanken über Universitäten in deutschem Sinn*, in *Sämmtliche Werke*, vol. III/1 (Berlin: Georg Reimer, 1846), 580f. Cf.

to do so, however, they first need to establish the theoretical means to reach these ends. In Schleiermacher's day it had long been accepted that jurisprudence and medicine had defined theory for their practice. It was the aim of the methodological encyclopedia to do the same for theology.

Only recently have interpreters of Schleiermacher's thought come to appreciate the degree to which his vision of theology's methodological unity is focused by the continuity of ecclesial tradition.[14] Influential interpreters of Schleiermacher's thought such as Wilhelm Bender, Karl Barth, Emil Brunner, and Felix Flückiger have done much to promulgate the erroneous view that the subjective orientation of Schleiermacher's theology overlooks, and perhaps even denigrates, the importance of tradition for theological reflection.[15] In Schleiermacher's view, the theoretical and practical dimensions of the theological task derive their unity from a "certain mode of faith," from a particular confessional commitment. This commitment is not a lifeless abstraction but is defined, like the theology that gives it expression, by the historical ambit within which the ecclesial community makes and lives by the Christian salvational claims.

The theoretical justification of theology as a positive science, and so as a discipline worthy of the university, requires the theologian's attention to the historical continuity of the tradition the theologian serves. In Schleiermacher's understanding, the theologian must first identify the definitive elements of that tradition. Second, the theologian must elucidate the tradition's past and delineate its shape in the present. Third, the theologian must establish principles for the proper guidance of the tradition in the present and into the

---

Farley, *Theologia*, 85f.; Hans W. Frei, "Barth and Schleiermacher: Divergence and Convergence," in *Barth and Schleiermacher: Beyond the Impasse?* ed. J. O. Duke and R. F. Streetman (Philadelphia: Fortress Press, 1988), 76f.; Erich Schrofner, *Theologie als positive Wissenschaft: Prinzipien und Methoden der Dogmatik bei Schleiermacher* (Frankfurt am Main: Peter D. Lang, 1980), 66–70.

14. See, for example, B. A. Gerrish, *Tradition and the Modern World: Reformed Theology in the Nineteenth Century* (Chicago: Univ. of Chicago Press, 1978), 13–48.

15. Especially pertinent among Bender's several studies is "Schleiermachers Lehre vom schlechthinigen Abhängigkeitsgefühl im Zusammenhang seiner Wissenschaft," in *Jahrbücher für deutsche Theologie*, 16 (Gotha: Rudolf Besser, 1871): 79–146; Emil Brunner, *Die Mystik und das Wort: Der Gegensatz zwischen moderner Religionsauffassung und christlichem Glauben dargestellt an der Theologie Schleiermachers* (Tübingen: J. C. B. Mohr [Paul Siebeck], 1924); Felix Flückiger, *Philosophie und Theologie bei Schleiermacher* (Zollikon-Zurich: Evangelischer Verlag AG, 1947); for Barth, see Introduction, n. 7.

future. This triadic definition of the theological task takes shape in the *Brief Outline* as three general areas of theological study: respectively, philosophical, historical, and practical theology. With these rubrics Schleiermacher offered an alternative to the more customary fourfold pattern of the theological encyclopedia, and with this triadic division he accorded to the historical dimension of theology an importance previously unknown in the history of the discipline. One can best achieve an appreciation for this new orientation by examining Schleiermacher's understanding of historical theology and its relationship to the other theological subdisciplines.

The first area of theological inquiry in Schleiermacher's schema bears an unfortunate title. Understood in contemporary usage, "philosophical theology" might give the false impression that its work is taken up with the reasonable criticism of the doctrine of God and the claims of faith. In Schleiermacher's understanding, the task of philosophical theology is circumscriptive: it attempts to define and preserve the essence of Christianity.[16] Philosophical theology takes its point of departure "from above Christianity in the logical sense of the word, that is, in the general concept of a pious community or a community of faith."[17] This spatial imagery does not intend to suggest that the theologian adopts an impartial, extra-ecclesial position at arm's length from the tradition. Schleiermacher argued throughout his career that the theologian's work is only legitimate to the degree that it represents, and in so doing speaks from within, a particular church. Schleiermacher's metaphor "from above" intends to convey the critical posture the theologian must adopt with respect to tradition if the theologian's vocational responsibilities are to be discharged faithfully. The work of philosophical theology moves in two directions and issues in the tasks of polemics and apologetics.

Schleiermacher's treatment of these theological subdisciplines inverts the conventional understandings of their activities. Polemics is the negative side of philosophical theology.[18] As criticism directed toward the historical manifestation of a given tradition, polemics seeks to identify spurious expressions of Christian faith that arise

16. For a discussion of Schleiermacher's efforts to delineate the essence of Christianity in his theological project, see Stephen Sykes, *The Identity of Christianity: Theologians and the Essence of Christianity from Schleiermacher to Barth* (London: SPCK, 1984), 81–101.

17. Schleiermacher, *Kurze Darstellung*, § 33, 14.

18. Ibid., 23, n. 2.

within the visible boundaries of the church. "There are," Schleiermacher points out, "no fewer diseased conditions in historical individuals than in organic," a simple recognition on his part of the occasional appearance of heresy in the history of Christianity.[19] Employing a motif from Schelling's early philosophy, Schleiermacher argues that diseased conditions in Christianity are departures from its very "idea."[20] Reason abstracts this idea from the multiplicity of historical data which legitimately represent the Christian tradition in its integrity. The idea of Christianity stands as a supraphenomenological norm with respect to which the task of polemics judges the authenticity of the tradition as it unfolds in history.

If polemics is oriented "completely inwardly" as it sifts the tradition for deviations from its essence, apologetics assumes a "totally outward" direction in its attempt to offer a positive definition of that essence.[21] Since the idea of Christianity, or of a specific Christian church for that matter, can never attain pure expression as a historical datum, the work of the theologian as an apologist is never ending. In Schleiermacher's rather nuanced view, apologetics clarifies the essence of Christianity to those both inside and outside the church. The aim of apologetics is not the conversion of unbelievers. The defense of Christian truth is at most an indirect consequence of its primary task of articulating the idea of Christianity in an intellectually respectable manner. By comparatively juxtaposing the many and imperfect historical manifestations of the Christian idea, the theologian as apologist gradually progresses toward a fuller appreciation of its unity, which the theologian must then communicate to the church and the broader culture in which it stands.[22]

19. Ibid., § 35, 15. For a discussion of Schleiermacher's understanding of heresy, see Klaus-Martin Beckmann, *Der Begriff der Häresie bei Schleiermacher* (Munich: Christian Kaiser, 1959).

20. Schleiermacher, *Kurze Darstellung*, § 34–35, 14–15. Schelling expounds his view on the ideal-real antithesis most clearly in *On University Studies*, trans. E. S. Morgan (Columbus: Ohio Univ. Press, 1966), 83–91. For a discussion of the relationship between the absolute and history in the broader context of Schelling's system, see his *System of Transcendental Idealism (1800)*, trans. P. Heath (Charlottesville: Univ. of Virginia Press, 1978), 199–214.

21. Schleiermacher, *Kurze Darstellung*, § 41, 18.

22. Cf. Schleiermacher, *Kurze Darstellung*, § 39, 16: "As one is a member of an ecclesial community only by virtue of one's conviction of the truth of the mode of faith propagated in the community, so also must the orientation of church leadership . . . be directed toward the clarification of this conviction by means of communication."

Schleiermacher's encyclopedia defines polemics and apologetics as exercises in theological heuristics. Their respective concerns encourage the theologian to seek the essentially Christian amid the vicissitudes of time and space and in so doing to articulate a normative spectrum within which theological reflection can be legitimately pursued. These exercises, however, are useless if conducted as ends in themselves. Practical theology is the *terminus ad quem* of the theological enterprise, not only as implemented in the ministerial life but also as the final area of investigation in Schleiermacher's threefold division of theological encyclopedia. While philosophical theology defines and preserves the essence of Christianity, practical theology promotes it by formulating principles for the nurture of Christian life in the church and the state. "As a theological discipline," Schleiermacher notes, "the form of philosophical theology must be determined by its relationship to church leadership."[23] But to be effective, church leadership requires "knowledge of [the church's] situation at any given time which, since [the church] is a historical entity, can only be conceived as a product of the past."[24] This knowledge is the proper domain of historical theology, the area of theological study that forms the center of Schleiermacher's encyclopedia, and, in his view, balances the theoretical and practical sides of theology. Historical theology "presents every point of time [in the tradition] in its true relation to the idea of Christianity," and in this exercise is "not only the foundation of practical theology but also the verification of philosophical theology."[25] Historical theology is the "actual corpus of theological study."[26] Its endeavors center on the historicity of the Christian idea, which philosophical theology defines and practical theology promotes.

Historical theology assumes responsibility for communicating a knowledge of the entire Christian tradition, its past and its present. As one might expect, a task of such proportions requires a theological division of labor. The subdisciplines of exegesis and church history

23. Schleiermacher, *Kurze Darstellung*, § 38, 16. Schleiermacher pursued the subject matter of this final section of the encyclopedia in his later university lectures, selections of which have recently been translated into English. See Friedrich Schleiermacher, *Christian Caring: Selections from "Practical Theology,"* ed. J. O. Duke and H. Stone, trans. J. O. Duke (Philadelphia: Fortress Press, 1988).
24. Schleiermacher, *Kurze Darstellung*, § 26, 11.
25. Ibid., § 27, 11.
26. Ibid., § 28, 11.

elucidate the Christian past; the former focusing on the portrayal of Christian origins in the tradition's canonical writings,[27] the latter on "the total development of Christianity since it has been established as a historical phenomenon."[28] The subdisciplines of dogmatics and church statistics present the contemporary shape of the tradition. It is under the rubric of dogmatics that Schleiermacher includes a consideration of the development of doctrine.

DOCTRINAL DEVELOPMENT
AND VALIDITY

Schleiermacher defines dogmatics as "the knowledge of doctrine now valid [*geltenden*] in the Evangelical church."[29] The ecclesial context of the dogmatician's work specified in this definition highlights Schleiermacher's efforts to situate theology within a circle of faith. A "dogmatic treatment of doctrine," he insists, "is . . . impossible without individual conviction."[30] Dogmatics, however, must not be a forum for the theologian's personal views. Its validity is measured not by its style, structure, or the reputation of its author but by the faithfulness with which it articulates the faith experience of the church the theologian serves. It is the dogmatician's task to bring this pious experience to doctrinal expression.

Schleiermacher outlined his understanding of this procedure in more detail in the introduction to his own contribution to dogmatics, *The Christian Faith*. As the immediate experience of the God-consciousness finds itself conjoined existentially with mediate, historical modifications of self-consciousness, a diversity of pious experience originates subjectively in the individual. The life of piety takes on a social dimension as those who share similar determinations of salvational experience form a church. The more fundamental of these experiences, such as the consciousness of sin and the consciousness of grace, when expressed as the doctrinal proposition (*Lehrsatz*) and its explanation, make up the content of dogmatics—a content that, Schleiermacher insists, must be ecclesially representative and intellectually sound.[31]

27. See ibid., § 103–48, 43–58.
28. Ibid., § 149, 58. Cf. § 149–94, 58–73.
29. Ibid., § 195, 73.
30. Ibid., § 196, 74.
31. Schleiermacher, *Der christliche Glaube*, § 1–6, 8–47. For overviews of

Every student of the *Glaubenslehre* knows that Schleiermacher defines the task of dogmatics in that work as the doctrinal presentation of the "circumstances of the Christian, pious inner life [*Gemütszustände*]," [32] and that he sees this task carried out in the doctrinal account of the inner life as "descriptions of human states of life, concepts of divine attributes and modes of action, or as pronouncements on the constitution of the world." [33] But all too often this delineation of the dogmatic task is cited as evidence of Schleiermacher's subjectivism, his inordinate attention to states of consciousness as a basis for Christian doctrine, and his utter disregard for traditional norms to adjudicate the adequacy of the theologian's work. These criticisms may be understandable in light of the novelty of Schleiermacher's theological program and the ways in which it was conceptually structured and expressed. Measured against the substance of Schleiermacher's views, however, especially their concern for the historical context of Christian doctrine, these criticisms finally are unwarranted. [34]

It would be more appropriate to understand Schleiermacher's conception of the dogmatic task by analogy with romantic explanations of artistry. In describing the communal experience of the church, the dogmatician is much like a theological artist whose work is a particular aesthetic contribution within an infinite spectrum of expressive possibilities. Like the artist, the dogmatician must be sensitive to the ever-changing historical setting within which portraiture—whether in metaphors, colors, or, as in this case, doctrines— is ventured. The dogmatician must possess empathy for the ecclesial tradition within which pious experience flourishes if dogmatics is to capture the nuances of its present state and through such articulation

---

Schleiermacher's execution of the project of dogmatics in the *Glaubenslehre*, see Hans-Joachim Birkner, "Beobachtungen zu Schleiermachers Programm der Dogmatik," *Neue Zeitschrift für systematische Theologie und Religionsphilosophie* 5 (1963): 119–31; Wolfgang Trillhaas, "Der Mittelpunkt der Glaubenslehre Schleiermachers," *Neue Zeitschrift für systematische Theologie und Religionsphilosophie* 10 (1968): 289–309; Richard R. Niebuhr, *Schleiermacher on Christ and Religion: A New Introduction* (New York: Charles Scribner's Sons, 1964), 137–73.

32. Schleiermacher, *Der christliche Glaube*, § 15, 105.

33. Ibid., § 30, 163.

34. Hans-Joachim Birkner maintains that the significance of Schleiermacher's theology lies "not in its radical redefinition of the theological task," but that "in its conception it disclosed a new approach to the Protestant doctrinal tradition" ("Beobachtungen zu Schleiermachers Programm der Dogmatik," 131).

bring to clarity the conditions, hopes, and ministerial needs of the church's faith.[35]

Schleiermacher assumes that the theologian's presentation of Christian doctrine, like artistic production, takes shape within a normative tradition that judges and is judged by its most recent, creative contributions. In the case of dogmatics, this tradition stipulates canons by which ecclesial sensibility abides and that this sensibility inevitably tempers to the present circumstances of historical faith. This process does not simply involve the aimless redescription of ecclesial experience from moment to moment or from generation to generation. The ecclesial tradition, past and present, possesses strong, though not utterly determined, expectations for the proper execution of the dogmatic task. "Doctrine," Schleiermacher states in the encyclopedia, "develops itself, on the one hand, through continual reflection upon the Christian self-consciousness in its different moments and, on the other hand, through the effort to fix its expression more strictly and in the direction of greater agreement."[36] Steady progress toward this dual goal confirms the validity of the dogmatician's work.

Schleiermacher's definition of dogmatics in the encyclopedia qualifies doctrine admissible to the dogmatic system by the adjective *geltend*. This choice of word in the second edition of 1830 was not casual; it is found not only in both editions of the *Brief Outline* but also in the definition of dogmatics given in both editions of *The Christian Faith*.[37] The word is of great importance in Schleiermacher's

35. Schleiermacher delineates this applicative side of dogmatics as follows: "Dogmatic theology has value for the leadership of the church first, by showing in what respects and up to what point the principle of the contemporary [*laufenden*] period has developed itself on all sides and how the seeds of improved formulations yet to blossom in the future are related to this principle. At the same time, dogmatics gives to practical activity the norm for popular expression in order to prevent the return of old confusions and to anticipate new ones" (*Kurze Darstellung*, § 198, 75–76.)

36. Schleiermacher, *Kurze Darstellung*, § 177, 67.

37. The first edition of the *Kurze Darstellung* gives the following definition of dogmatics: "dogmatischen Theologie . . . hat es eben zu tun mit der zusammenhangenden Darstellung des in der Kirche jetzt grade geltenden Lehrbegriffs" (*Kurze Darstellung*, 74, n. 1). The first edition of the *Glaubenslehre* states as its opening proposition: "Dogmatische Theologie ist die Wissenschaft von dem Zusammenhange der in einer christlichen Kirchengesellschaft zu einer bestimmten Zeit geltenden Lehre" (*Der christliche Glaube nach den Grundsäzen der evangelischen Kirche im Zusammenhange dargestellt*, vol. 1 [Berlin: Georg Reimer, 1821], § 1, 1). The second edition offers a single, inconsequential change of word, substituting *gegebenen* for *bestimmten* (§ 19, 119).

theological vocabulary. It does not merely stipulate a quality for admissible doctrine but points to a *criterion* on the basis of which one judges the legitimacy of doctrine. Unfortunately, this evaluative connotation has been all but lost in the reception of Schleiermacher's work in the English-speaking world. The English translations of the *Brief Outline* and *The Christian Faith* render *geltend* as "current" and "prevalent" respectively. In these readings, dogmatics—to use Terrence Tice's translation of the encyclopedia definition—is "the knowledge of doctrine now current in the evangelical Church"[38] In all fairness to the logic of this translation, "currency" felicitously evokes the temporal backdrop against which Schleiermacher envisages doctrinal expression. Yet, in all the definitions, reference is made independently of the word *geltend* to the temporality of doctrinal formulation (for example, the word *now* [*jetzt*] in Tice's translation above), thus implying a redundancy in the translation of *geltend* as "current" or "prevalent." The ideas of "currency" and "prevalence" are too neutral to convey what Schleiermacher intends, since they might suggest that the acceptability of doctrine is governed by its mere appearance in a historical period. Schleiermacher's understanding of polemics as doctrinal criticism is based on the presupposition that doctrinal validity and doctrinal currency are not the same. The fact of heresy in a particular historical period, for example, does not legitimate the value of its teaching.

Schleiermacher's use of the word *geltend* conveys his understanding that a judgment must be made about the legitimacy of doctrine—a judgment that evaluates its adequacy as an expression of Christian pious experience in the present moment. Perhaps this evaluative connotation to *geltend* has prompted its translators to choose their milder renderings. In a note to his translation of the *Brief Outline*, Tice directly states that he chose to render *geltend* by "current" "because it is neutral and its meaning can be more easily supplied in context."[39] It seems that the translation of *geltend* by the word "valid" has been avoided because it would be difficult to reconcile this reading with customary assumptions about Schleiermacher's understanding of theological authority. If Schleiermacher's approach to the theological

38. Schleiermacher, *Brief Outline on the Study of Theology*, 71. Cf. Schleiermacher, *The Christian Faith,* 88: "Dogmatic theology is the science which systematizes the doctrine prevalent in a Christian Church at a given time." The editors' preface identifies the translator as J. Y. Campbell.

39. Schleiermacher, *Brief Outline on the Study of Theology*, 72, n. 2.

enterprise is as subjectively grounded as is often thought, then on what basis could he insist upon the validity of particular doctrines or of doctrinal collocations as such? The rise of biblical criticism in Schleiermacher's day, and through several of his own writings, shattered theological consensus regarding the authority of Reformation hermeneutics. After the Enlightenment the principle of *scriptura sui interpres*, like the biblical text itself, could be invoked as a support for theological opinion but not as a certain and final word on its validity. Moreover, the evangelical church that Schleiermacher represented had no explicit magisterial office to serve as a court of appeal for the proper resolution of theological disagreement.

For Schleiermacher doctrinal validity is neither a quality that can be absolutely fixed nor a normative constant with respect to which doctrinal expression must be aligned. Rather, doctrinal validity is an ideal that may be approximated dialectically but never reached. Anticipating an image found in Schleiermacher's 1818 letter to the philosopher F. H. Jacobi, we might best picture the encyclopedia's conception of doctrinal construction as an ellipse,[40] the foci of which represent two tendencies in the valid development of doctrine: orthodoxy and heterodoxy. These tendencies fix the shape of the theoretical construct that Schleiermacher offered in the encyclopedia to account for the process of doctrinal development. "Each element of doctrine," he observed, "construed with the intention of adhering to what is already generally recognized, together with the natural consequences of the same, is orthodox; each element of doctrine construed in the tendency of keeping doctrine mobile [*beweglich*] and of making room for other modes of comprehension is heterodox."[41] In Schleiermacher's exposition of their meaning, orthodoxy and heterodoxy are not labels conveying the theologian's judgment on the acceptability or unacceptability of particular entries in the dogmatic system but mutually related qualities of doctrine that together capture the vitality of the tradition of faith.

40. Friedrich Schleiermacher, *Aus Schleiermacher's Leben: In Briefen*, vol. 2, ed. L. Jonas and W. Dilthey (1860; reprint, Berlin: Walter de Gruyter, 1974), 351. In this important letter, Schleiermacher describes his mind-set as an ellipse, the foci of which are reason and feeling. Cf. Albert L. Blackwell, *Schleiermacher's Early Philosophy of Life: Determinism, Freedom, and Phantasy* (Chico, Calif.: Scholars Press, 1982), 88–92. For a discussion of the ellipse as a romantic image, see Marshall Brown, *The Shape of German Romanticism* (Ithaca, N.Y.: Cornell Univ. Press, 1979), 127–79.

41. Schleiermacher, *Kurze Darstellung*, § 203, 77–78.

Schleiermacher does not tie the validity of Christian doctrine to its orthodox element. Such an identification would understand validity in a static fashion, much in the manner of the textbooks of Protestant scholasticism whose reputation had been compromised by Schleiermacher's day. The orthodox and heterodox elements of doctrine are "equally important"[42] in the expressive work of the dogmatician. The orthodox element of doctrine represents its "true unity"[43] and its abiding loyalty to the fundamental expressions of Christian faith that have defined the tradition from ancient to modern times. Yet the orthodox element of doctrine cannot stand alone as a representation of Christian fundamentals except as an empty abstraction. In the words of Dietz Lange, Schleiermacher's insistence on the historical character of dogmatics means that the "conception of a timeless, unchangingly valid Christian doctrine is a fiction."[44] Orthodoxy is completely meaningless if considered apart from its dialectical relationship to heterodoxy.

Heterodoxy does not describe professedly ecclesial views which in fact depart from Christian essentials. As our discussion of the heuristic concerns of polemics has shown, Schleiermacher was prepared to recognize the possibility of doctrinal aberration, though he reserved the designation of heresy for such positions. Heterodoxy is that element of doctrine without which there would "still be no conscious and free mobility"[45] in the development of doctrine. The heterodox dimension of doctrine captures the present determination of Christian faith in history and highlights the relationship of the most recent sensibilities of the tradition to the time-honored orthodox expressions of the past. Heterodoxy is the exploratory spirit in contemporary doctrine. It yearns to set sail from the familiar waters of its orthodox haven but only in order to plot a pioneering course through the uncharted seas of the tradition's present vitality and relevance. Heterodoxy is not a quality of doctrine to be avoided but an essential trait of all valid doctrine.

The mobile tendency in doctrine, however, does not alone constitute its validity. Doctrinal validity cannot be tied to either tendency

---

42. Ibid., § 204, 78.

43. Ibid.

44. Dieter Lange, "Neugestaltung christlicher Glaubenslehre," in *Friedrich Schleiermacher 1768–1834: Theologe—Philosoph—Pädagoge*, ed. D. Lange (Göttingen: Vandenhoeck & Ruprecht, 1985), 92.

45. Schleiermacher, *Kurze Darstellung*, § 204, 78.

in its constitution; its normativeness is dialectical and constantly posed anew by the current, though ever-revisable, relationship between orthodoxy and heterodoxy. Each doctrinal tendency isolated from the other leads to doctrinal dissolution. Heterodoxy drifts without direction from its orthodox settings when one "introduces philosophical propositions into Christian doctrine without also desiring to demonstrate, through reference to the canon [of scripture], that they also belong to the Christian consciousness."[46] Orthodoxy ossifies when one "does not desire to fix doctrine beyond the utterances of primitive Christianity."[47] The theologian's failure to appreciate the dialectical relationship between doctrine's orthodox and heterodox elements compromises the validity of theological construction. Such a failure results in skewed understandings of ecclesial tradition in which its truth is portrayed *either* as its past *or* as its present: "Every dogmatician who either innovates or who exalts what is old in a one-sided manner is only an imperfect organ of the church. The falsely heterodox dogmatician will pronounce even the most appropriate orthodoxy false, and the falsely orthodox dogmatician will inveigh against even the mildest and most inevitable heterodoxy as a destructive innovation."[48] "Knowing the changes that the relation of both tendencies undergoes," Schleiermacher insists, "belongs essentially to the understanding of the development of doctrine."[49] In this model, doctrinal validity—to employ two complementary images from the letter to Jacobi—is an *Oscillation* between the tradition's recognized past and unfolding present or a *Schweben*, a hovering, in which doctrinal validity floats above and between its orthodox and heterodox poles, never settling on one or the other but constantly being redefined by the events of the present moment and their continuity with the past.[50]

46. Ibid., § 181, 68–69.
47. Ibid., § 181, 68.
48. Schleiermacher, *Kurze Darstellung*, § 208, 79. In the *Glaubenslehre*, Schleiermacher introduces the orthodoxy-heterodoxy relationship only to reject an antithetical juxtaposition of the terms and the meanings they convey. Without reference to the theoretical model he constructs in the encyclopedia, Schleiermacher points to the misunderstanding he claims is associated with these words in the history of doctrine (*Der christliche Glaube*, § 25, 145–46).
49. Schleiermacher, *Kurze Darstellung*, § 182, 69.
50. For a discussion of the image of *Schweben* in Schleiermacher's thought, see Jack Forstman, *A Romantic Triangle: Schleiermacher and Early German Romanticism* (Missoula, Mont.: Scholars Press, 1977).

DISCERNMENT AS A THEOLOGICAL SKILL

Schleiermacher's revisioning of the concept of heterodoxy in the encyclopedia evinces his commitment to the historical character of dogmatic theology. Since ecclesial experience is thoroughly historical and subject to the conditions of temporality, the doctrinal expression of that experience must reflect its transient dimension if justice is to be done to the present apprehension of Christian truth. How, though, is one to capture in language the present shape of ecclesial experience? How does the dogmatician formulate something as elusive as the present determination of Christian faith shared by a particular church? Schleiermacher recognized two means toward this end: one scientific, the other artistic.

The first involves the work of church statistics, a theological subject matter new to the nineteenth century and on which Schleiermacher was among the first to lecture. Schleiermacher conceives church statistics as a discipline auxiliary to dogmatics, as a *Hilfswissenschaft* that offers dogmatics a "knowledge of the social [*gesellschaftlichen*] situation in all different parts of the Christian church."[51] Church statistics assembles any factual information that currently bears on the identity of a particular church. Scientifically or critically assessed, this data contributes to an understanding of the most recent "state of faith." By comparing and evaluating different modes of ecclesiastical polity, ecumenism, church–state relations, and creedal formulations, church statistics provides objectifiable evidence for the dogmatician's efforts to grasp the elusive manifestations of the tradition unfolding in the present moment.

Yet the dogmatician finds a more fruitful resource for accomplishing this task in the less tangible realm of personal ability. In constructing a dogmatics, the theologian draws on the very skills that define the theological vocation. Some of these skills are technical in character, such as competency in biblical languages, knowledge of Christian history and the organizational prowess required for effective pastoral leadership. But the most important ability for dogmatics is the theologian's interpretive sensibility as a discerner of the "Christian spirit in its movement."[52] Schleiermacher understands the able dogmatician to be one whose presentation of Christian doctrine

51. Schleiermacher, *Kurze Darstellung*, § 195, 74.
52. Ibid., § 188, 71.

voices an insightful discernment of the ecclesial community's affective life. This encounter between a church's experience as a whole and the empathetic appropriation of that experience by one of the community's theologically talented members is the subjective point of departure for the task of dogmatics.

Like so many of the important topics included in the *Brief Outline*, Schleiermacher's treatment of the skill of discernment is too brief to satisfy the reader's interest in this important idea. The only direct reference to discernment as a skill occurs in Schleiermacher's observation that a "dogmatic presentation is more perfect to the extent that it is divinatory as well as assertory." While the assertory character of dogmatics is exhibited in "the reliability of its individual opinion," the divinatory character of dogmatics is manifested in "the clarity of its conception of the entire situation [of the ecclesial community]."[53] The skill of theological divination or discernment is not a criterion for membership in the church. Schleiermacher abides by the classical Reformation understanding of the church as a community to which one gains entry by faith alone. Theological discernment is not an extraordinary form of faith that ranks the theologian above other believers. It is an ability that the dogmatician must put to use in service to the church if its contemporary belief is to be articulated and understood within the larger setting of its developing tradition. Without the workings of theological divination and the expression of its discernment in doctrinal form, the living heterodoxy in contemporary belief would never be clarified for the church, and its understanding of tradition would be fixed on the repetition of lifeless formulas from a bygone time. We can amplify the encyclopedia's terse description of theological discernment by considering two of Schleiermacher's other works, the lectures on *Hermeneutics* and his *Open Letters to Dr. Lücke*.

As was true of the subject matter of theological encyclopedia, Schleiermacher lectured on hermeneutics throughout his career. The lectures on hermeneutics, however, unlike those on encyclopedia, were not published by Schleiermacher himself but appeared posthumously in an edition compiled by his student Friedrich Lücke for the *Sämmtliche Werke* in 1838. A later critical edition by Heinz Kimmerle published in 1974 follows the Lücke edition in making the

53. Ibid., § 202, 77.

lectures of 1819 central to his presentation of the material, as they will be to ours.

In the lectures of 1819, Schleiermacher defines hermeneutics as "the art of understanding," not merely "the presentation of what has been understood."[54] Schleiermacher conceived this art as a general theory and in so doing departed from the customary treatment of hermeneutics in his day as a host of regional theories with special applications to biblical or classical texts. Although Schleiermacher was willing to rank hermeneutics with the philosophical sciences, he judged as erroneous any approach to its undertaking that would seek understanding only in thought. Understanding presupposes an inseparable relationship between speaking and thinking and is, indeed, the "coinherence of these two activities."[55] Speaking is "the medium for the communality of thinking"; thinking "matures through inner speech and, to that extent, speech is only the developed thought itself."[56] Accordingly hermeneutics must weigh the contributions of both thinking and speaking to the act of understanding if the interpretive theory it offers is to do full justice to its subject matter. To this end Schleiermacher proposes that the interpreter address both the "outer" or grammatical and "inner" or technical dimensions of the hermeneutical enterprise. Although distinguishable, grammatical and technical interpretation are as interrelated as the acts of speaking and thinking of which they respectively give account.

Grammatical interpretation situates the text in the "linguistic sphere common to the author and the author's original public."[57] This exercise brings precision to the text's language as a precondition of its understanding. The interpreter relies on various means to reach this hermeneutical goal. Grammatical interpretation may appeal to historical knowledge, sociocultural studies, dictionaries, concordances, contemporaneous writings and the author's larger canon in order to formulate the linguistic meaning of the text. Even though it is fundamental to the art of interpretation, grammatical interpretation can never be completed. The closure of grammatical understanding would require "a perfect knowledge of language"[58] but also

54. Fr. D. E. Schleiermacher, *Hermeneutik*, ed. H. Kimmerle (Heidelberg: Carl Winter Universitätsverlag, 1974), 75. English edition, *Hermeneutics: The Handwritten Manuscripts,* ed. H. Kimmerle, trans. J. Duke and J. Forstman (Missoula, Mont.: Scholars Press, 1977).

55. Schleiermacher, *Hermeneutik*, 77.

56. Ibid., 76.

57. Ibid., 86.

58. Ibid., 78.

the completed contributions of technical interpretation, itself an end-less process.

The designation of the second aspect of interpretation as "tech-nical" mistakenly suggests the more instrumental or mechanical side of understanding that Schleiermacher associates with linguistic analy-sis in grammatical interpretation. Schleiermacher's use of the term *psychological* as a synonymn for *technical* more accurately conveys his understanding of this dimension of hermeneutics. Psychological, like grammatical, interpretation looks beyond the details of the text for its unity. In psychological interpretation, however, "the unity of the work, the theme, is perceived as the principle moving the author, and the main features of the composition are perceived as the author's particular nature revealed in that movement."[59] Focusing on the sub-jective purposes of the author, psychological interpretation concerns itself with what is peculiar to a given text as the product of an individual mind. It examines the work in question in order to de-termine the governing role of the author's intention in the construc-tion of all its parts. This process involves two complementary meth-ods, comparison and divination: "The comparative method first posits the author to be understood as a general type and then seeks the author's uniqueness [*Eigenthümliche*] as the author is compared to others dealt with under the same general type. By transforming oneself, as it were, into others, the divinatory method seeks to ap-prehend the individual author immediately."[60]

Here we meet again, at least in name, the sensibility that Schleier-macher regarded as crucial for the theologian's contribution to the process of doctrinal development. Drawing on a stereotype current in his day and in ours, Schleiermacher describes divination as the "feminine power in human understanding," and one based on the assumption that "each person . . . possesses a receptivity for all oth-ers." Even the comparative method proceeds from the divinatory presupposition that "each person contains something minimal of everyone else and, consequently, divination is stimulated through comparison with oneself."[61]

The procedures of psychological interpretation, especially the role of the divinatory method, inevitably call to mind Schleier-macher's well-known description of the hermeneutical enterprise as

59. Ibid., 103.
60. Ibid., 105.
61. Ibid.

the task of "understanding the text first as well as, and then better than, its author."[62] This subjective side of Schleiermacher's interpretation theory has been highlighted in Hans-Georg Gadamer's influential work *Truth and Method* (1960). Gadamer locates Schleiermacher's original contribution to hermeneutics in the project of technical interpretation and its characteristic method of divination. But, in Gadamer's judgment, this "romantic hermeneutics" mistakenly envisages understanding as the ahistorical psychologizing of the text. It naively expects that an immediate, interpretive sensibility uniting authors across the ages will successfully circumvent the historical circumstances within which all legitimate acts of understanding actually occur.[63]

Gadamer presents Schleiermacher's position stereotypically as a foil for his own emphasis on the role played by tradition in interpretive acts of understanding. This juxtaposition necessarily downplays Schleiermacher's careful attention to the grammatical side of hermeneutics, as well as his insistence that neither grammatical nor psychological interpretation can claim primacy over the other. Schleiermacher understood the method of divination as an important, but not an exclusive, dimension of the hermeneutical enterprise. Most consequentially, Gadamer's exaggeration of the subjective aspect of Schleiermacher's theory overlooks the degree to which that theory mirrors the commitment to historicity and tradition exhibited in the hermeneutical assumptions of the *Brief Outline*. In Schleiermacher's view, the interpreter's understanding can supersede that of the text's author precisely because the interpreter has access to the tradition of meaning that postdates the interpreted text.

Gadamer's stereotypical presentation of Schleiermacher's theory of interpretation also misrepresents the specific discussion of divination offered in the lectures on *Hermeneutics*. Gadamer champions a tradition-based hermeneutics in which meaning is not located exclusively in authorial intention but is understood as a function of the text's meaningful, productive history. In this approach Gadamer believes he differs markedly from Schleiermacher, whose rival theory supposedly advocates a solipsistic, and nearly magical, relationship between a skilled interpreter and an author long dead. Gadamer

62. Ibid., 83.
63. Hans-Georg Gadamer, *Truth and Method,* trans. G. Barden and J. Cumming (New York: Crossroad, 1975), 153–92.

assumes that romantic divination, which he decries, is the interpreter's psychological ability to produce a "re-creation of the creative act."[64] He caricatures this creativity as the interpreter's immediate sympathy for the text's authorial purpose, regardless of the historical distance and cultural limitations that intervene. This view tends to conceive hermeneutics as an enterprise that transpires exclusively between the individualities of the interpreter and the interpreted author and as one involving only the interpretation of past texts.

Schleiermacher, however, understands divination as a talent cultivated through its exercise in the present and in settings that are communal by their very nature. Gadamer virtually ignores Schleiermacher's repeated claim in the mature lectures on *Hermeneutics* that psychological interpretation needs to be grounded firmly in grammatical interpretation, that is, in the communal structures of language and meaning.[65] Even the high reaches of interpretive genius are only possible, Schleiermacher insists, when the insights of divination are set in a fine balance with the results of grammatical analysis.[66]

In addition to his insistence that subjective insight be measured by the communal structures of grammar, Schleiermacher regards divination itself as a power ordinarily practiced in social relations set in the present. "The successful practice of the art of interpretation," Schleiermacher notes, "is based on a talent for language and a talent for the particular knowledge of people."[67] Schleiermacher provides a specific illustration of this application of discernment in his 1829 address to the Berlin Academy of Sciences, *On the Concept of Hermeneutics:*

> Who could associate with exceptionally gifted persons without being moved to listen between their words, just as we read between the lines of ingenious and compact books? Who would not judge a meaningful conversation . . . worthy of closer consideration by singling out its vital points, by trying to grasp its inner coherence, and by pursuing its subtle suggestions further? . . . Now should this art of observing and interpreting experienced, cosmopolitan, and politically shrewd persons . . . actually

64. Ibid., 164.
65. Ibid. But Gadamer qualifies this position in a later essay: Hans-Georg Gadamer, "The Problem of Language in Schleiermacher's Hermeneutic," in *Schleiermacher as Contemporary (Journal for Theology and the Church* 7), ed. R. W. Funk (New York: Herder & Herder, 1970), 81–82.
66. Schleiermacher, *Hermeneutik,* 79.
67. Ibid., 78.

be entirely different from the one we apply to books? . . . I think not.[68]

Indeed, this model of the conversation elucidates the talent of divination by considering its exercise in organic circumstances that are commonplace, social, and transpire in the present:

> But in particular, and in order to abide by the direct concerns of the interpreter of written works, I would urgently recommend diligence in practicing the interpretation of meaningful conversations. For the immediate presence of the speaker, the living expression that proclaims the participation of the speaker's entire spiritual being, the manner in which thoughts here are developed out of the common life—all this stimulates us far more than does the solitary consideration of an entirely isolated writing to understand a series of thoughts at once as a moment emerging out of life, and yet as a moment related to others that are different. This aspect of interpretation is marginalized most of all, and indeed usually neglected entirely, in explaining the author.[69]

Divination is an important aspect of the theory Schleiermacher proposes for interpreting the mind of a classical author. But he did not conceive the psychological dimension of hermeneutics as a craft applied only to the authorial intention of the ancient text. Although its skillful use is a "natural gift,"[70] the rudimentary talent of divination is as universal as the human trait of sensitivity to other persons and is practiced most frequently in ordinary social intercourse. The exemplary practice of discernment that Schleiermacher commends in his 1829 address to the Berlin Academy is an expression of his assumption that divination is a communal sensibility as well as an individual one. Its common basis in human nature provides at least partial foundations for the universality that Schleiermacher expected of a general theory of hermeneutics. This attention to divination in the later lectures on *Hermeneutics* can inform our understanding of the role of discernment in the method of dogmatics.

Schleiermacher's conception of doctrinal validity presupposes that both of its elements, the established orthodoxy of the Christian

68. Schleiermacher, "Ueber den Begriff der Hermeneutik, mit Bezug auf F. A. Wolfs Andeutungen und Asts Lehrbuch," in *Hermeneutik*, 130–31.
69. Schleiermacher, "Ueber den Begriff der Hermeneutik," in *Hermeneutik*, 131.
70. Schleiermacher, *Hermeneutik*, 78.

past and the heterodox faith of the contemporary ecclesial community, must be fathomed in their own right before their dialectical relationship can be appreciated. Understanding the church's authoritative scriptures and confessional documents, the bearers of its orthodox faith, clearly requires a hermeneutical act and so the contributions of the dogmatician's divinatory power. But Schleiermacher also makes the more novel claim that an understanding of the church's present faith requires no less an interpretive act. It is through the skillful application of the dogmatician's divinatory sensibility that the heterodox moment in the development of faith is enunciated lucidly and correctly. In effect the dogmatician "reads" the contemporary experience of the church as the interpreter reads an ancient text or as interlocutors in a conversation "read" each other. The dogmatician may and indeed must appeal in such a reading to the factual, objectively verifiable circumstances of present ecclesial life provided by the theological discipline of church statistics. Ecclesial, like exegetical, hermeneutics possesses a grammatical side. This grammatical interpretation, though, must be complemented by a psychological one in which the theologian's insight looks past the externals of ecclesial life and grasps their true importance for the living spirit of the community in its present state of development.

There is nothing mechanical in the final results of ecclesial interpretation properly conducted. Ecclesial experience in history, like the ingenious book or the gifted person, possesses a rich and complex meaning that cannot be comprehended if regarded only literally or phenomenally. Interpretation of the present state of the church insightful enough to issue in valid doctrine requires the dogmatician to discern the minds and hearts of the community of faith so that the work of the Holy Spirit among its members may be configured in language. This act of discernment, like the hermeneutical enterprise in general, is an art; its accomplishment requires the theologian—in Schleiermacher's image of the Berlin Academy address—to "read between the lines" of the contemporary experience of the church in order to apprehend its ongoing tradition.

Schleiermacher understood his own dogmatics, *The Christian Faith,* as an embodiment of the theoretical reflections of the *Brief Outline.* In his *Open Letters to Dr. Lücke* (1829), his published response to the earliest critics of the *Glaubenslehre,* Schleiermacher voiced his expectations for his dogmatics as a contribution to the development

of doctrine. Aside from the methodological discussions of its introduction, the *Glaubenslehre* drew its greatest share of criticism for its
general treatment of the God-world relationship in the first part of
the system of doctrine. Schleiermacher's consideration of creation,
preservation, and the divine attributes of eternity, omnipresence,
omnipotence, and omniscience as doctrines characteristic of all mon-
otheistic faiths led to the charge that he had engaged in philosophical
speculation under the guise of Christian theology. Even though the
doctrines of the first part of the theological system were not explicitly
expositions of the consciousness of sin and grace, Schleiermacher
maintained that they were genuinely Christian. In the *Open Letters*
he looked forward to the day when his own dogmatic presentation
of them would be widely regarded as such. His expression of hope
for the endurance of his achievement also articulates his understanding
of the theologian's divinatory power in the life of the contemporary
church:

> But if you ask me whether, according to my own views, the
> first part of my doctrine of God belongs yet specifically to my
> individual belief which indeed may exist in the church, but which
> according to my own theory yet deserves no place in dogmatics,
> I would answer negatively. If the usual treatment [of this doctrine]
> is actually church doctrine, then mine indeed is obviously het-
> erodox. But I am firmly convinced that it is a divinatory het-
> erodoxy that in due time will become orthodox, although cer-
> tainly not just because of my book and even if for the first time
> long after my death.[71]

All legitimate acts of theological divination properly yield heterodox results since they are directed toward the present. But, as
Schleiermacher observed to Lücke, the effects of theological discernment are not limited to the present. The divinatory heterodoxy
of today may become the grammatical orthodoxy of tomorrow, itself
standing in dialectical relationship to the heterodoxy of times to come.
By the same token, contemporary acts of theological discernment
frame the established orthodoxy in new perspectives that recall its
origin in the heterodox sensibilities of a time gone by and crystallize
its time-honored value for the contemporary church.

71. Friedrich Schleiermacher, *Ueber seine Glaubenslehre, an Herrn Dr. Lücke,* in
Sämmtliche Werke, vol. I/2 (Berlin: Georg Reimer, 1836), 603–4. English edition,
On the "Glaubenslehre": Two Letters to Dr. Lücke, trans. J. Duke and F. Fiorenza
(Chico, Calif.: Scholars Press, 1981).

TRADITION AND THEOLOGICAL
CREATIVITY

Through his regard for the historicity of Christian tradition, Schleier-macher contributed much to the apologetical program of the late eighteenth-century theological encyclopedists. He recognized that the most effective apologetics the church could practice in its often frustrating dialogue with the "cultured despisers" was one that agreed to meet the Enlightenment critique of Christianity on the battlefield of history chosen by the rationalists but that interpreted the historical character of theology to its own advantage. One might say that the principle of the development of doctrine emerged as an imaginative appropriation of the temporality of faith and its doctrinal expression for theological method. Moreover, the scientific aspirations of the theological encyclopedia influenced the focus of Schleiermacher's model of development. His commitment to a unitive, albeit fluid, conception of doctrinal validity reflects the encyclopedists' quest for the unity and integrity of theological knowledge. Clearly the para-digm of *Wissenschaft* posed by Schleiermacher's idea of doctrinal va-lidity is molded not by the presuppositions of natural science but by those of the discipline of history. Contrapuntally defined by the poles of orthodoxy and heterodoxy, Schleiermacher's conception of doc-trinal validity can be described neither as an abstract absolute nor as a compromising relativism. Schleiermacher assumes that doctrinal validity, like all modes of truth, is an unreachable ideal whose unity must be continuously sought amid the historical realities of ecclesial experience.

Schleiermacher conceived doctrinal development both as a de-scription of the workings of Christian tradition in history and as a theological task that must be accomplished by practitioners of dog-matic method. Especially in this second sense, his views on devel-opment call our attention to the importance of theological talent in this "hermeneutics of faith." Reflecting in the *Brief Outline* on the nature of the tradition's historical progress, Schleiermacher observes that "in each distinguishable [historical] moment, that in doctrine which originates from the immediately preceding epoch emerges as something most determined by the church; but that in doctrine through which the following course [of doctrinal development] is established issues from the work of individuals."[72] The entire church

72. Schleiermacher, *Kurze Darstellung* §199, 76. Cf. §251, 96.

may guard the transmission of its orthodox past to the subsequent generation of believers. But the individual theologian is responsible for discerning the faith of the contemporary church, expressing that experience doctrinally, reconciling this vital heterodoxy with the tradition's recognized orthodoxy, and guiding and promoting the tradition into the future. In Schleiermacher's view these are all dimensions of what we have described in this study as the task of theological authorship.

This analysis of Schleiermacher's notions of doctrinal development and divinatory skill has shown that the rampant subjectivism of which Schleiermacher has often been accused cannot be ascribed to his understanding of theological authorship. Schleiermacher never departs from the view that theological creativity is validated through the favorable judgment of the church's tradition. Should the theologian shirk this responsibility of speaking on behalf of the church, the resulting dogmatics would be a mere testimony of personal opinion and an uncreative failure as an exercise in ecclesial self-understanding.

Schleiermacher's theory maintains that theological creativity, as it originates in divinatory sensibility, plays an indispensable role in the development of Christian tradition. He rejects any conception of theological responsibility that identifies service to the church with the theologian's mere defense of classical orthodoxy. Such a view of responsibility would explicitly deny the relevance of the past for the present, which is highlighted through the creativity that Schleiermacher insists be a part of the dogmatic enterprise. Moreover, Schleiermacher refuses to understand theological responsibility as a search for an implicit, albeit hidden, orthodoxy in the church's contemporary faith. For Schleiermacher "present orthodoxy" is a contradiction in terms. Doctrine may be judged orthodox only in retrospect. From the creative talent of theological authorship issues the church's present self-understanding—valid doctrine—that transient center of the conversation which the talented theologian conducts with the orthodox past. Divinatory sensibility constitutes the depth and range of the theologian's voice in this dialogue. Were this voice silenced, the dialogue between orthodoxy and heterodoxy would immediately cease.

As shall be seen in chapter 3, Schleiermacher cast his understanding of the theologian as a creative agent in the mold of the romantic conception of the hero. This notion has proven to be problematic in the history of theology and a poor model for a contemporary exercise of theological authorship. Nevertheless, Schleiermacher's consideration of some of the basic traits of authorship itself—the first of its kind in the Christian tradition—provides a necessary and valuable starting point for reflection on the exercise of authorship in modern theology.

Chapter Two

Authorship in Romantic Catholic Theology

*L*ISTINGS of Schleiermacher's contributions to theology rarely mention his reflections on doctrinal development. Newman's name has come to be associated so closely with this idea that the theories of an earlier generation of German theologians on this topic, among which Schleiermacher's was the first, have been eclipsed by the detailed historical exposition of the *Essay on the Development of Doctrine*. This has proven to be especially true in the Catholic tradition. Newman penned the *Essay* while still an Anglican, just prior to his entry into the Catholic Church. Yet this work has been embraced by Catholic theology in the twentieth century as an exemplary exposition of the principle of doctrinal development. Although Newman's work entirely deserves this accolade, it is not the first Catholic theory that merits high praise, even if the *Essay* is regarded as the work of Newman the Roman Catholic theologian and later cardinal. That honor belongs to the German theologian Johann Sebastian Drey.

Drey, born in 1777 and ordained to the priesthood in 1801, was appointed professor on the small Catholic faculty at Ellwangen in 1812. In 1817 the Ellwangen faculty was transferred to Tübingen, where a Protestant theological faculty of some reputation had flourished since the sixteenth century. The antagonism and cooperation ensuing from this relationship provided a context for the Catholic Tübingen school's particular brand of theology. Drey's system provided an intellectual matrix for this school. He was among the founders of the still-influential *Tübinger theologische Quartalschrift,* which began publication in 1819. By the time of his retirement from the university in 1846, Drey had cultivated the next generation of Catholic Tübingen theologians, who promulgated his theological vision. He died in 1853.

Although Drey has long been recognized as the founder of the Catholic Tübingen school, his importance in the history of modern theology has been overshadowed by the work of his well-known student, Johann Adam Möhler. Möhler's *Unity in the Church* (1825) and *Symbolics* (1832) were influential in their own day and were quickly regarded as representative of the Tübingen approach to Catholic theology. It was Drey, however, who first united the speculative tendencies of traditional Catholic thought and the Romanticism of his own time in a theological style that continues to be characteristic of the Catholic Tübingen school to the present day.[1]

1. The most significant contributions to the secondary literature on the Catholic Tübingen school in general have been made by Josef Rupert Geiselmann, especially *Die katholische Tübinger Schule: Ihre theologische Eigenart* (Freiburg: Herder, 1964); *Lebendiger Glaube aus geheiligter Überlieferung: Der Grundgedanke der Theologie J. A. Möhlers und der katholischen Tübinger Schule* (Freiburg: Herder, 1966); "Die Glaubenswissenschaft der katholischen Tübinger Schule in ihrer Grundlegung durch Johann Sebastian v. Drey," *Theologisches Quartalschrift* 111 (1930): 49–117; "Das Übernatürliche in der katholischen Tübinger Schule," *Theologisches Quartalschrift* 143 (1963): 422–53; Bernhard Welte, "Beobachtungen zum Systemgedanken in der Tübinger katholischen Schule," *Theologisches Quartalschrift* 147 (1967): 40–59.

Notable among the German secondary literature specifically on Drey are Franz Schupp, *Die Evidenz der Geschichte: Theologie als Wissenschaft bei J.S. Drey* (Innsbruck: Universität Innsbruck, 1970); Wolfgang Ruf, *J. S. von Dreys System der Theologie als Begründung der Moraltheologie* (Göttingen: Vandenhoeck & Ruprecht, 1974); Max Seckler, "Johann Sebastian Drey und die Theologie," *Theologisches Quartalschrift* 158 (1978): 92–109. Abraham P. Kustermann, *Die Apologetik Johann Sebastian Dreys (1777–1853): Kritische, historische und systematische Untersuchungen zu Forschungsgeschichte, Programmentwicklung, Status und Gehalt* (Tübingen: J. C. B. Mohr [Paul Siebeck], 1988); Eberhard Tiefensee, *Die religiöse Anlage und ihre Entwicklung: Die religionsphilosophische Ansatz Johann Sebastian Dreys (1777–1853)* (Leipzig: St. Benno, 1988).

Recently there have been several studies on Drey in English. Of greatest importance is Wayne L. Fehr, *The Birth of the Catholic Tübingen School: The Dogmatics of Johann Sebastian Drey* (Chico, Calif.: Scholars Press, 1981). Fehr's book is a very balanced presentation of Drey's theological system and may be consulted for a bibliography of Drey's writings and secondary literature. Two other book-length

Among the traits typical of Tübingen theology are an appreciation for the historicity of divine revelation and a developmental understanding of the meaning of that revelation in doctrinal tradition. Here the focus will be on Drey's discussion of the second of these traits, the development of doctrine. It is most common for commentators to elucidate Drey's views on the historicity of doctrine by way of Schelling's influence on his later and massive *Apologetik* (1838–47). The concern here, however, will be with the degree to which the literary genre of theological encyclopedia provided a context for Drey's exposition of the theory of doctrinal development and the disciplinary assumption that theologians function as authors within the tradition. Thus, some of the issues raised in the last chapter's discussion of the literary genre of theological encyclopedia will be treated in greater detail. Moreover, the earlier theory of doctrinal development proposed by Schleiermacher in the *Brief Outline* will be shown to have provided an important resource for Drey's own reflections on doctrinal development and theological authorship. In this respect this chapter considers Schleiermacher's influence on a significant aspect of modern Catholic theology.[2] Finally, the birth of the romantic paradigm will be assessed in the encyclopedic matrix of the late eighteenth and early nineteenth centuries.

———————————

studies have attempted to situate Drey in the intellectual context of his time. Thomas F. O'Meara, *Romantic Idealism and Roman Catholicism: Schelling and the Theologians* (Notre Dame, Ind.: Univ. of Notre Dame Press, 1982) considers Drey as one of the first Catholic thinkers of the nineteenth century to recognize the value of Schelling's early philosophy for a theological interpretation of history. Gerald A. McCool, *Catholic Theology in the Nineteenth Century: The Search for a Unitary Method* (New York: Seabury Press, 1977), examines Drey within a broader survey of nineteenth-century theological method, but McCool bases his presentation of Drey entirely on secondary literature. For brief overviews of Drey's theological project, see Joseph Fitzer, "J. S. Drey and the Search for a Catholic Philosophy of Religion," *Journal of Religion* 63 (1983): 231–46; James Tunstead Burtchaell, C.S.C., "Drey, Möhler and the Catholic School of Tübingen," in *Nineteenth Century Religious Thought in the West*, vol. 2, ed. N. Smart, et al. (Cambridge: Cambridge Univ. Press, 1985), 111–39.

2. To the best of my knowledge there are only two studies that examine Schleiermacher and Drey side by side and in depth: Nic. Schreurs, "J. S. Drey en F. Schleiermacher aan het Begin van de Fundamentele Theologie: Oorsprongen en Ontwikkelingen," *Bijdragen: Tijdschrift voor filosofie en theologie* 43 (1982): 251–88; Bradford E. Hinze, "Doctrinal Criticism, Reform and Development in the Work of Friedrich Schleiermacher and Johann Sebastian Drey" (Ph.D. diss., Univ. of Chicago, 1989).

FROM CHURCH HISTORY TO
HISTORICAL THEOLOGY

While the literary genre of theological encyclopedia originated in German academic lecture halls of the eighteenth century as introductory courses offered to divinity students, its methodological project was continued in British and American seminaries throughout the nineteenth and into the early twentieth century. The period after the First World War witnessed the decline of this particular approach to theological method, although it is noteworthy that contemporaries of the stature of Rudolf Bultmann and Gerhard Ebeling offered lecture courses on theological encyclopedia.[3]

Our theological forebears' encyclopedic approach to their discipline's method has been explored in Edward Farley's *Theologia: The Fragmentation and Unity of Theological Education*.[4] In addition to sketching the history of the theological encyclopedia, Farley argues that its project contributed to the loss of theology's unity and to its eventual demise as an ecclesial science. The encyclopedic division of theology into the fourfold pattern of exegesis, church history, dogmatics, and practical theology—each with its attendant propaedeutic, canons of expertise, and auxiliary methods—shattered the precritical unity of theological knowledge and encouraged the conceptualization of theology as an amalgam of technical abilities. According to Farley, the search for the unity of theological knowledge gradually was supplanted by the goal of clergy education. The mastery of theological skills only served as means to the end of professional clerical practice. In Farley's terms, this "clerical paradigm" of theological education replaced the medieval, and for Farley more valuable, model of theology as an intellectual *habitus*, as personal, sapiential understanding. The theological encyclopedia may have begun in a quest for methodological coherence but ended, Farley contends, in the present-day failure to appreciate what is truly distinctive about theological reflection. For Farley the history of the theological encyclopedia catalogs the progressive eclipse of theological substance by methodological form.[5]

3. Rudolf Bultmann, *Theologische Enzyklopädie*, ed. E. Jüngel and K. Müller (Tübingen: J. C. B. Mohr [Paul Siebeck], 1984); Gerhard Ebeling, *Studium der Theologie: Eine enzyklopädische Orientierung* (Tübingen: J. C. B. Mohr [Paul Siebeck], 1975).

4. Edward Farley, *Theologia: The Fragmentation and Unity of Theological Education* (Philadelphia: Fortress Press, 1983).

5. One reviewer has observed that "while not palpably in the literary form of

While I have great admiration for Farley's provocative book, I think that his interest in tracing the growing professional concerns of academic theology diverts his attention from an important dimension of the encyclopedic literature. In his desire to show where the theological encyclopedia has led us, Farley tends to overlook the concerns, motivation, and even hope with which the early theological encyclopedists embraced their task. The encyclopedists of the late eighteenth and early nineteenth centuries may have laid the foundation for the post-Enlightenment shift from theology as sapiential wisdom to theology as the skills of a clerical vocation, but in terms of their own aspirations they are best understood as apologists. The encyclopedists sought the unity and integrity of theology in a carefully structured method capable of justifying their discipline against the onslaught of Enlightenment criticism. The theological encyclopedia may have led, as Farley claims, to the fragmentation of *theologia*, but it originated as a defense of the credibility of theological method. Such a defense, however, required an effective response to the Enlightenment's criticism of the foundations of theological knowledge—scripture or tradition or both. Enlightenment rationalism argued that these revelatory sources of theological knowledge forfeited any rightful claim to truth by virtue of their appeal to supernatural authority.

Ironically both Enlightenment rationalism and premodern theology, in spite of their mutual disdain, shared the assumption that the most meaningful truth was ahistorical and unchanging. Rationalism traced these characteristics to the timelessly regular operations of univeral reason; Protestant Orthodoxy to the supernaturally inspired biblical text; Tridentine Catholicism distinctively to a supernaturally informed ecclesial tradition. It is a matter of fact that the supernaturalistic foundations of premodern theology could not withstand the force of rationalistic criticism.[6] As the seriousness of this criticism became clear, theologians were faced with three courses of action: ignore the criticism, no matter how cogent, and renew one's

---

the lamentation, [Farley's *Theologia*] contains the characteristics of a lament: a spiritual inquietude, an unrest, a sense of loss attached to the uncertain hope that theology can once again become the 'sapiential wisdom' it once was" (P. Joseph Cahill, "Theological Education: Its Fragmentation and Unity," *Theological Studies* 45 [1984]: 334).

6. In another work Farley refers to this phenomenon as the "collapse of the house of authority" (*Ecclesial Reflection: An Anatomy of Theological Method* [Philadelphia: Fortress Press, 1982], 3–168).

theological commitment to the authority of traditional supernaturalism; admit the cogency of the criticism, and understand one's
original confidence in theology as at best a well-intentioned but erroneous stage preceding one's rational awakening; admit the cogency
of the criticism while affirming the legitimacy of the precritical theological vision, if not its simple claims to authority traditionally understood. The first two courses demanded allegiance to a more or
less traditional model of truth as a timeless and therefore changeless
relation. The third course required the reconciliation of truth and
historical development. This was the course chosen by Schleiermacher and, as we shall see, by Drey in their individual contributions
to theological encyclopedia.

As mentioned earlier, the theological encyclopedias of the late
eighteenth and early nineteenth centuries divided the whole of theological science into a fourfold pattern of study comprising the disciplines of exegesis, church history, dogmatics and practical theology.[7] One of the significant departures in this curricular pattern from
pre-Reformation and pre-Tridentine conceptions of theology was a
recognition of the importance of history for the study of divinity.
This shift was signaled by the study of church history as a discrete
discipline. Church history, as a branch of theological science, had its
beginnings in the apologetics and polemics practiced by the Catholic
and Protestant traditions in their respective efforts to justify or con-
demn the religious upheavals of the sixteenth century. In this regard
church history is a child of the Reformation and Counter-
Reformation; in the theological division of labor it was first called
upon to provide data for the legitimacy of one tradition and the
spuriousness of another.[8]

7. The fourfold division of theological study was solidified in the German
academic tradition of theological encyclopedia but can be traced back to the Protestant
theologian Hyperius's *De theologo, seu de ratione studii theologici* (1556). See Farley,
Theologia, 24. It is important to realize that the fourfold pattern was not structurally
presented in a consistent manner. Farley points out that although the content of the
fourfold pattern remains consistent throughout the history of the theological encyclopedia, formal consistency in the presentation of that content was only achieved
through the influence of Hagenbach's encyclopedia, first published in 1833 (101f).
For a discussion of the various ways several of the early Catholic encyclopedists
structured their works, see William E. McConville, "Franz Anton Staudenmaier:
Historical Theology and Theological Encyclopedia" (Ph.D. diss., Vanderbilt Univ.,
1984), 178–81.
8. Cf. Albert C. Outler, "The Idea of 'Development' in the History of Christian

In the early years of the genre of theological encyclopedia, church history was treated either as a subdiscipline in its own right or under a larger rubric devoted to history in general. Samuel Mursinna's *First Lines of Theological Encyclopedia* (1764), for example, ranks church history among a great variety of disciplines, such as biblical languages, rhetoric, philosophy, and general history, all of which are considered to be necessary propaedeutic to theology proper.[9] In his *Encyclopedia of the Theological Sciences* (1798), Johann A. H. Tittmann considers church history as a specific subdivision of "the auxiliary knowledge provided by history," which includes particular forays into topics as wide-ranging and disparate as the "history of the human spirit," "the history of nations," the principles of "historical criticism," and the "history of religion."[10] Marianus Dobmayer's *System of Catholic Theology* (1807) lists biblical studies, history, and philosophy as the subsidiary disciplines of Catholic theology and, in a manner similar to Tittmann's approach, situates church history among the "historical disciplines" that take specific shape in secular as well as in religious histories.[11] The new responsibilities of church history in these schemas were defined by the defensive posture assumed by the encyclopedists in their often strained conversation with Enlightenment rationalism.

But the encyclopedists quickly discovered that the discipline of church history contributed little of value to the advancement of their apologetic position. At their best, apologetics drawing on the resources of church history corrected the gross caricatures of Christian tradition that Enlightenment harangues often produced. At their worst, they begged the apologetic question of their own time by

---

Doctrine: A Comment," in *Schools of Thought in the Christian Tradition*, ed. P. Henry (Philadelphia: Fortress Press, 1984), 7–8. Cf. Adolph Harnack, *History of Dogma*, vol. 1, trans. N. Buchanan (New York: Dover Publications, 1961), 25f. Jaroslav Pelikan maintains that theological sensitivity to history emerged in the context of sixteenth-century Protestant interconfessional disputes. Jaroslav Pelikan, *Historical Theology: Continuity and Change in Christian Doctrine* (Philadelphia: Westminster Press, 1971), 38–39.

9. Samuel Mursinna, *Primae lineae encyclopaediae theologicae in usum praelectionum ductae*, 2d. ed. (Halae Magdeburgicae, 1784), 264f.

10. Johann A. H. Tittmann, *Encyklopädie der theologischen Wissenschaften* (Leipzig: Weidmannische Buchhandlung, 1798), 278–313.

11. Marianus Dobmayer, *Systema theologiae catholicae*, vol. 1 (Solisbaci Typis Seideliani, 1807), xiv–xvi.

arguing from the historical fact of the Christian tradition to its truth.[12] Neither approach, however, effectively parried the critical thrusts of the rationalists.

A more fruitful type of apologetics was foreshadowed in a subtle terminological change that gradually took shape in the encyclopedists' theological vocabulary. By the end of the eighteenth century, the encyclopedic division until then treated generally as the "historical disciplines" and specifically as "church history" began to be called "historical theology." This terminological shift can be seen explicitly in the Göttingen theologian G. J. Planck's *Introduction to the Theological Sciences* (1794–95). In this work Planck treats historical theology as one of the principal divisions of theology proper along with exegetical theology and systematics.[13] For Planck historical theology is distinguishable from the discipline of history itself, which he regards as the most important of theology's auxiliary sciences.[14] But this difference lies only in historical theology's narrower focus, in historical theology's regional application of the skills and knowledge of universal history. While the study of universal history "increases [the theologian's] intellectual range" and "makes the fullest extension of this perspective possible and then gradually habitual,"[15] historical theology draws on these wider vistas in order to bring sharper definition to the temporal events of the Christian tradition. Thus, in Planck's understanding, there is no difference between the task of historical theology and the traditional task of church history.

Like Planck, Johann E. C. Schmidt positions historical theology as the first area of theological study in his *Theological Encyclopedia* (1811), a classic example of the fourfold pattern in its subsequent attention to exegetical, systematic, and practical theology. Schmidt understands the task of historical theology largely to coincide with that of church history, though the concerns of the former are somewhat broader than those of the latter. Historical theology envisages "the destiny of Christianity."[16] This speculative task is accomplished

12. For an example of this approach, see Johann Fr. Kleuker, *Grundriss einer Encyklopädie oder der christlichen Religionswissenschaft*, 2 vols. (Hamburg: Friedrich Perthes, 1800–1801).

13. G. J. Planck, *Einleitung in die theologische Wissenschaften*, vol. 2 (Leipzig: S. L. Crusius, 1795), 183f.

14. G. J. Planck, *Einleitung in die theologische Wissenschaften*, vol. 1 (Leipzig: S. L. Crusius, 1794), xiii.

15. Ibid., 1:260.

16. Johann E. C. Schmidt, *Theologische Encyclopädie* (Giessen: G. F. Heyer, 1811), 3.

not by imagining the direction of its future course through time but by understanding Christianity as the goal of a progressive development stretching from the first inchoate religious sensibilities through more sophisticated religious ideas and traditions to the refinement of its present historical form.[17] In Schmidt's view historical theology is not simply reducible to church history because it must establish apologetic grounds for the integrity of church history, in his case by the triumphalistic argument that the essentially religious nature of humankind reaches its culmination in the history of Christianity. But aside from this speculative introduction, the lion's share of the task of historical theology in Schmidt's encyclopedia is devoted to church history traditionally understood.

In the pre-Schleiermacherian encyclopedias, then, this terminological shift from church history to historical theology was little more than formal, indicating at most the encyclopedists' intention to bring the knowledge of church history within the ambit of theology itself.[18] Although both Planck and Schmidt introduced the new designation of historical theology to the schematic outline of encyclopedia, neither claimed constructive potential for this theological subdiscipline. Both understood the definitive work of historical theology to be the representation of an accurate chronicle of the Christian past and saw its knowledge simply as a source of confessional identity. Schleiermacher, however, gave historical theology a more responsible charge.

In Schleiermacher's *Brief Outline*, a truly theological appropriation of history does not merely sketch the chronological setting, whether ecclesial or extra-ecclesial, in which reflection on theological themes takes place. History is the sphere in which the meaning of

17. Ibid., 4–14.

18. Johann Fr. Kleuker articulated some of the ambivalence and even hostility that some members of his theological generation felt toward the new rubric of "historical theology." Kleuker devotes 270 pages in the final section of his two-volume encyclopedia to the history of Christianity, with particular reference to its history as a church. Kleuker sarcastically refers to this section as "so-called historical theology." He feels obliged to mention the new term but criticizes it, preferring to describe this concluding section as "the history of Christianity and of the Christian knowledge of religion [*Religionswissenschaft*] in its application" (*Grundriss einer Encyklopädie oder der christlichen Religionswissenschaft*, vol. 2 [Hamburg: Friedrich Perthes, 1801], 203–5. In Kleuker's opinion, the term *historical theology* is "inappropriate and . . . hardly suitable to its object" (*Grundriss einer Encyklopädie oder der christlichen Religionswissenschaft*, vol. 1 [Hamburg: Friedrich Perthes, 1800], 5).

salvation unfolds and to which the theologian's creative efforts must attend if the development of doctrine is to become coherent for the church. To the degree that Schleiermacher accepts the Enlightenment's claim for the limitations of human knowledge, the church's historical experience is the foundation of the theological enterprise, and historical theology occupies a central position among the various subdisciplines that this enterprise comprises.

Historical theology relies to some extent on the findings of the traditional discipline of church history. But in Schleiermacher's view these findings are put to the service of a constructive hermeneutics of the Christian tradition. The theological author does not simply consider the possible ways in which past tradition informs the present. Through acts of imaginative construction, the theological author must illuminate the continuity between what has transpired and what might be cultivated in the life of faith as it progresses through time. The task of historical theology involves the theologian's peering through the surface opaqueness of events great and small in the tradition in order to determine both the relevance of the doctrinal past for the present and future directions for ecclesial life suggested by the living heterodoxy of contemporary faith.

It was this romantic revision of the traditional role of the discipline of church history and its classification in the encyclopedic literature that suggested an imaginative reconciliation of truth and historical development. This romantic appraisal of history gave rise to the first methodological treatment of the principle of doctrinal development in Schleiermacher's encyclopedia, a notion that entailed the authorial contributions of the theologian to a Christian tradition now conceived as a fluid rather than static reality. This historical apologetics provided a basis for Drey's theological reflections on doctrinal development and theological authorship.

JOHANN SEBASTIAN DREY'S HISTORICAL THEOLOGY

In 1819 Drey published his *Brief Introduction to the Study of Theology with Reference to the Scientific Standpoint and Catholic System*,[19] a work whose lengthy title announced its author's dual commitment to the

19. Johann Sebastian Drey, *Kurze Einleitung in das Studium der Theologie mit Rücksicht auf den wissenschaftlichen Standpunct und das katholische System* (1819; reprint, ed. F. Schupp, Darmstadt: Wissenschaftliche Buchgesellschaft, 1971).

intellectual rigor of critical analysis and the established tradition of Catholic theological reflection. The opening pages of Drey's encyclopedia adumbrate the understanding of revelation that informs his more rarefied, technical considerations of the encyclopedic outline. "All faith and all knowledge," Drey proclaims in the *Brief Introduction*'s first proposition, "rests on the obscurely felt or clearly conceived assumption that everything finite . . . not only has proceeded from an eternal and absolute ground but also is yet, with its temporal existence and life, rooted in this primal ground and borne by it."[20] The fullest truth of experience lies in its abiding, causal relationship to God's creation and preservation of the world, ongoing occurrences that, from the perspective of faith, coalesce with the events of nature and history. This insight can be dulled by daily cares or lost in the pretensions of a narcissistic ego. But however myopic the intellectual and emotional vision of a particular moment may be, the divine causality remains at work in the mind and heart, its meanings and purposes dimly apprehended in a religious impulse that Drey ascribes to human nature as such. This "inclination, tendency, striving" that religion is seeks the truth of the divine in human history.[21] Drey describes this impulse as a yearning of the inner life "to know the relationship of all . . . things to God"[22] and sees this knowledge embodied concretely in both the order of the universe itself and a supernatural revelation affirmed as the divine plan within a historical religious tradition.

Wayne Fehr has rightly stressed the degree to which Drey's conception of revelation was shaped by his dialogue with the Enlightenment.[23] Drey found the Enlightenment's rejection of supernatural revelation unacceptable but appreciated its expectation that the most profound human truth be apprehensible through the ordinary workings of the mind.[24] The intellect, he claims, possesses the ability to consider the universe "purely as revelation, purely as the work and property of God."[25] Its notions, though, remain a

20. Ibid., § 1, 1.
21. Ibid., § 9, 5.
22. Ibid., § 10, 5.
23. Fehr, *The Birth of the Catholic Tübingen School*, 23f.
24. Abraham Kustermann argues more forcefully than other Drey scholars for the consonance between the spirit of Enlightenment rationalism and Drey's theological project, particularly as represented by his later *Apologetik*. See Kustermann, *Die Apologetik Johann Sebastian Dreys (1777–1853)*.
25. Drey, *Kurze Einleitung*, § 18, 10.

formal, incomplete, and inferior stage in the conceptualization of divine truth. In opposition to the Enlightenment, Drey insists that the fallenness of the human condition requires the prevenience of a supernatural revelation, although he avoids the tendency on the part of traditional confessionalism to conceive of the supernatural as largely foreign to the historical.

The famous essay of the Enlightenment philosopher G. E. Lessing, *The Education of the Human Race* (1780), served as a prototype for Drey's understanding of revelation, though the shades of contrast between Lessing's essay and Drey's encyclopedia are more instructive than their similarities. The opening sections of Drey's *Brief Introduction* reverse the historical stages proposed by Lessing for fixing the proper relationship between natural and supernatural knowledge of God. Lessing, like Enlightenment rationalism in general, judged the claims of traditional supernaturalism to be antiquarian expressions of a truth primitively fathomed. Historically exhausted, they had been superseded by a natural knowledge of God capable of thinking the traditionally forbidden thoughts of human autonomy, the coinherence of providence and the natural laws, and a secular future in which the church's authority had yielded its claims to the power of reason. Following the same lines of historical development to different conclusions, Drey argues that the Christian tradition represents the most advanced stage in the education of the human race, a process unfolded in time and culture as humankind is slowly nurtured in its understanding of God's presence in and fulfillment of history. Drey portrays revelation as the increasingly clearer manifestation of the divine will in the ideas, concepts, and doctrines of the Christian tradition. This developing revelation brings particular shape and growing precision to the natural impulse to apprehend the relationship between the infinite and the finite, as primitive religious aspirations achieve the conceptual sophistication of historical tradition. For Drey, then, this revelational pedagogy moves toward a richer understanding of the church's tradition, and not, as it does for Lessing, to an age of the "new eternal gospel" in which ecclesial tradition has been rendered obsolete by the awakening of the rationalist temperament.[26]

26. See Gotthold Lessing, "The Education of the Human Race," in *Lessing's Theological Writings*, trans. H. Chadwick (Palo Alto, Calif.: Stanford Univ. Press, 1956), 96. For a discussion of Lessing's influence on Drey, see Arno Schilson, "Lessing und die katholische Tübinger Schule," *Theologisches Quartalschrift* 160 (1980): 267–70.

Theology is an attempt to bring understanding to this educative process, which Drey likes to describe as the unfolding of the idea of the Kingdom of God in history. Theology is the "purely intellectual pursuit of religion."[27] Like any intellectual discipline, it "originates according to the necessary laws of human nature in its entirety," the very laws through which "human nature brings greater clarity to its otherwise obscure feelings" and "seeks to establish, in the permanence of concepts, what would otherwise be transitory."[28] Theology is "the construction of religious faith through [an act of] knowing."[29] Drey insists that the noetic construction involved in theological reflection be responsible to the cultural circumstances in which Christianity currently dwells, as well as to the church that the theologian serves. "We regard as essential," Drey states, "a specifically scientific construction of theology according to the spirit of our time and according to the present situation not only of theology but also of Christianity itself."[30]

Both the spirit of culture and the particularities of ecclesial life supply the content of theological reflection in Drey's view, though ecclesial existence remains by far the more important of the two. The church is the "true basis of all theological knowledge," for only within it does the theologian encounter "the empirically given substance" of theology. Within the church, "the theologian's concepts first achieve reality"; outside its boundaries those same concepts "diverge into airy, contentless speculation."[31] Drey, then, understands ecclesial faithfulness as a prerequisite of all theological undertakings. His commitment to this position is embodied in the distinctively Catholic content of the *Brief Introduction*. In spite of the formal nature of its methodological concerns, Drey's encyclopedia remains an unabashedly confessional piece of theological writing.

The body of the *Brief Introduction* is divided into three principal sections: historical propaedeutic, scientific theology, and practical theology. The distinctive aspect of Drey's theological program lies above all in the task he assigns to the discipline of scientific theology. Drey conceives of the qualifying adjective *wissenschaftlich* in terms of

27. Drey, *Kurze Einleitung*, § 38, 23.
28. Ibid.
29. Ibid., § 45, 27.
30. Ibid., § 56, 34.
31. Ibid., § 54, 33.

the model of *Wissenschaft* presented in Schelling's early work, especially his *Lectures on the Method of Academic Study* (1803). Schelling claims that authentic knowledge or *Wissenschaft* occurs in the intellectual synthesis of the ideal and the real. Taken as a general epistemological statement, this description of the constitution of knowledge could apply to critical and postcritical philosophers as different as Kant, Fichte, Schleiermacher, and Hegel. Schelling, however, specifically attempts to portray human knowledge within the divine scheme of things, and applies the colors of his epistemology to a canvas stretched between created and uncreated reality. Acts of knowing emerge from the noetic synthesis of the ideal and the real, a synthesis that mirrors the ontological identity of God and history. Underlying Schelling's epistemology is a monistic metaphysics in which the world is understood as a mode of the divine being itself. As creation is the realistic appearance of God's ideal existence, history is the temporal manifestation of the divine ideas. For Schelling, knowing is at once a transcendental and historical act by means of which human consciousness fathoms the divine mind. Both its ideal and real dimensions contribute to the apprehension of divine truth, though Schelling maintains that such truth is grasped only contingently through history. The noetic synthesis of the ideal and the real characteristic of proper thinking elevates the relativity of history to the intellectual necessity of absolute knowledge. Schelling regards *Wissenschaft* as nothing less than the conceptual apprehension of the divine ideas.

Drey's conception of scientific theology relies to a great extent on the epistemology of Schelling's romantic idealism. For Drey, proper theological knowledge is an intellectual synthesis of the all-embracing divine idea of the Kingdom of God, the manifestations of which continually appear in history. The constructive goal of scientific theology is to raise the relativity of historical faith to the epistemic necessity of the theological concept. Theology that is truly *wissenschaftlich* attains a level of conceptual determinateness and stability that participates in the inner necessity of the divine idea.[32] Yet Drey balances this obviously speculative approach to theological method with a historical one. While Schelling's monism enables him

32. For a detailed explanation of Drey's conception of scientific theology, see Schupp, *Die Evidenz der Geschichte*, 130–44; Fehr, *The Birth of the Catholic Tübingen School*, 73–176.

to avoid the Cartesianism of his idealist precursors and to take history more seriously than they, historical knowledge remains for him but an inferior stage anticipating the logical necessity of legitimate science. As a Catholic theologian, Drey presupposes that history is the medium of divine revelation. The truth of ecclesial tradition is an indispensable foundation for theological concepts, which, rather than overcoming, articulate and preserve their historical roots. The truth of scientific theology may take conceptual form, but its substance is the self-revelation of God in history.

The first section of the *Brief Introduction* provides Drey with an occasion to reflect on the importance of history and historical understanding for theological reflection, for here he examines the historical propaedeutic to scientific theology. In fact, Drey understands the entire subject matter of the first section of the encyclopedia—which includes exegesis, biblical philology, hermeneutics, and theoretical considerations of the nature of history—to constitute the work of historical theology in general.[33] It is under the rubric of historical theology proper, however, that Drey sketches the theological understanding of history on which he bases his theory of doctrinal development.

Drey follows Schleiermacher in rejecting the full theological value of chronological history, even when its subject matter is church history. The chronicle presents facts accurately but is unable to grasp the overarching meaning of successive events. In his discussion of historical theology in the *Brief Outline*, Schleiermacher speaks of the need to complete chronological history with an interpretive overview of historical data aiming at "the particular spirit of the whole, perceived as a movement."[34] Drey's direct indebtedness to Schleiermacher's encyclopedia can be seen in his commitment to this notion of tradition, although Drey articulates this romantic view of history even more forcefully. The chronicles on which the history of Christianity is based are "indispensable" and "of the greatest usefulness" for a larger understanding of the historical enterprise.[35] But in and

33. "Indeed, to conceive and present [Christianity in its entirety] in a purely historical fashion is the business of historical theology or, as I call it, historical propaedeutic" (Drey, *Kurze Einleitung*, § 107, 73).

34. Friedrich Schleiermacher, *Kurze Darstellung des theologischen Studiums zum Behuf einleitender Vorlesungen*, ed. H. Scholz (1910; reprint, Darmstadt: Wissenschaftliche Buchgesellschaft, 1973), § 150, 59.

35. Drey, *Kurze Einleitung*, § 218, 147.

of themselves they are deficient. A theological interpretation of factual occurrences requires what Drey calls a "higher concept of history." Such a view perceives the passing of time as "the striving and weaving of *a single spirit*, which breaks forth from the spiritual currents of an age to form its own particularity; which *through the power of its influence* draws everything into its circle, shaping the malleable according to itself and destroying all resistance."[36]

While all events of historical consequence require the coherence provided by this perspective, those of the Christian tradition actually encourage their interpretation in this manner. By its very nature, Christian tradition "designates, strictly and exactly, the spirit from which it derives all of its developments."[37] That unity of the tradition, everything about it that is particular and essential, must occupy the attention of historical theology. But the unity of the tradition, the heart of its faith and the common core of the church, only appears as a historical development that courses purposively through time and culture. Such a developmental understanding of history was foreign to those who lived even a generation earlier than Drey. Yet he insists that any historical presentation of Christianity that begins with a different view of history "contradicts Christianity, is unchristian and untheological."[38]

This "higher concept of history" governs Drey's understanding of historical theology in the *Brief Introduction*. He notes that there is a distinctively Catholic perspective on this theological subdiscipline which he locates in the presupposition that for "the understanding

36. Ibid., § 175, 118.
37. Ibid.
38. Ibid. Franz Schupp claims that the conception of history espoused by the Catholic Tübingen school resulted primarily from the influence of German idealism ("Die Geschichtsauffassung der Tübinger Schule und in der gegenwärtigen Theologie," *Zeitschrift für katholische Theologie* 91 [1969]: 152). This judgment is perfectly acceptable as long as it does not overlook Schleiermacher's influence on Drey. In another article Schupp argues cogently that, contrary to frequent characterizations, Romanticism can be defined not by its proponents' devotion to experiential immediacy but by the rejection of the immediate, ahistorical character of Enlightenment reason in favor of the principle of historical mediation ("Reflexion zwischen Aufklärung und Romantik," *Zeitschrift für katholische Theologie* 95 [1973]: 325). Assuming the aptness of Schupp's characterization, it would be fair to say that Drey's "higher concept of history" is an expression of the definitive concerns of the romantic temperament.

of Christianity, its further development is just as important and necessary an object as its primitive history."[39] Drey clarifies this conception of ecclesial tradition in his discussion of historical theology proper, which centers on a distinction he makes between the inner and outer history of Christianity. The outer history of Christianity comprises the "history of [its] destiny."[40] It examines the struggle between Christianity and culture and is accessible to believer and unbeliever alike as the narrative of world history. The inner history of Christianity issues from the interpretation of those historical appearances "in which the productivity of Christianity freely emerges, in which its spirit immediately expresses itself and takes shape as phenomenal reality."[41] Only the believer can appreciate Christianity's inner history, for its truth can be seen only through the eyes of the church's shared faith.

Apologetical concerns motivate Drey's distinction between the inner and outer history of Christianity, a distinction he hopes will rescue the truth claims of Christianity from Enlightenment criticism. His conception of historical theology understands history as a course plotted by the ever-renewed encounter between humankind and the all-embracing truth of Christian tradition fixed in its central idea of the Kingdom of God. This idea appears historically in innumerable forms, its progressive development always yielding thought, action, and community, which mold its essential traits to the circumstances of hour and place. For Drey the truth of the Catholic doctrinal tradition is embodied in and as this development. In his view the inner spirit of Catholicism, its most sublime truth, is found neither in world history nor even in church history but only in the ecclesial tradition that historical theology recognizes and scientific theology constructs.

DOCTRINAL DEVELOPMENT AND LIVING TRADITION

The inner or essential history of Christianity evinces the meaning of tradition both doctrinally and devotionally, two approaches that Drey distinguishes respectively as the history of Christian ideology and the history of Christian ecclesial society (*Kirchengesellschaft*). Doctrine is the ideal side of theological knowledge and provides the intellectual

39. Drey, *Kurze Einleitung*, § 174, 118.
40. Ibid., § 180, 121.
41. Ibid., § 177, 119.

underpinnings for the devotional life of the church, the realistic dimension of theological knowledge. In Drey's view only a developmental account of doctrine can be true to the history of Christianity, the subject matter of historical theology. But Drey does not understand the theologian's attention to doctrinal development only as a descriptive enterprise. Doctrinal development is a constructive task accomplished in the work of scientific theology, one that calls for the creative use of theological talent.

In his earlier writings and lectures, Drey was most fond of using organic images and metaphors to conceptualize both the history of theology and doctrinal development. His first published essay, *Revision of the Present Situation of Theology* (1812), outlines a speculative history of theology from medieval scholasticism to his own time. His narrative charts what he sees as the gradual and unfortunate surrender of theology's mystical spirit and scientific form to the recent encroachments of intellectual lifelessness: literalism, empiricism, and naturalism. Drey argues that only a view of history as a living organism can restore lost vitality to theology and the doctrinal tradition of the church.[42] Drey's lecture notes from 1812–13, published posthumously under the title "Ideas on the History of the Catholic System of Dogma," employ a variety of tropes—aesthetic, geometric, natural scientific, and, following Lessing, pedagogical—to depict doctrinal development, but here too biological metaphors predominate. Theology requires a systematic approach to history that is possible only if a temporal event can be conceived as "a development from a kernel and seed," itself the "seed of many other developments."[43] The Catholic system of dogma can truly be expounded only from the perspective of the "living element [*Lebenspunkt*] of its history."[44] A simple chronicle of the doctrinal formulas of the past is incapable of this conceptualization, which requires that the theologian perceive "the whole [of history] as enlivened [*belebt*] by an inner spirit."[45]

42. Johann Sebastian Drey, "Revision des gegenwärtigen Zustandes der Theologie," in *Revision von Kirche und Theologie: Drei Aufsätze*, ed. F. Schupp (Darmstadt: Wissenschaftliche Buchgesellschaft, 1971), 3–26, esp. 13–15, 17, 22. English edition, "Toward the Revision of the Present State of Theology," in *Romance and the Rock: Nineteenth-Century Catholics on Faith and Reason*, ed. J. Fitzer (Minneapolis: Fortress Press, 1989), 60–73.

43. Johann Sebastian Drey, "Ideen zur Geschichte des katholischen Dogmensystems," in *Geist des Christentums und des Katholizismus*, ed. J. R. Geiselmann (Mainz: Matthias Grünewald, 1940), 240–41.

44. Ibid., 241.

45. Ibid., 238. For a discussion of the theological use of such tropes, see Wilhelm

Several years later, however, for the pages of the *Brief Introduction to the Study of Theology*, Drey chose a more technical, dialectical illustration of the process of doctrinal development. A synoptic presentation of this model and the explanation of doctrinal development offered by Schleiermacher in his encyclopedia will illustrate Drey's direct reliance on the *Brief Outline* for the exposition of his theory.

As explained in the previous chapter, Schleiermacher conceives of doctrinal development as a dialectical exchange between two elements in all valid doctrinal expression: orthodoxy and heterodoxy. "Each element of doctrine," Schleiermacher states, "construed with the intention of adhering to what is already generally recognized, together with the natural consequences of the same, is orthodox; each element of doctrine construed in the tendency of keeping doctrine mobile [*beweglich*] and of making room for other modes of comprehension is heterodox."[46]

To this passage, Drey's reception of the same bipolar model stands as a striking parallel: "a complete system of [doctrinal] concepts that is thought of not as dead tradition from a time gone by but as the development of a living tradition necessarily bears within it a twofold element: a *fixed* aspect and a *mobile* aspect."[47]

Both Schleiermacher and Drey agree that doctrine does not represent a static truth that is in but not of history. Doctrines from past times possess the sort of stability that accompanies any historical facticity. But both theologians refuse to understand Christian tradition as the unchanging communication of doctrines formulated in the past from generation to generation. Both conceive the doctrinal tradition as a hermeneutical interplay between past and present faith in which the stable or received aspect of doctrine is enlivened by the contemporary faith of the church, and the abiding aspects of the tradition's present mobility eventually form the doctrinal stability received by future generations of believers. Both Schleiermacher and Drey consider the mobile aspect of doctrine to be indispensable to the meaningful expression of Christian truth. Drey, however, was

---

Maurer, "Der Organismusgedanke bei Schelling und in der Theologie der katholischen Tübinger Schule," *Kerygma und Dogma* 8 (1962): 202–16.

46. Schleiermacher, *Kurze Darstellung*, § 203, 77–78.

47. Drey, *Kurze Einleitung*, § 256, 170. Karl-Heinz Menke has noted Drey's reliance on Schleiermacher's dialectical model of development: "Definition und speculative Grundlegung des Begriffes 'Dogma' im Werke Johann Sebastian von Dreys (1777–1853)," *Theologie und Philosophie* 52 (1977): 188.

unwilling to follow entirely the lead set by Schleiermacher in his treatment of the doctrinal past.

According to Drey, the fixed aspect of doctrine is "that which is *completed* [*Abgeschlossene*] through previous development."[48] Doctrine that has reached conceptual completeness is designated "dogma," and Drey regards this completeness as the church's "single, objectively . . . valid criterion of Christian *truth*."[49] This understanding of normativeness sounds, and in many respects is, rather traditional. As dependent on Schleiermacher as Drey was for the broad strokes of his theory of doctrinal development, he clearly parted company with Schleiermacher in his understanding of validity. For Schleiermacher, doctrinal validity is a relational notion defined by both the orthodox and heterodox tendencies in current doctrinal expression. Schleiermacher refuses to equate doctrinal validity with the fixed or, in his terminology, orthodox aspect of doctrine. Valid doctrine is shaped by the ever-changing relation between the orthodox past and the heterodox present and configured by the talented theologian in a dogmatic presentation of doctrine that expresses the faith of a particular Christian church. By comparison, Drey's conception of validity is less fluid. In fact, his definition of validity as the completeness of received dogma or the church's deposit of orthodox faith seems to commend a classical norm for theology at odds with the romantic view of history that Drey otherwise makes the center of his theology. The theme of doctrinal mobility, on which Schleiermacher's encyclopedia again proved instructive, provided Drey with a category for describing the place of contemporary belief in normative Catholic tradition.

The mobile aspect of doctrine, Drey states, is "that in the development which is yet conceiving [doctrinal truth]."[50] While it is still mobile, the theological concept lacks the fixity of dogma. Its historical course has not reached its destination of completeness, and its truth continues to develop. Drey observes that "insofar as disagreement prevails concerning it among investigators in the church and in the academy [*Schule*] it is called *scholastic opinion* [*Schulmeynung*] [or] *theological opinion*."[51] This designation of the mobile aspect of

48. Drey, *Kurze Einleitung*, § 256, 170.
49. Ibid., § 258, 171.
50. Ibid., § 256, 170–71.
51. Ibid., § 258, 171.

doctrine as "opinion," however, is not pejorative. We should recall that the doctrinal mobility that theological opinion articulates is a vital constituent of tradition. Neither should Drey's distinction between dogma and theological opinion be taken to suggest that dogma exhausts the tradition's truth. In spite of the disagreement that characterizes theological opinion, Drey claims that "it can in itself still be Christian truth, which only is not yet developed to the level that it can be universally recognized as such in the church."[52] Such truthful opinion is "implicit dogma," whose further development to completeness may lead to universal ecclesial recognition of its truth and thus to its redefinition as "declared dogma."[53] "Therefore, and because," Drey maintains, "it is the nature of the Christian doctrinal concept always to develop itself more clearly . . . , opinions are not merely a contingent, but a necessary object of dogmatic-moral inquiries and presentations."[54]

We should note Drey's willingness to affirm the authority of completed doctrine or dogma and be aware of the degree to which this affirmation exceeds the authority that Schleiermacher was willing to grant to the category of orthodox doctrine in his own model of development. Drey, however, is able to affirm traditional authority without accepting a classical notion of theological responsibility. Dogma is not an immutable expression of divine truth. Its completeness is that of conceptual clarity achieved by the church, not of an ahistorical enshrinement that resists reinterpretation. In Drey's theory of development, dogma functions as an ecclesial guideline for theological speculation. Apart from its heuristic relationship to the mobile aspect of doctrine, dogma would not share in the vitality of tradition.

This definition of orthodoxy clarifies the regulative role Drey assigns to dogma in his theological encyclopedia. Orthodoxy is the "striving to preserve the completed aspect in the doctrinal concept and to construct the mobile aspect in the sense of the completed aspect and in agreement with it."[55] The corruption of orthodoxy may take the form of either heterodoxy or hyperorthodoxy. Heterodoxy stems from failure to respect the dogmatic guideline; it is the "striving

52. Ibid., § 258, 171–72.
53. Ibid., § 257, 171.
54. Ibid., § 258, 172.
55. Ibid., § 260, 173.

to make the fixed aspect mobile or to construct the mobile in opposition to the fixed."[56] Hyperorthodoxy is best conceived as theological complacency; it is the attitude of "one who finally negates all mobility of the doctrinal concept, since such a person either denies it generally or raises opinion to the level of dogma."[57] Living or orthodox tradition possesses both fixed and mobile aspects, each of which complements the other. A one-sided presentation of the fixed aspect results in an empty symbolics, a petrified documentation of the dogmatic past. A one-sided presentation of doctrine's mobile aspect results in a wandering scholasticism, fanciful theological speculation without normative guidance. "True dogmatics," Drey asserts, "is neither mere symbolics nor mere scholasticism, but the joining of the two."[58]

The extent to which Drey adapts Schleiermacher's theological vocabulary illustrates his sensitivity to the novelty of the theory of development for a tradition committed to the doctrinal and theological heritage of Trent. While Schleiermacher uses the term *orthodoxy* for the accepted doctrines of the past, Drey refers to such doctrines as the *fixed* aspect of living tradition and defined orthodoxy as the legitimate relationship between past and present doctrine. Schleiermacher expresses this relational balance between past and present as "doctrinal validity," intending, no doubt, to avoid the implication that validity can be found only in the old dogmatics of Protestant orthodoxy.[59] Drey speaks of doctrine's validity only in terms of its orthodoxy, using the language of the classical paradigm to express a decidedly romantic conception of doctrine. He is also unwilling to follow Schleiermacher in designating the mobile aspect of doctrine as heterodoxy. Although this term has positive connotations for Schleiermacher as an expression of the vitality of the doctrinal present, Drey reserves the term for doctrinal corruption.

56. Ibid.
57. Ibid.
58. Ibid., § 263, 175.
59. In the preface to the first volume of his later *Apologetik*, Drey distances himself even further from Schleiermacher by criticizing the inability of his understanding of doctrinal validity to distinguish clearly in the present moment between essential and unessential elements in the content of Christianity. Johann Sebastian Drey, *Die Apologetik als wissenschaftliche Nachweisung der Göttlichkeit des Christentums in seiner Erscheinung*, vol. 1 (1838; reprint, Frankfurt am Main: Minerva, 1967), iv–v.

The differences between Schleiermacher's and Drey's dialectical models are not merely semantic. Although both positions conceive doctrinal validity as an intersection between past and present faith, Schleiermacher's utterly relational model does not recognize the possibility of doctrinal completeness which Drey ascribes to dogma. Using terms suggested by Brian Gerrish, we might say that Schleiermacher regards the historical object of theological reflection as *ein Werdendes*, while for Drey it remains *ein Gewordenes*.[60] The heuristic role of dogma in Drey's theory of development lends a degree of objectivity to his conception of doctrinal validity that distinguishes it from Schleiermacher's and indirectly voices his commitment to an ecclesial tradition that respects the authority of the magisterium. A consequence of his approach is that the power he accords to theological talent is qualified by a visible, institutional authority that stands as a criterion for the theologian's constructive efforts. His somewhat more modest view on the power of theological talent, however, did not prevent Drey from supporting the basic notion of theological authorship that he found in Schleiermacher's encyclopedia.

THE RELIGIOUS SENSE AS
ECCLESIAL DISCERNMENT

Drey's "higher concept of history" might give the impression that doctrinal development is the inexorable movement of a common spirit that creates the symbolic world independently of individual human actions. Such is not the case. The theologian "as a teacher in the church is called to cooperate" in the process of doctrinal development.[61] Drey maintains that "the impulse to further developments and to the clear determination of [doctrinal] concepts . . . can only proceed from individuals."[62] Theological opinion stimulates the development of doctrine, as individual insight apprehends the meaning

60. The comparison Gerrish offers between Schleiermacher and Newman applies as readily to Schleiermacher and Drey: "But there remains an apparent difference between Schleiermacher's notion of development and, say, the notion later put forward by John Henry Newman, who had no thought of discarding dogmas but only of showing how they came to be. If for Schleiermacher the datum of reflection was *ein Werdendes*, for Newman it was, so to say, *ein Gewordenes*" ("From 'Dogmatik' to 'Glaubenslehre': A Paradigm Change in Modern Theology," in *Paradigm Change in Theology*, ed. H. Küng and D. Tracy, trans. M. Köhl [New York: Crossroad, 1989], 163).

61. Drey, *Kurze Einleitung*, § 258, 172.

62. Ibid., § 259, 172.

of the ecclesial present and suggests creative ways of understanding its relationship to established tradition. Like Schleiermacher, Drey thinks of the development of doctrine as a theological task, though he devotes far more space than Schleiermacher did to a discussion of the talent from which this task proceeds.

Theological talent, Drey notes, possesses many of the same characteristics of academic talent in general and has similar uses. It requires the "talent of historical and philosophical construction," "no ordinary memory" for comprehending large measures of historical information, "no ordinary power of reasoning and acumen" for distinguishing between the true and the false, "no ordinary power of judgment" in all these matters, and the "entirely individual gift" of communicating the results of these skills effectively.[63] Like all accomplished scientific inquiry, theology requires an extraordinary ability that Drey calls a "lively sense for the true."[64] This sense is the gift of insight or discernment. Dwelling in the heart as zeal and guiding the intellect as commitment, it takes on a specifically theological cast in what Drey calls the sense for the holy or the religious sense. This disposition cannot be identified with religiosity in general or with the capacity to be affected by religious feelings, since these qualities are quite ordinary both within and outside the church. The religious sense is the talent by means of which the theologian divines the meaning of ecclesial tradition, especially the continuity between its most recent expressions and those of its past. It is, Drey observes,

> that organization of the spirit by virtue of which the lively sense for the holy, as well as the respect and love for it, has attained such a dominance over the remaining intellectual and moral powers that they willingly serve the dominating sense with their entire activity; that, for example, the understanding, the power of judgment, and the imagination seek no other objects of their concern than the religious or those related to the religious; that the powers striving practically toward the outside world set for themselves no other goal than the dissemination of religion, the furthering of religiosity.[65]

The religious sense requires such theological singlemindedness or concentration if it is successfully to discern the truth of God developing historically in the church. Every able theologian possesses this ability, which establishes the very possibility of the theological task.

63. Ibid., § 100, 67.
64. Ibid., § 101, 67.
65. Ibid., § 102, 69.

As was true of Schleiermacher's conception of theological divination, Drey's reflections on the religious sense can be appreciated
more fully when placed in the context of his understanding of hermeneutics. According to Drey, the lion's share of the exegete's work
involves painstaking attention to detail as the text is examined gram-
matically, historically, and as an expression of its author's individuality. In coming to an initial appreciation of its meaning, the exegete
must attend to the letter of the text and the nuances of its language,
as well as to its sociocultural setting and historical circumstances.
The exegete must also consider the author's ideas as more than products of received language and history, as ideas that may veer from
the usual directions of their time and culture and set new courses in
the history of thought. Interpretation of this sort proceeds method-
ically and requires abilities of the exegete that can be refined by
practice and augmented by study.

The art of interpretation, though, aims at a deeper understanding
of the text achieved through "a special talent whose deficiency cannot
be replaced by principles and rules."[66] In the act of interpretation,
Drey observes, one "must situate oneself in the place of the author,
transform oneself, so to speak, into the author, and now construct
[*construieren*] anew what the author originally produced. This is called
the process of reconstruction [*Nachconstruieren*], and in this ability
. . . to transform oneself into an unfamiliar author lies the vocational
call of the interpreter to [the exegetical] office."[67]

This description calls to mind Schleiermacher's understanding
of psychological interpretation, specifically the role played by the
talent of divination in hermeneutics. Like divination, the process of
reconstruction transcends the more analytic levels of understanding
by entering into sympathetic relationship with the authorial mind
behind the text. Empathy, however, is only an initial stage in this
process. The goal of reconstructive interpretation is not only to reach
back into history to grasp an authorial intention hidden to conventional readings but to propose creative ways in which that past meaning might be brought to life for contemporary understanding.

Just as Schleiermacher envisioned a theological application of
hermeneutical talent, so too did Drey. Theological study, Drey
claims, possesses objective conditions defined by the mastery of technique and the enhancement of the theologian's skills through practice.

66. Ibid., § 161, 109.
67. Ibid.

But theological study presupposes "other, more subjective conditions" that stem from "the personal relationship of the student to the discipline [*zu seiner Wissenschaft*]."[68] While proficiency in theological skills can increase through training, the subjective conditions of theological study issue from a vocational calling (*Beruf*) too original to be cultivated by technical means. For Drey this calling, like all vocations, is an "inner natural qualification" and abides in "the conditions through which one who undertakes a task is given the possibility of success."[69] Vocational calling is the gift of talent. And any vocational talent for scientific study, theology included, "lies in those characteristics without which one can neither transform, through a free reconstructing [*Nachconstruieren*], the dead and externally given heap of concepts into a living knowledge in the individual nor bring this living knowledge to actuality in some other sphere."[70]

Drey thinks of the mental process of *Nachconstruieren*, of bringing life to dead concepts, as the talent that motivates all scientific inquiry. It is an imaginative act, the freedom of the insightful mind to rescue the past from formulaic or merely factual understandings of its meaning. As an imaginative act, however, reconstructive interpretation is neither solipsistic nor divorced from pertinent evidence, divergent views, or disciplinary canons. Its creativity is not the product of fantasy but flourishes precisely in the renewal it brings to a tradition of meaning.

Talent for reconstructive interpretation motivates theological inquiry no less than scientific inquiry in general. The living tradition of the church draws its energy from the commitment of its members. But the understanding of that commitment through the ages rests on the theologian's ability to imagine creative relationships between the fixed and mobile aspects of doctrine. In Drey's view true orthodoxy is the expression of such theological creativity engaged in the task of doctrinal development. The theological process of *Nachconstruieren*, of bringing life to the ecclesial doctrines of times past, is not a matter of fanciful speculation. Reconstructive interpretation that results in the development of doctrine is not the work of a theologian isolated from the church but the exercise of theological talent within and on behalf of the ecclesial community. The very

68. Ibid., § 99, 66.
69. Ibid.
70. Ibid., § 99, 66–67.

tradition from which such acts of the imagination emerge and whose faith they reflect owes its historical coherence to the power of the theologian's insight.

One cannot overestimate the importance of the religious sense within Drey's account of theological talent, particularly as the religious sense applies its discerning powers to the task of reconstructive interpretation. For Drey the meaningful reconstruction of the doctrinal tradition is an ongoing task. Its open-ended character is defined by the historicity of faith and so by the theologian's constant need to discern the most recent development in ecclesial experience that can rightly be described as contemporary faith. This act of discernment is necessary if the results of reconstructive interpretation are to be relevant at all to the believing community. Theological reconstruction begins in an act of hermeneutical sympathy as the theologian's understanding grasps the spirit of the doctrinal past. But it is completed in the imaginative renewal of fixed doctrine for the mobile or living faith of the church. The theologian's apprehension of the present state of faith is just as important a moment in Drey's theory of reconstruction as the theologian's empathy toward the past, for the theologian's ability to fathom the nature of contemporary faith establishes the goal of the reconstructive task.

The talent of the religious sense, then, is exercised in the interrelated activities of ecclesial discernment and doctrinal reconstruction. The theological vocation exists in one who possesses this talent in such a way that "it becomes possible to assimilate the substance of theology as a living knowledge and, in a practical direction, to apply this knowledge fruitfully and beneficently in the church."[71] The religious sense, Drey observes, "and indeed the Christian form of the religious sense, is as much a necessary characteristic of the good theologian as it is of the exegete."[72] In Drey's judgment the good theologian serves the church as a creative author, recognizes the value of imagination for the theological task, and measures theological responsibility by faithfulness both to the fixed dogmas of the past and to the contemporary faith of the church.

Drey's discussion of the theological subdiscipline of polemics includes some interesting observations on this notion of theological responsibility. "Human beings," Drey claims, "can distance themselves from the truth itself either by falling away from it or by lagging

71. Ibid., § 99, 67.
72. Ibid., § 173, 116.

behind it [*Zurückbleiben hinter ihr*]."[73] This last phrase is one of the most remarkable in the history of the Catholic tradition, for it is the first Catholic recognition of the inadequacy of a classical model of truth for post-Enlightenment theology. Lagging behind the truth, Drey explains, is "inertia, the consequence of the expiring activity of the [religious] principle in its progressive development."[74] This conception of error illumines Drey's subsequent discussion of doctrinal mobility in the *Brief Introduction* and directly complements his notion of hyperorthodoxy. Theological inertia is the inactivity or complacency of theological talent seduced by the ever-present temptation to find truth only in received dogma and thus to forsake its vocational responsibility. Through the activities of ecclesial discernment and reconstructive interpretation, the theologian overcomes such inertia and resists such temptation and does so by exercising the talent of authorship on which the church depends for the self-understanding that it calls tradition.

THE NEW TEXTBOOKS AND THE ROMANTIC PARADIGM

In his early writings Drey turned in several ways to the romantic movement as a resource for his theory of development. First, Drey found in Schelling's romantic idealism a metahistory that introduced the themes of process and development to the static idealism of the Fichtean ego. Second, the vitalistic imagery of the *Lebensanalogie*, which pervaded romantic literature of all sorts, provided Drey with noetic categories, vocabulary, and tropes for depicting a more dynamic understanding of the Christian tradition. Third, and often overlooked, is Drey's romantic approach to historical theology as a constructive enterprise, one distinguishable from a traditional presentation of church history. By the time Drey began to lecture on theological encyclopedia, Schleiermacher's *Brief Outline* was the only contribution to this genre that could serve as a precedent for a romantic understanding of theological method.

But why did the romantic paradigm of theological responsibility first emerge in the literary genre of theological encyclopedia? And why has this paradigm endured until the present day, albeit in forms different from the distinctively romantic ones in which its creators

73. Ibid., § 240, 162.
74. Ibid.

first cast its assumptions? I would like to suggest answers to each of these questions in turn.

Mindful of Kuhn's discussion of the role of textbooks in defining and promulgating the assumptions of a new paradigm, I would propose that reflection on the origins of the romantic paradigm might fruitfully take its point of departure in the history of the encyclopedic genre in which Schleiermacher and Drey first expressed their ideas on theological construction, doctrinal development, and authorship.

In name, though neither in structure nor content, the theological encyclopedia imitated the massive *Encyclopédie* of the eighteenth-century *philosophes* Denis Diderot and Jean Le Rond d'Alembert, the first volume of which appeared in 1751.[75] Quite unlike the expected latter-day collection of informative and objectively written entries, the *Encyclopédie* presented a philosophical stance on the present state and future course of intellectual achievement. Its epistemology, ethics, and humanistic anthropology sought to demythologize the traditional bastions of social and ecclesial authority and, in so doing, to promote the Enlightenment quest for autonomous knowledge. Its philosophical agenda aside, the *Encyclopédie* articulated a general expectation emerging in intellectual circles about the proper constitution of knowledge. It was this spirit, rather than the letter, of the *Encyclopédie* that survived in the subsequent history of the encyclopedic movement. Whether that history took the form of alphabetically arranged compendiums of which the *Encyclopedia Britannica* of 1771 is the first and best example, or the form of the methodological encyclopedias that began to appear in disciplines like theology and philosophy,[76] the encyclopedic approach was committed to the self-conscious investigation of the nature, the limitations, the breadth, and the unity of knowledge, however defined. Its critical temperament announced

75. *Encyclopédie, ou dictionnaire raisonné des sciences, des arts et des metiers, par une société de gens de lettres . . .* , 35 vols. (Paris, 1751–80). For a discussion of the modern encyclopedia movement, see Robert Collison, *Encyclopedias: Their History throughout the Ages* (New York: Hafner, 1964).

76. Kant, for example, lectured ten times on the topic of *philosophische Enzyklopädie*. Among the published philosophical encyclopedias of this time are Johann Georg Büsch, *Encyclopädie der historischen, philosophischen und mathematischen Wissenschaften* (Hamburg: Heroldsche Buchhandlung, 1775); Karl Heinrich Heydenricks, *Encyclopädische Einleitung in das Studium der Philosophie* (Leipzig: Weygandsche Buchhandlung, 1793). For a sketch of the philosophical encyclopedia as a literary genre, see William Gerber, "Philosophical Dictionaries and Encyclopedias," in *The Encyclopedia of Philosophy*, vol. 6 (New York: Macmillan, 1972), 179–80.

a departure from the epistemic and methodological approaches of previous generations and provided a context for the birth of new, and the revision of old, disciplines.

As Kuhn points out, the assumptions of a new paradigm are communicated in textbooks, which articulate the standards for normal science conducted under their auspices. In this light the contributions to the encyclopedia movement can be understood as textbooks promulgating new and general assumptions regarding the legitimate qualities of knowledge and its proper organization. The assumptions of the encyclopedia movement as such were not specific to a particular discipline. Generally speaking, the encyclopedia movement provided the textbooks with a new paradigm of epistemic integrity. The methodological encyclopedias focused these concerns specifically on disciplinary issues. That theology embraced the encyclopedic format seems somewhat surprising, since the critical spirit that imbued the encyclopedia movement was hostile to the commitments of theology. Nevertheless the theological encyclopedia became a forum for addressing the critical spirit apologetically, as well as for shaping it into a form that served, rather than undermined, theological assumptions.

Just as the classical paradigm of theological responsibility came to expression in the scholastic commentaries, compendiums, and collocations of the premodern period, the romantic paradigm found articulation in the genre of the encyclopedia as theologians struggled with the new assumptions about knowledge, method, and disciplinary integrity. This is not to say that the task of theological encyclopedia entailed commitment to the romantic paradigm of theological responsibility. The early encyclopedists did not espouse the romantic paradigm. But their concern with the problem of disciplinary integrity provided a matrix for a new understanding of both the theological project and the theological vocation. It is in the shift from church history to historical theology in the encyclopedias of the late eighteenth and early nineteenth centuries that we witness the birth of the romantic paradigm. The encyclopedias of Schleiermacher and Drey fulfilled the expectations of early encyclopedists like Planck, Tittmann, and Schmidt, for they proposed a constructive approach to the discipline of historical theology that raised the apologetics practiced by the early encyclopedists to a level of sophistication of which they were incapable.

The question of why this paradigm has retained currency to the present day can only be answered partially at this point in our study. The next chapter will detail the problematic features of the romantic paradigm as it was first articulated in the work of Schleiermacher and Drey and will consider the ambivalent history the paradigm has had in the Roman Catholic tradition. But in spite of these difficulties in its conception and history, the romantic paradigm voices presuppositions about the nature of theological responsibility that have been simply indispensable since the time of the Enlightenment.

Although not all that the Enlightenment has bequeathed subsequent generations remains in place, the antagonism it initiated between theology and culture has rarely diminished in the post-Enlightenment world. Whether that world is described as modern or postmodern, its cultural assumptions have judged the integrity of the theological enterprise negatively. The romantic paradigm emerged in response to this judgment as an apologetic approach to the theological task, one founded on presuppositions enabling the dialogue between theology and culture that thinkers like Schleiermacher and Drey considered crucial if their discipline were not to be reduced to a historical curiosity whose time had passed. To the degree that theology continues to face similar challenges to its disciplinary integrity posed by the Enlightenment heritage, the apologetical concerns of the romantic paradigm continue to determine the agenda of modern theology, even when particular theologies sharing the paradigm's basic assumptions question specific ways in which those assumptions are applied.

The romantic paradigm of theological responsibility insisted on bringing cultural experience into the ambit of theological reflection and on seeing theology as a revisable enterprise committed to the renewed construction of the experience of the church in history. Since the time of Schleiermacher and Drey, all but fundamentalist theologians have recognized the historicity of faith, the development of its doctrinal expression, and the need to give theological account of the variable, as well as the common, dimensions of ecclesial experience in the modern world. Theology could no more retreat from these assumptions and perspectives than its practitioners could now embrace the worldview expressed in the classical paradigm.

The constellation of theological perspectives that make up the romantic paradigm also entailed a different understanding of the theological practitioner, one tied as closely to modern sensibilities as the themes considered above. The acceptance of historical experience as a resource for the theological enterprise required that theological talent be conceived largely as the power of imagination, whose historical object embraced not only scripture and the established tradition of the past but also the developing experience of the church in culture. For the first time in the Christian tradition, theologians conceived their vocational practice to involve a personal creativity responsive to the historical creativity that they believed to be at work in ecclesial tradition. Under the romantic paradigm, theologians came to be understood as purveyors of meaning whose talent was discharged in the discernment and expression of the living faith of the ecclesial community. The originators of the romantic paradigm described this talent in somewhat different ways—as divination expressed in a dogmatic presentation for Schleiermacher, as the religious sense put to the service of doctrinal reconstruction for Drey. In both cases, authorship, broadly understood, is an apt way of portraying this talent because it conveys a sense for the creative dimension of their enterprise on which theologians now began to insist, and connotes, in its description of the practitioner, something of the authority theologians now began to lay claim to in the exercise of their vocational duties.

As shall be seen more specifically in the next chapter, early nineteenth-century conceptions of creativity and genius shaped the understanding of theological authorship at least in the early years of, and perhaps indirectly throughout, the history of the romantic paradigm. I will argue that in spite of some problematic features of its early nineteenth-century formulation, the notion of authorship expresses assumptions about the theological task that are fundamental to a Catholic understanding of the role of the theologian in the church.

Part Two

Authority
and
Creativity

Chapter Three

Catholic Reception of Creative Authorship

THE EARLY nineteenth-century readers of Schleiermacher's and Drey's encyclopedias might easily have come to the conclusion that their novel views on theological authorship would only endure on the printed page but not in the vocational commitments of subsequent generations of theologians. This opinion has proved to be both true and false. It has proved true in the sense that the specific categories in which Schleiermacher and Drey framed their notions of authorship have remained tied to their own time and culture, expressions of an early German Romanticism that, from the perspective of later modern and postmodern sensibilities, overestimated the contribution of individual talent to tradition. It has proved false in the sense that the modern period in general has judged the contributions of the individual imagination to be necessary to human acts of meaningful construction, whether theological, literary, political, or some other. That individual insight and voice contribute creatively to the ongoing search for truth is by now axiomatic to the modern temperament itself and to the self-understandings of disciplines as different as literature, physics, history, and mathematics. In this respect contemporary commitment to the notion of theological authorship reflects the endurance of this originally romantic idea. The value of creativity for theological reflection has largely remained a disciplinary and vocational assumption since the emergence of the romantic paradigm nearly two hundred years ago.

This distinction between theological authorship and early nineteenth-century expressions of this talent often has not been made with sufficient care in the history of modern theology. It has been much more common to conflate the expressions of authorship that we find in theologians like Schleiermacher and Drey on the one hand and the notion of authorship itself on the other. Whenever theological authorship has been reduced to early nineteenth-century expressions of its power, the result has been at least misgivings about the integrity of theological talent and the suspicion that its exercise all too readily produces subjectivistic theologies unfaithful to the Christian tradition. In the Protestant tradition, Barth's lifelong and influential criticism of liberal theology might well be understood in terms of his distrust of the notion of authorship, as might George Lindbeck's postliberal rejoinder to what he calls the theological approach of "experiential-expressivism." In the Catholic tradition the testy relations between theologians and the magisterium in the years following the Second Vatican Council evince this same suspicion. At most this conflation has resulted in the outright rejection of individual talent as a dimension of the theological vocation. This stance is typified by the theological heritage of Vatican I, which extends from the council through the antimodernist polemic of the early twentieth century to Vatican II. The Catholic tradition's rejection of theological authorship throughout most of the modern period is the subject of this chapter; the suspicion of authorship in the work of the Protestant theologian George Lindbeck and its viability as a position for Catholic theology is the subject matter of the next.

This chapter will begin by examining the specifically romantic manner in which the talent of theological authorship was first expressed. Here the discussion of Schleiermacher and Drey will be continued by exploring the intellectual background to their views on theological creativity. Although differing subtly in their conceptions of authorship, these theologians shared an understanding of the theological vocation that is best appreciated in the broader climate of early nineteenth-century Romanticism. Philosophical and literary illustrations from the work of their precursors and contemporaries will enable an appreciation of how Schleiermacher and Drey conceived of theological talent at work and, more important, the negative consequences of their conceptualization for the history of modern theology. Attention will be drawn, then, to the Roman Catholic reception of the notion of authorship, a process marked by a troubled history that continues to our own day. The explicitly romantic conception of authorship threatened traditional expectations on the part of the Catholic hierarchy regarding the proper exercise of theological responsibility. Although the magisterium has reversed its initial rejection of theological authorship, it continues to be wary of the role of theological talent in the church. Finally, the contemporary value of the notion of theological authorship will be considered. If this ability is indeed indistinguishable from its early nineteenth-century conceptualization, then theological authorship is by now a historical relic, interesting perhaps as a footnote in the history of theology but no longer a tenable assumption of the discipline. This, however, is not the case. Theological authorship is an assumption that continues to inform the theological task. Its claim that theologians are imaginative authors reflects an understanding of the creative process that is simply taken for granted in modern culture, including that dimension of culture that theology is. This chapter will conclude by proposing ways in which theological creativity might be understood as talent in service to the church.

THE ROMANTIC THEOLOGIAN
AS HERO

As noted in the Introduction, Romanticism is an intellectual and artistic movement that defies precise definition. The suggestion of even a partial list of its general characteristics—such as an attention to the role of imagination, a distrust of the formalism of an earlier classicism, a holistic or synthetic regard for the relationship between self and world, or self-conscious reflection on the power of creativity—can easily elicit examples of similar traits in the works of writers and artists that clearly predate or postdate even the most generous historical boundaries one might assign to the romantic movement. Delimiting the themes of Romanticism becomes a less demanding project if one relinquishes the task of definition and remains satisfied with a description of family resemblances. In spite of the different stages that arguably can be distinguished in the romantic movement, this approach is practicable as long as it is grounded in particulars and aware of the modesty and necessary incompleteness of its enterprise. I would like to consider one romantic theme in such a way here, the self-understanding of the artist or, broadly understood, author that emerged in the early stages of the romantic movement. This general conceptualization of the talented individual's role in creative endeavor will shed light both on the vocational under-standing of the theologian advanced by Schleiermacher and Drey and on many of the suspicions that have been directed toward the romantic paradigm in the course of its history.

Literary movements and genres of all sorts have produced var-iations on the theme of the heroic figure, a character presented in myth, poem, or narrative plot whose virtue, sensibility, exploits, or destiny distinguishes the individual from the mass of ordinary human expectations and accomplishments. Romanticism is no exception. While there are pronounced differences between Novalis's Heinrich von Ofterdingen, Goethe's Werther or Faust, Shelley's Prometheus or Byron's Don Juan, these characters, and others like them, possess enough common traits to justify the consideration of the romantic hero as a literary type. Walter Reed distinguishes three traits of the heroic character in romantic literature. "The Romantic hero," Reed asserts, "is not a simple being, but one involved in a set of relationships both dialectical and dynamic." First, though neither divine nor im-mortal, the romantic hero stands in "a privileged relation with the supernatural . . . or, as is more usual in Romanticism, the natural supernaturalism of the created world." Second, the hero is "related as an actor is to an audience, as an extraordinary person is to the ordinary members of his society." Third, in addition to the "gods" and society, the romantic hero stands in relation to personal identity. The hero must "live up to, or decline from, an inherited heroic ideal." Bound to the movement of history, the romantic hero's identity "is never completely fixed but in a process of evolution or devolution" as the hero struggles to remain true to existential or aesthetic com-mitments.[1]

These traits of the heroic character are readily apparent in the vocational ideal of authorship set out by Schleiermacher and Drey. For them the theologian stands in a privileged relation to the devel-oping meaning of divine revelation in ecclesial experience. The the-ologian is distinguished from the church at large by discerning sen-sibility, expressive talent, and heuristic abilities, though it is primarily for the ecclesial audience that the theologian's extraordinary voca-tional duties are discharged. Without the effective application of theo-logical talent, the historical development of the tradition would either

1. Walter L. Reed, *Meditations on the Hero: A Study of the Romantic Hero in Nineteenth-Century Fiction* (New Haven, Conn.: Yale Univ. Press, 1974), 10.

languish or wander aimlessly. Those unhappy possibilities establish a context within which the theologian's struggle for self-identity takes place. Faced on either side of professional responsibility by the minimalist temptation of torpid imitation and the maximalist temptation of fanciful innovation, the theologian struggles, heroically one might say, to remain faithful to a vocational ideal ever redefined by time and circumstance.

As striking as the comparison may be between Reed's generic sketch of the hero in romantic literature and the vocational self-understanding of the romantic theologians, it is quite unlikely that Schleiermacher and Drey molded their understanding of theological authorship on character portrayals in romantic literature. In addition to the absence of literary evidence to establish such an influence, it is improbable that the few romantic characters presented to the reading public in the first decade of the nineteenth century would have provided sufficient definition for the particular vocational understanding proposed by Schleiermacher and appropriated in its broad strokes by Drey. How then might we account for the close similarity between Reed's description of the ideal romantic character and the vocational self-understanding of the theologians?

Perhaps the most unique aspect of the heroic character in Romanticism is its development as the fictional representation of the creative enterprise itself. While the hero was portrayed in classical literature as a champion struggling with the gods, in early medieval literature as the saint wrestling temptation, and in late medieval and Renaissance literature as the knight engaging opponents, the early romantics endowed the hero with the qualities and purpose of the creative agent, of the author broadly understood.[2] This identification between fictional characterization and the author's vocational ideal is possible because the early romantics understood the artist not only as the creator of heroic characters but also and primarily as a hero. Unlike the heroes of earlier literary periods, the romantic hero was created in its author's own image and likeness, as an expression of the artist's own complex and creative relationships with the spheres of the transcendent, the social, and the self. This heroic configuration

2. See Victor Brombert, "The Idea of the Hero," in *The Hero in Literature*, ed. V. Brombert (New York: Fawcett, 1969), 11–21. See also the essays in the collection *Concepts of the Hero in the Middle Ages and the Renaissance*, ed. N. T. Burns and C. J. Reagan (Albany: SUNY Press, 1975).

of the author is an important expression of romantic consciousness itself and provides a context for understanding the origin of theological authorship.

Although the literary type of the hero possesses a genealogy that dates back to the beginnings of literature, the idea of the artist as hero has a smaller family tree rooted in the middle of the eighteenth century, a period that witnessed a spate of treatises on the topics of originality and genius.[3] The titles of Edward Young's *Conjectures on Original Composition* (1759), William Duff's *Essay on Original Genius* (1767), Alexander Gerard's *An Essay on Genius* (1774), Courtney Melmoth's *The Tears of Genius* (1774), and Elizabeth Gilding's *The Breathings of Genius* (1776) testify to the eighteenth century's growing fascination with the process of intellectual creativity. This flurry of attention to the power of imagination in the English-speaking world was prompted by the epistemological investigations of the British philosopher John Locke (1632–1704). Locke argued that ideas were the product of sense experience and insisted that the residual Platonism of the doctrine of innate ideas was philosophically untenable. But an unnuanced understanding of Locke's commitment to empiricism, encouraged perhaps by his jolting image of the mind as a *tabula rasa*, obscures the power he accorded to the mind in establishing sophisticated relationships between ideas. "In this faculty of repeating and joining together its *ideas*," he argues in his *Essay Concerning Human Understanding* (1690), "the Mind has great power in varying and multiplying the Objects of its Thoughts, infinitely beyond what *Sensation* or *Reflection* furnished it with: But all this still confined to those simple *Ideas*, which it received from those two Sources, and which are the ultimate Materials of all its Compositions."[4]

Although minimalist in its approach, Locke's associationist theory of creativity inaugurated a tradition of reflection on the imagination that began in Great Britain and continued in Germany in the

3. The following consideration of the late eighteenth-century writers on imagination—Duff, Gerard, Tetens, and Kant—relies largely on the historical lines sketched by James Engell in his excellent study *The Creative Imagination: Enlightenment to Romanticism* (Cambridge, Mass.: Harvard Univ. Press, 1981). Engell's interest in the connection between British and German traditions is particularly helpful for contextualizing the views of Schleiermacher and Drey. For a discussion of eighteenth-century developments in the concept of imagination that takes into account the French tradition, see Roland Mortier, *L'Originalité: Une Nouvelle Catégorie esthétique au siècle des lumieres* (Geneva: Librairie Droz, 1982).

4. John Locke, *An Essay Concerning Human Understanding*, ed. P. H. Nidditch (Oxford: Clarendon Press, 1975), 91.

course of the late eighteenth century. His insistence that mental activity be anchored solidly in both sensibility and intellection led him to denigrate the faculty of imagination as a chimera. Locke's understanding of an associative power of the mind, however, capable of producing and reproducing ideas, suggested an intellectual operation that a later generation of thinkers would invest with far greater abilities.[5]

The Scottish philosopher William Duff (1732–1815) and theologian Alexander Gerard (1728–1795) at once advanced and criticized Locke's relatively static theory of noetic combination in theories of the imagination that depicted this faculty as an intellectual function *sui generis*. Duff's *Essay on Original Genius* presents the imagination as the source of genius, as the talented mind's ability to weave the disparate threads of knowledge into a unified whole. Duff describes the imagination as a "plastic power [capable] of inventing new associations of ideas, and of combining them with infinite variety."[6] The imagination is endowed with the ability "to present a creation of its own, and to exhibit scenes and objects which never existed in nature."[7] From its resiliency and versatility issue acts of mental creation that establish the subtle artistry of genius. Gerard's *Essay on Genius* augments the power of the imagination by incorporating the traditional role of judgment into its scope. Unlike Duff, who portrays it only as a faculty for holding the imagination in check,[8] Gerard also considers judgment an extension of imaginative power itself. For Gerard judgment is no longer "a power to control and subordinate imagination" but "a complementary aid to perfect" its creative work.[9] Gerard's commitment to the notion of a "comprehensive imagination"[10] is evinced in his development of a detailed epistemology of creativity. The pages of the *Essay on Genius* are filled with lengthy explanations of the role played by all facets of experience—the senses, passions, reason, and memory—in the process of imaginative activity. Like Duff, Gerard regarded imagination as the matrix of inventiveness and as the wellspring of all that is original.

5. Engell, *The Creative Imagination*, 18.
6. William Duff, *An Essay on Original Genius and Its Various Modes of Exertion in Philosophy and the Fine Arts, Particularly in Poetry (1767)*, ed. J. L. Mahoney (Gainesville, Fla.: Scholars' Facsimiles & Reprints, 1964), 7.
7. Ibid.
8. Ibid., 9.
9. Engell, *The Creative Imagination*, 82. Cf. Alexander Gerard, *An Essay on Genius (1774)*, ed. Bernhard Fabian (Munich: Wilhelm Fink, 1966), 36–38.
10. Gerard, *An Essay on Genius (1774)*, 38.

The pioneering efforts of Duff and Gerard to speak of the imagination as a creative impulse in its own right were continued in Germany by Johann Nicolaus Tetens (1736–1807), a professor of philosophy at Kiel, and by Immanuel Kant (1724–1804). Both Tetens and Kant were influenced by Duff and especially by Gerard. The important role accorded to the idea of a productive imagination in their respective epistemological theories was influential in mediating the earlier, British discussions of creative genius to the first generation of German romantic thinkers. Although Gerard suggested a taxonomy of imaginative powers, both he and Duff tended to speak only of particular dispositions of the imagination toward genius in one field or another. Tetens and Kant built on this foundation by delineating a well-defined hierarchy of imaginative faculties and their respective operations.

In the opening pages of his two-volume *Philosophical Inquiries Concerning Human Nature and Its Development* (1777), Tetens labels the highest exercise of imagination the "poetic faculty" (*Dichtungsvermögen*). Not merely the source of verbal artistry but a universal ability that "expresses itself in numerous fashions," the poetic faculty is the power by which the inspired mind separates and assembles commonplace images into "new creations" of the intellect.[11] First steps toward its highest reaches are made in the imaginative formation of images through what Tetens calls the "faculty of perception" and in the association of more complex ideas through the imaginative play of "phantasy." But in Tetens's view these subordinate exercises of imagination find their fulfillment in the spontaneous productivity of the poetic faculty, the imagination's most fruitful employment and "an essential ingredient of genius."[12]

In the *Critique of Pure Reason* (1781) Kant followed Tetens in distinguishing between higher and lower capacities of the imagination (*Einbildungskraft*). For Kant the empirical imagination is grounded in intuition, the array of images offered by sensibility. Bound to the phenomenal world of appearances, it is at work in the mental activities of "recognition, reproduction, association, [and] apprehension."[13] A

11. Johann Nicolaus Tetens, *Philosophische Versuche über die menschliche Natur und ihre Entwicklung*, vol. 1 (Leipzig: M. G. Weidmann, 1777), 24, 25.
12. Ibid., 1:107.
13. Immanuel Kant, *Critique of Pure Reason*, trans. N. K. Smith (New York: St. Martin's Press, 1965), 147.

higher function of the imagination lies in its synthetic power considered a priori, in abstraction as it were, apart from the particular images that the lower imagination is able to conjure from sensibility. The transcendental faculty of the imagination is the formal capacity of the mind to unite the discrete productions of the empirical imagination. Since this unity establishes the mind's coherent creation of images, the synthesis effected by the transcendental faculty of the imagination conditions "the very possibility of all experience."[14] The foundation supplied by the transcendental to the empirical imagination achieves its consummate expression in the spirit of genius that Kant portrays in the *Critique of Judgment* (1790) as the "happy relation" between the free productivity of imagination and the more disciplined structures of human understanding.[15]

This brief overview of late eighteenth-century Enlightenment thinkers makes clear that the romantics had no monopoly on the notions of imagination and creativity. Not only did Duff, Gerard, Tetens, Kant, and others among their contemporaries address the topic of the imagination but they did so in a way that called attention to the scope of its power by establishing its integrity within the faculties of the human mind. This rich tradition of reflection on the workings of the imagination moved in the direction of romanticism as it encountered the new, organic understandings of nature and history that began to emerge at the turn of the nineteenth century. Schelling's philosophy, which directly influenced Coleridge, Schleiermacher, Hegel, and Drey, was one of the earliest and boldest expressions of this organic interpretation of reality.[16] His specific reflections on the place of creativity in the historical process constitute an important moment in the lineage of the heroic conception of the artist.

Schelling's first thematic consideration of an organic view of history appears in his *System of Transcendental Idealism* (1800). In this work Schelling introduces the idea of historical development to his earlier, panentheistic efforts to explain the natural world as an expression of the divine life in the *First Sketch of a System of Natural*

14. Ibid., 133.
15. Immanuel Kant, *Critique of Judgment*, trans. J. H. Bernard (New York: Hafner, 1966), 160.
16. For a discussion of organicism in the early German romantic tradition, see M. H. Abrams, *The Mirror and the Lamp: Romantic Theory and the Critical Tradition* (New York: Oxford Univ. Press, 1953), 201–13.

Philosophy (1799). According to the *System of Transcendental Idealism*, "history as a whole is a progressive, gradually self-disclosing revelation of the absolute."[17] It is the point of intersection between God and the world, a stage on which human nature enacts the divine purposes, which, Schelling claims, are accessible to reason, will, and imagination. The notion of history entails "the concept of an infinite progressiveness [*Progressivität*]."[18] By freely striving to embody the ideal of the divine life in thought and action, human nature fashions the truth of history and its directed movement through time and culture.

Such an explanation of human creativity within the vicissitudes of history required a modification of eighteenth-century understandings of the artistic enterprise and the power of genius. As nuanced as their views on the imagination may be, Duff, Gerard, Tetens, and Kant tended to explain the imagination as a power of sensitivity through which relational life is brought to the mind's otherwise isolated and disjointed experience. All four understood the rudimentary assemblage of concepts and images with which the imagination plays as a product of sensibility, and so as a staid, lifeless representation of the mind's encounter with the natural world. The imagination stirs these fixed ingredients into an animated combination, into an original whole unanticipated in its parts. Genius, in their view, is extraordinary talent exercised at the heights of noetic experience, above, so to speak, the sensible realm of perception and observation. This is not to say that these explorers of genial talent severed its abilities from the more commonplace dimensions of experience in the natural world. Each held in his own way that genius can fashion its insights only by raising the initially mechanical products of sensibility to unanticipated levels of meaning; each maintained that the masterpieces of creative artistry stand among the objects of the natural world as testimonies to their primitive power of inspiration. But Duff, Gerard, Tetens, and especially Kant tended to see the consummate exercise of such talent as a bestowal of creative, original energy upon the dry predictability of the natural world.[19]

17. Friedrich Schelling, *System des transscendentalen Idealismus*, in *Schellings Werke*, vol. 2, ed. M. Schröter (Munich: C. H. Beck'sche Verlagsbuchhandlung, 1958), 603.
18. Ibid., 2:592.
19. Although this idea of creative imputation is clearest in Kant's conception of the transcendental faculty of the imagination, it is implicit in the earlier work of Duff and Tetens and explicit in the work of Gerard. Cf. Gerard, *An Essay on Genius*

Genius, they believed, is a vital force that issues completely from the side of the human and that the empirical worlds of nature and history can only receive.

The romantics modified this Enlightenment conception of the workings of the imagination and genius. Their organic understanding of nature and history assumed that historical experience was charged with meaningful possibilities and that time and culture were dynamic spheres in which such possibilities could develop into actual expressions of truth. Whether this truth was conceived as human or divine, organic thinking wove its extraordinary or supernatural character into the fabric of the finite world. The human experience of nature and history was no longer regarded merely as raw, empirical data on which imagination might confer its higher vision but as the vehicle of an evolving truth and a source itself of imaginative insight. In the theories of imagination proposed by the romantics, an act of creative vision required sympathetic consonance with the developing creativity of the natural and historical realms. The sophisticated associationism of Duff, Gerard, Tetens and Kant demanded a still greater sophistication in a romantic setting as the imagination's creative juxtaposition of ideas now presupposed its felicitous rapport with the development of historical truth.

The grounding of imagination in nature's and history's own creative realities produced intensified claims for the power of the imagination and a related modification in the notion of genius. Among many possible examples, Schelling again serves as a good illustration. The imagination, in his view, stands stretched between the real and ideal realms and mediates between them. Although this observation could just as well characterize the views of the Enlightenment thinkers, Schelling's romantic understanding of nature and history tempers its meaning. Genius, for Schelling, is the highest exercise of the imagination. It is an "obscure concept" (*dunkeln Begriff*), "an incomprehensible power . . . which brings objectivity to the conscious."[20] This objectivity is the work of art that the artist completes by uniting the unconscious productivity of the natural

---

(1774), 29: "It may be questioned, whether, in some very peculiar cases, [imagination's] power extends not even to the formation of a simple idea. But it is certain that, when it only exhibits simple ideas which have been derived from the senses, it confers something original upon them, by the manner in which it exhibits them."

20. Schelling, *System des transscendentalen Idealismus*, in *Schellings Werke*, 2:616.

realm and the conscious productivity of genial talent. Genius is the ability to mediate, to unite into a single whole, the conscious forces of human subjectivity and the unconscious forces of nature and history, each different expressions of the divine nature itself.[21] The genial or artistic imagination achieves this result by a process analogous to the divine creativity, an idea Schelling expresses strikingly in his 1802–03 lectures on the *Philosophy of Art*:

> This eternal concept of human nature in God as the immediate cause of its productions is what is usually called genius . . . , the divine indwelling in human nature. It is, so to speak, a piece of the absoluteness of God. Each artist can thus produce only to the degree that the artist's own nature is bound, in the eternal concept, to God. Now the more the artist already intuits the universe in this union, and the more organic the artist is, and the more the artist joins the finite to the infinite, the more productive [is the artistic genius].[22]

Although Duff, Gerard, Tetens, and Kant marveled at the workings of genius, none made such strong claims for its power or envisioned the creative process in such extravagant terms. Schelling, of course, does not speak for the romantic tradition. His explicitly gnostic account of genius as a divine ability, his exposition of the existential dialectic in panentheistic terms, and his explicit philosophical idealism cannot be regarded as typically romantic. The aspects of Schelling's exposition of creativity that bespeak the most commonly shared romantic assumptions about genius can be found in his commitment to immediate, developing experience as the locus of truth and beauty, his efforts to explain artistic endeavor in correspondingly organic terms, and his understanding of genius as the ability to mediate between the visionary power of individual imagination and the broader, communal resources for artistic vision that lie in nature, history, and society.

This heightened sense of the power of artistic creativity became emblematic of the romantic temperament and took shape in a strong notion of authorship as nuanced in its expression as the creative concerns of individual romantic thinkers. To be struck by the various ways in which romantic authorship could be described one need only

21. Ibid., 2:616–18.
22. Friedrich Schelling, *Philosophie der Kunst*, in *Schellings Werke*, 3:480.

think of Coleridge's formidable notion of the "creative, and self-sufficing power of absolute *Genius*,"[23] of Wordsworth's more temperate description of the poet as one "possessed of more than unusual organic sensibility [who] had also thought long and deeply,"[24] of Blake's apocalyptic conception of "the Poetic Genius which is every where call'd the Spirit of Prophecy,"[25] of Friedrich Schlegel's paean to the artist-priest "who desires nothing on earth but to fashion the finite into the infinite,"[26] or of Shelley's triumphant claim that poets "are the unacknowledged legislators of the World."[27] In spite of their differences, these conceptions of authorship depict the personal exercise of artistic talent in heroic terms and can be commonly portrayed by Reed's earlier-cited characterization of the heroic character's relationships to the "gods," society, and the self.

By virtue of talent alone the heroic artist occupies a privileged position in relation to the world of truth and beauty, at once transcendental and enmeshed in the dynamic forces of nature and history. The artistic imagination mediates this world to society, the ordinary company of men and women, which is moved to a state of appreciation, confusion, paradox, or even betterment as it is faced with the artist's original vision. The heroic artist's vocational responsibility is thus defined, and ever redefined, by the exercise of personal talent. Like the literary heroes of previous ages, the romantic artist undertakes a quest, in this case a creative journey demanding the productive exercise of the imagination in the face of the opposing and reactionary forces of classicism, empiricism, and common sensibility. In a fashion parallel to the quests of the ancient or medieval heroes who sought to snatch fire from the heavens or to possess the Holy Grail, the heroic artist seeks the proper exercise of imaginative creation, a talent precious in its ability to see and to speak the true meaning of the

23. Samuel Taylor Coleridge, *Biographia Literaria*, in *The Collected Works of Samuel Taylor Coleridge*, vol. 7, part 1, ed. J. Engell and W. J. Bate (Princeton, N.J.: Princeton Univ. Press, 1983), 31.

24. William Wordsworth, "Preface of 1800," *Lyrical Ballads 1798*, ed. W. J. B. Owen (New York: Oxford Univ. Press, 1969), 157.

25. William Blake, "All Religions Are One," in *The Complete Poetry and Prose of William Blake*, ed. D. V. Erdman (Berkeley: Univ. of California Press, 1982), 1.

26. Friedrich Schlegel, "Ideen," in *Friedrich Schlegel: Kritische Schriften* (Munich: Carl Hanser, 1964), 90.

27. Percy Bysshe Shelley, "A Defence of Poetry," in *Shelley's Poetry and Prose*, ed. D. H. Reiman and S. B. Powers (New York: W. W. Norton & Co., 1977), 508.

human situation within the currents of history. While romantic authors embodied the quest motif both in literary themes and in the exploits of their characters, these were expressions of a vocational self-understanding that was formed gradually in the course of several decades of reflection on the nature and power of genius.

Schleiermacher and Drey formulated their views on theological authorship in the context of this relatively short but rich tradition of reflection. Their efforts to sketch the methodological outlines of their discipline prompted them to address the issue of theological responsibility by embracing the intellectual presuppositions of their time on personal creativity and its role in the construction of meaning. In fact Schleiermacher's and Drey's commitment to the tradition of the genial imagination was so explicit that they even employed its vocabulary to describe accomplished theological endeavor. In Schleiermacher's view the theologian who breaks new ground by venturing beyond the common fare of disciplinary knowledge possesses "virtuosity." He judges that only through such work can the theologian seek "the completeness of a particular discipline" and avoid being "only a bearer of tradition, which is the most inferior and least important [professional] activity."[28] For Drey "the *decisive* vocational call to theology" dwells in the individual whose "understanding, judgment and imagination" are completely occupied with religious concerns, whose "spiritual organization . . . could, by way of analogy, be called *religious genius*."[29]

Certainly there is a family resemblance shared by the romantics in general and the theologians in particular on the issue of authorship. We might examine the lines of kinship more closely by investigating the degree to which the theologians advocated the strong notion of heroic authorship held by their counterparts in other fields. Examining this point might best be attempted by reformulating it in terms of the issue of authority at stake in the entire project of Romanticism. If understood in reference to the artist, Reed's second trait of the romantic hero—the hero's relationship to society—can be of help here.

28. Friedrich Schleiermacher, *Kurze Darstellung des theologischen Studiums zum Behuf einleitender Vorlesungen*, ed. H. Scholz (1910; reprint, Darmstadt: Wissenschaftliche Buchgesellschaft, 1973), § 17, 19; 7, 8.

29. Johann Sebastian Drey, *Kurze Einleitung in das Studium der Theologie mit Rücksicht auf den wissenschaftlichen Standpunct und das katholische System* (1819; reprint, ed. F. Schupp, Darmstadt: Wissenschaftliche Buchgesellschaft, 1971), § 102, 69.

Its ascription of authority to individual talent or genius could only stir an ambivalence on the part of the romantic temperament toward the accepted, authoritative canons of society. This ambivalence is, in Thomas McFarland's apt phrase, the manifestation of an "originality paradox" and stems from the struggles of the romantic mind to distinguish its strong claims to originality from the customary truths of the past and the present.[30] While tradition and community are undoubtedly the matrix of originality, they pose a dual menace to its innovative claims by threatening to quench the fire of insight in the waters of predictable conformity or to expose its claims to novelty as pretension, as merely the recent echoes of ancient voices. The originality paradox itself frames the tensions within the heroic understanding of authorship. More particularly, it is an expression of the romantic version of the quest motif, the troubled tension between the free play of individual imagination and the conservative forces of tradition and community. The romantic conception of genius as the ability to mediate between the visionary power of individual imagination and the organic resources for artistic vision that lie in nature, history, and society accentuated the originality paradox by defining tradition and community as at once the object of genial mediation and the resistant critic of romantic imagination.

One of the most resilient caricatures of the romantic tradition insists that its representatives dealt with the ambivalence of the originality paradox by denying the authority of tradition outright and, in an act of utter assertion, proclaiming the legitimacy of individual vision.[31] In this parody of romantic originality, the artist judges the heritage of tradition and community to be so vacant of meaning that it must be ignored as the imagination creates a world of aesthetics, purpose, and values *ex nihilo*. This, of course, was a position held by none of the romantics. Even the most ardent advocates of strong authorial voice assumed that the artist's vision is responsible to the tradition and community in which the imagination works, its originality inescapably tempered by the social framework of authority

30. Thomas McFarland, *Originality and Imagination* (Baltimore: Johns Hopkins Univ. Press, 1985), 1–30.

31. Martin Kemp gives expression to this caricature in his attempt to sketch the boundaries that separate renaissance from romantic genius: "we are still [in the sixteenth century] some way from the autonomous genius of the Romantic period, accountable only to itself and disdainful of normality" ("The 'Super-artist' as Genius: The Sixteenth-Century View," in *Genius: The History of an Idea*, ed. P. Murray [Oxford: Basil Blackwell, 1989], 49).

with which it grapples. Like all of the romantics, the theologians can only unjustly be accused of creative solipsism.

Some romantics wrestled with this ambivalence by accentuating the power of the artist's authorial voice, concomitantly minimizing, though not negating, the role of tradition and community in the creative project. This was the path chosen by romantics like Schelling, Novalis, Blake, and Friedrich Schlegel, who so stressed the power of the creative imagination that they portrayed genius as divinely inspired or as divinity itself. In this strain of Romanticism, the strength of authorial voice seeks to restate the meaning of intellectual tradition by embracing it within the immediacy of the romantic vision. Its customary meaning transfigured in the fantastic images and concepts of a new mythology, tradition sacrifices its classical authority and subordinates its established self-understanding to the authority of the artist. As much as the theologians were committed to the indispensability of theological creativity, their respect for ecclesial tradition would not permit the acceptance of a notion of authorship that accorded this degree of power to the individual theological voice. Schleiermacher and Drey, along with other romantics like Goethe and Keats,[32] dealt with the ambivalence of the originality paradox by following a more moderate course, stressing the importance of developing tradition as the measure of original insight and insisting upon a more balanced, mediatorial understanding of the authorial voice. In this approach the artist's ambivalence is not fixated in the desire to remake the classical tradition but is motivated by the concern that original vision and tradition be properly reconciled.

Like all the romantics, Schleiermacher and Drey struggled to find conceptual categories to give account of the assumptions of the modern era, especially its commitment to the idea of historical change and the place of human creativity within that process. Historical theology, the development of doctrine, and theological authorship are examples of such categories. From a classical perspective, these ideas seemed traitorous for a discipline in which tradition was perceived as fixed and authority identified with the once-spoken voice of the divine author. Schleiermacher and Drey, and following their lead, modern theology in general, did not reject the authority of scripture and tradition but made some room beside them for the

32. Engell, *The Creative Imagination*, 277–78. For Goethe, cf. Michael Beddow, "Goethe on Genius," in *Genius*, 106.

living voice of the theologian as a qualified authority in its own right. They insisted on the contributions of authorship to the process of theological construction not in order to subvert the ecclesial tradition that shaped their faith but to recognize its power in the life of the church and the need to interpret its entire truth, present as well as past, to the contemporary Christian community.[33]

The expression of this vocational ideal in terms of the model of heroic authorship, however, presented special difficulties to the romantic theologians, difficulties that were not faced as pointedly by romantics who exercised their artistry in other disciplines. As they conceived of theological responsibility as a heroic quest in which original insight struggled to enunciate a truth resisted by conservative ecclesial powers, the theologians vied with a classicism that was more identifiable, stable, and centralized than the classicism of their counterparts. This was especially true within the Catholic tradition, where the conflictual model could easily be construed as a struggle for authority between the theologian and the institutional church. The following section will address this issue by considering the reception of the notion of theological authorship by the teaching authority of the Roman Catholic Church since the romantic era. This will entail an examination of the ambivalence of the originality paradox from an institutional rather than a subjective perspective.

THEOLOGICAL AUTHORSHIP AND THE MAGISTERIUM

Among matters of concern cited in the *Final Report* of the November 1985 Extraordinary Synod in Rome was the persistence of friction

33. Two studies on the young Schleiermacher provide evidence for postulating a consistency between the type of Romanticism he embraced in his early years and the conception of theological authorship later formulated in his encyclopedia. Jack Forstman's *A Romantic Triangle: Schleiermacher and Early German Romanticism* (Missoula, Mont.: Scholars Press, 1977) argues that the Schleiermacher of the *Speeches* advocated a moderate Romanticism that sought to encounter the experience of the infinite within the limitations of the finite. This type of Romanticism stood in contrast to the approach adopted by his early compatriots Friedrich Schlegel and Novalis, which portrayed artistic vision as a transcendental flight from the finite. Albert Blackwell's *Schleiermacher's Early Philosophy of Life: Determinism, Freedom, and Phantasy* (Chico, Calif.: Scholars Press, 1982) proposes the term *active quietism* (253) to describe Schleiermacher's early reflections on the role of the imagination in artistic endeavor. Blackwell, like Forstman, understands this position as a moderate alternative within the spectrum of possible romantic stances. Unfortunately, comparable literary sources through which to consider Drey's early views on this issue do not exist.

between the magisterium and theologians.[34] The document notes that "theology is specifically necessary to the life of the church today" and appreciatively recognizes "what has been done by theologians to elaborate the documents of Vatican Council II and to help toward their faithful interpretation and fruitful application in the post-conciliar period." In quite a different tone, however, the document expresses "regret that the theological discussions of our day have sometimes occasioned confusion among the faithful" and suggests the remedy of "communication and a reciprocal dialogue between the bishops and theologians" in order to insure "the building up of the faith and its deeper comprehension."

The concerns raised here focus on the nature of theological responsibility, a matter that has occupied both the magisterium and theologians in recent years. This issue has not been merely a theoretical one. Actual conflicts between the magisterium and theologians such as Hans Küng, Edward Schillebeeckx, Leonardo Boff, Charles Curran, and Matthew Fox have made the issue of theological responsibility a point of debate and questioning on the part of the whole church. One might perceive the occasional tension between the magisterium and theologians as a struggle to define the legitimate boundaries of teaching authority in the church, to determine the proper share that the magisterium and the theologians each contribute to the task of church teaching. This issue has been of special concern to both parties in the years following the Second Vatican Council. The fact that the council was in most respects a model of cooperation between the magisterium and theologians raised the expectation that good relations between these constituencies would flourish in the postconciliar church. That expectation has not been entirely fulfilled.

I would like to suggest that the history of tension between the magisterium and theologians in the Roman Catholic tradition of the nineteenth and twentieth centuries might best be understood in terms of the paradigm shift outlined in the Introduction.[35] The romantic

34. The full title of the document, released in Latin on December 9, 1986, is *The Church, in the Word of God, Celebrates the Mystery of Christ for the Salvation of the World.* An English translation appears in *Origins* 15, 27 (December 19, 1985): 444–50. Citations from the document are from section II.B.a.3.

35. According to Yves Congar, conceptions of magisterial authority in the church have been fluid, though a watershed in the definition of such authority occurred in the early nineteenth century. Congar states that in "the Fathers, in the Middle Ages and up until the 1820s and 1830s, *magisterium* means simply the situation,

paradigm of theological responsibility did not immediately win the loyalty of the entire ecclesial community. It found itself in conflict with its classical predecessor as adopted at Trent, affirmed at Vatican I, and promulgated throughout the modernist controversy and its aftermath until Vatican II. In spite of recent evidence that the magisterium has recognized the main features of the romantic paradigm, its continued suspicion of the paradigm's understanding of theological authorship often has affected adversely its relationship to the theological community at large.

By the middle of the nineteenth century, the historical theology introduced to Catholic thought by Drey and the Tübingen school increasingly found itself under question by Vatican theologians and the magisterium itself. As Thomas O'Meara has observed, the rise of neoscholasticism in the middle of the century led to the eclipse of historical theology for generations of Catholic theologians.[36] While it is tempting to understand Josef Kleutgen's attack on Tübingen theology in his *Theology of Earlier Days* (1853) or Pius IX's *Syllabus of Errors* (1864) as reactionary statements of commitment to the theological styles of the past, it is important to recognize that the conservative Roman theology of this time did not always simply reiterate the assumptions of the classical paradigm in its sixteenth-century expression. Roman theology and the magisterium remained suspicious of the new tendencies of modern theology but found certain

---

the function or the activity of someone who is in the position of *magister*, that is, of authority in a particular area" ("A Brief History of the Forms of the Magisterium," in *Readings in Moral Theology No. 3: The Magisterium and Morality*, ed. C. E. Curran and R. A. McCormick, S.J. [New York: Paulist Press, 1982], 318). In another article, Congar specifies that "the expression 'the magisterium' in its current usage was introduced by eighteenth-century theology but especially by German canonists at the beginning of the nineteenth century" ("A Semantic History of the Term 'Magisterium,' " in *Readings in Moral Theology No. 3*, 306). Cf. Michael D. Place, "Magisterium and Theologians: Historical Perspectives. Trent to the First Vatican Council," *Chicago Studies* 17 (1978): 225–41. The present sketch of the troubled relations between the magisterium and the notion of theological authorship should begin with the observation that the emergence of the modern connotation of the magisterium as a discrete and authoritative hierarchical body is directly contemporaneous with the emergence of the romantic paradigm of theological responsibility. The fact that the new paradigm of theological responsibility and the new understanding of institutional teaching authority struggled for their senses of identity and purpose in relation to each other helps to explain their mutual ambivalence.

36. Thomas F. O'Meara, *Romantic Idealism and Roman Catholicism: Schelling and the Theologians* (Notre Dame, Ind.: Univ. of Notre Dame Press, 1982), 188–99.

of its aspects compatible with the magisterial understanding of ecclesial authority espoused by the classical paradigm since the late Middle Ages. The organic view of history and tradition expressed in the notion of doctrinal development, for example, could be and was invoked to lend support for the proclamations of the dogmas of the Immaculate Conception in 1854 and papal infallibility in 1870.[37] The idea of an organic tradition helped to explain the very possibility of offering explicit definition in recent times to what had always been the implicit, if undefined, faith of the church.[38] Such explanations of developing tradition, however, were recognized only on an ad hoc basis and only to justify an exclusively institutional definition of ecclesial authority.[39]

37. Edgar Hocedez, S.J., *Histoire de la théologie au XIXe siècle*, vol. 2 (Paris: Desclée de Brouwer, 1952), 374.

38. The best example of this approach is found in the work of Charles Passaglia, who introduced an organic perspective to the conservative theology that flourished in Rome under the pontificate of Pius IX. See Hocedez, *Histoire de la théologie au XIXe siècle*, 2:356. Cf. Jan H. Walgrave, *Unfolding Revelation: The Nature of Doctrinal Development* (Philadelphia: Westminster Press, 1972), 335.

39. Ironically, John Henry Newman remained under a cloud of suspicion during most of his years in the Roman communion even though his *Essay on the Development of Christian Doctrine* remains the most sophisticated expression of a theory of development compatible with a largely institutional disposition toward the exercise of ecclesial authority. This is not to say that the exposition of such a viewpoint was Newman's intention in the *Essay*. He wrote the *Essay* to bring theoretical order to the problem of traditional change and continuity which he met in his studies of early church history and patristics, an exercise that increasingly came to chart his intellectual and spiritual journey toward the Church of Rome. The result, however, was a theory of development that could be invoked by others with relative ease to support an exclusively institutional definition of teaching authority in the church. That the *Essay* was not used in this way can be explained by the personal suspicion under which Newman was held under the pontificates of Pius IX and Pius X, in spite of his elevation to the cardinalate under Leo XIII. See Gary Lease, "Newman: The Roman View," in *Newman and the Modernists*, ed. M. Weaver (New York: Univ. Press of America, 1985), 161–82.

Newman's theory occasionally describes the development of doctrine in organic terms, but it more regularly uses the noetic metaphor of development as the clarification of an idea. Newman conceives of this process as one that is "homogeneous, expanding and irreversible" (Nicholas Lash, *Newman on Development: The Search for an Explanation in History* [Shepherdstown, W.V.: Patmos Press, 1975], 65). The development of doctrine through the ages, he assumes, is better explained in terms of communal structures, institutions, and embracing ideas than in terms of the significant contributions of individuals. Unlike Schleiermacher and Drey, Newman does not recognize the special contributions of theologians to this process in the *Essay*. He does not portray the development of doctrine as issuing from the creative

The romantic paradigm's description of doctrinal development differs from this institutional use of organic explanation by virtue of its insistence upon the theologian's important, and indeed indispensable, contributions to ecclesial tradition through the exercise of personal talent. Even when willing to embrace an organicism shaped by its concern for an utterly centralized authority, the magisterium and its favored theology of neoscholasticism remained suspicious of any conception of doctrinal development that allowed the theologian to serve as an authorial interpreter of the experience of the church. Prior to the modernist controversy, this suspicion was voiced indirectly in the magisterium's condemnations of Georg Hermes, Anton Günther, Antonio Rosmini, and Jakob Frohschammer for the roles they allowed for various forms of subjectivity, whether rational or intuitive, in the enterprises of theology and philosophy.[40] It would

---

interplay between the fixed belief of the past and the vital belief of the present but from an impulse at work in the entire tradition for growth in its understanding and refinement in its articulation of divine truth. The historical movement of this impulse can be witnessed most clearly in the ancient church's battles with heresy. But Newman could also receive the news of the impending proclamation of the dogma of the Immaculate Conception in 1854, nine years after the publication of the *Essay*, as a confirmation of his theory. See Paul Misner, *Papacy and Development: Newman and the Primacy of the Pope* (Leiden: E. J. Brill, 1976), 121.

Newman's theory of development bears the marks of a historian's mind and is not troubled by the sorts of apologetic and constructive issues faced by Schleiermacher and Drey. Indeed, Newman's *Essay* emphasizes the corporate character of doctrinal evolution, and Newman looks primarily to the institutional church, with its desire for homogeneity in matters of belief, for the legitimating authority of true development: "If the very claim to infallible arbitration in religious disputes is of so weighty importance and interest in all ages of the world, much more is it welcome at a time like the present, when the human intellect is so busy, and thought so fertile, and opinion so indefinitely divided. The absolute need of a spiritual supremacy is at present the strongest of arguments in favour of its supply" (John Henry Newman, *An Essay on the Development of Christian Doctrine* [London: James Toovey, 1845], 127). In a passage added to the third edition of 1878, which undoubtedly takes into account the conciliar definition of papal infallibility, Newman observes that development "is carried on through and by means of communities of men and their leaders and guides; and it employs their minds as its instruments, and depends upon them, while it uses them" (*An Essay on the Development of Doctrine*, 6th ed. [Notre Dame, Ind.: Univ. of Notre Dame Press, 1989], 38). With the publication of the 1877 edition of the *Via Media*, Newman began to highlight the importance of theological reflection and the work of the *schola theologorum* within the authoritative life of the church. His principal exposition of the theory of doctrinal development in the *Essay*, however, even in its 1878 edition, did not address the issue of theological authorship. See Misner, *Papacy and Development*, 158–73.

40. Anton Günther is particularly noteworthy for our purposes because he also

be interesting, moreover, to consider the tacit agenda in Vatican theology from Pius IX's encyclical *Qui Pluribus* (1846) to Vatican I's *Dei Filius* (1870) as an attempt to suppress modern claims to authorship by defending the consonance between metaphysical reasoning in the Thomistic tradition and a faith moored in the established dogmas of the church.

The period between Vatican Councils I and II witnessed the magisterium's outright rejection of theological authorship. This rejection is nowhere made as clearly and forcefully as it is in the encyclical of Pius X, *Pascendi dominici gregis* (1907).[41] This text caricatures and condemns the romantic insistence on creative authorship in the historical theology of the modernists at the turn of the twentieth century. No ecclesial document focuses so explicitly on what is considered to be the misappropriation of theological responsibility and attacks so vigorously the modern conception of the theologian. There are, of course, reasons for this. The modernists sought the same romantic reconciliation of truth and history ventured by Drey and the Catholic Tübingen school in the first half of the nineteenth century. Their situation was rendered far more precarious, however, by the conciliar definition of the prerogative of infallibility (1870), the required adoption of a scholastic model of theological education at the insistence of *Aeterni Patris* (1879), and the generally conservative atmosphere of the post–Vatican I church.

---

explicitly addresses the issue of theological responsibility. In this regard he follows Drey closely in viewing the theologian as a creative contributor to ecclesial tradition. Orthodox doctrine, in Günther's view, cannot be identified with the established dogmas of the past; it is a synthesis between the "constant" (*ein Beharrliches*) and "mobile" (*ein Bewegliches*) elements in doctrinal tradition. The former is the doctrine's "given object" and represents the established formulas of the past; the latter is the doctrine's "learning subject" and represents the developing belief of the church in the present historical moment. The theologian's task is not merely to preserve the completed doctrine of the past but to develop the orthodox tradition by "bringing the mobile element of doctrine into unison with its constant element." This harmony must be established by steering a middle course between the Scylla of heterodoxy and the Charybdis of hyperorthodoxy, threats to proper doctrinal development posed by sheer theological innovation on the one hand and the lifeless repetition of established dogma on the other (*Vorschule zur speculativen Theologie des positiven Christentums*, in *Dr. Anton Günther's gesammelte Schriften*, vol. 2 [1882; reprint, Frankfurt am Main: Minerva, 1968], 278–83).

41. The translation of *Pascendi dominici gregis* employed here appears in *The Papal Encyclicals 1903–1939*, ed. C. Carlen, (Wilmington, N.C.: McGrath, 1981), 71–98; *Acta Sancta Sedis* 40: 593–650. References to the encyclical's numbered paragraphs are cited instead of page numbers.

What amounts to the encyclical's outright horror in the face of the modernist's commitment to a developmental understanding of religious truth is the source of its passionate condemnation. Modernism, *Pascendi* claims, is "the synthesis of all heresies . . . , the sap and substance of them all."[42] In the judgment of the encyclical, modernism's challenge to the steadfast truths of the scholastic tradition and its repudiation of patristic wisdom have resulted in a pseudo-theology destructive of the one, true faith. Its affirmation of an experiential approach to revelation, and its assumption that this subjective truth and its dogmatic expression are in a constant process of evolution, have vitiated the normative safeguards for theological reflection that are in the possession of the magisterium[43] and have eroded the stability expected of genuine theological science.[44]

The notion of theological authorship first advocated by Schleiermacher and Drey, and subsequently by later generations of theologians, had its provenance in a consciousness of the historicity of faith, one that portrayed doctrinal development as a dialectical movement through time and culture that the theologian purposively fosters. *Pascendi* specifically rejects this conceptualization of development and does so by offering a caricatured portrayal of the talent of theological authorship:

> Hence, studying more closely the ideas of the Modernists, evolution is described as resulting from the conflict of two forces, one of them tending towards progress, the other towards conservation. The conserving force in the Church is tradition, and tradition is represented by religious authority, and this both by right and in fact; for by right it is in the very nature of authority to protect tradition, and in fact, for authority, raised as it is above the contingencies of life, feels hardly, or not at all, the spurs of progress. The progressive force, on the contrary, which responds to the inner needs lies in the individual consciences and ferments there—especially in such of them as are in most intimate contact with life.[45]

This "pernicious doctrine which would make of the laity the factor of progress in the Church" is condemnable not only because of its

42. *Pascendi*, 39.
43. Ibid., 8–15, 23, 25.
44. Ibid., 45, 46.
45. Ibid., 27.

deficient notion of truth and populist understanding of authority but also because of the directive power it accords to theological sensibility. The progress of the tradition, the encyclical chidingly observes, supposedly occurs as the "individual consciences of some of them act on the collective conscience, which brings pressure to bear on the depositaries of authority, until the latter consent to a compromise."[46]

In a manner departing from the customary style of ecclesiastical condemnations, *Pascendi* devotes its zealous criticism to a psychological analysis of the modernist "personality" considered in its many aberrations—as philosopher, believer, historian, critic, apologist, and reformer—though it is in the caricatured portrait of the modernist as theologian that we discover the magisterium's explicit rejection of the notion of romantic authorship. Brusquely conflating theological authorship and its heroic conceptualization, *Pascendi* condemns what it sees as the autonomy of the supposed theological genius, authorized by personal talent and engaged in a quest for the ongoing truth of tradition that ability alone is capable of accomplishing:

> What is imputed to them as a fault they [modernist theologians] regard as a sacred duty. Being in intimate contact with consciences, they know better than anyone else, and certainly better than the ecclesiastical authority, what needs exist—nay, they embody them, so to speak, in themselves. Having a voice and a pen, they use both publicly, for this is their duty. Let authority rebuke them as much as it pleases—they have their own conscience on their side and an intimate experience which tells them with certainty that what they deserve is not blame but praise. Then they reflect that, after all, there is no progress without a battle and no battle without its victim, and victims they are willing to be like the prophets and Christ Himself. They have no bitterness in their hearts against the authority which uses them roughly, for, after all, it is only doing its duty as authority. Their sole grief is that it remains deaf to their warnings, because delay multiplies the obstacles which impede the progress of souls, but the hour will most surely come when there will be no further chance for tergiversation, for if the laws of evolution may be checked for a while, they cannot be ultimately destroyed.[47]

As any authentic quest necessarily entails the overcoming of obstacles, the theological author does not seek the final demise of

46. Ibid.
47. Ibid.

the magisterium's authority and thus "it is part of their [the modernists'] system that authority is to be stimulated but not dethroned."[48] Such a view of theological authorship masks "an incredible audacity,"[49] the reflection of "pride which fills Modernists with that confidence in themselves and leads them to hold themselves up as the rule for all."[50] It is this same pride which leads them to the presumptuous judgment that *"we are not as the rest of men,* and which, to make them really not as other men, leads them to embrace all kinds of the most absurd novelties."[51]

Gabriel Daley's judgment that modernism "never possessed the cohesion that its enemies bestowed on it"[52] applies to virtually all of the ideas of modernists such as Alfred Loisy, Friedrich von Hügel, and George Tyrell, with the possible exception of the notion of theological authorship. As different as their particular concerns may be, all made the historicocritical method central to their conceptions of the theological enterprise and assumed that the theologian's creative judgments contribute to the development of doctrine and thereby to the health of the tradition. In this regard *Pascendi*'s determination of the issue at stake in the controversy between the theologians and the magisterium is faultless. This is not to say, however, that the encyclical's depiction of theological authorship is warranted. For our purposes the question of the encyclical's truthful portrayal of the modernist position is not at issue. As in all caricatures, truth and falsity become strange partners in *Pascendi* and meet only in a context of exaggeration and distortion.

What is at issue in the present analysis is the text's reception of the romantic understanding of theological responsibility and how that reception has contributed to the state of relations between the magisterium and theologians in the twentieth century. In reaffirming the classical paradigm of theological responsibility, the encyclical ignores the reasons for theological claims on behalf of authorial talent. The encyclical does not recognize the urgency of offering an effective theological response to the Enlightenment or the need to account for

48. Ibid.
49. Ibid.
50. Ibid., 40.
51. Ibid.
52. Gabriel Daly, *Transcendence and Immanence: A Study in Catholic Modernism and Integralism* (Oxford: Clarendon Press, 1980), 117.

the development of doctrine and the historicity of faith or the increasing appeal in the eighteenth and nineteenth centuries to the individual imagination as a explanation of creative agency. *Pascendi* perceives theological authorship only as a threat to the truth of the ages, which stands under the protection of the teaching office of the church. In *Pascendi* the modernists' commitment to the exercise of theological talent is indistinguishable from the centuries-old portrayal of the heretic as an apostate who brazenly asserts solitary speculations in opposition to the universal faith. In the climate of *Pascendi*, which lasted throughout the greater part of the twentieth century, "[t]he theologian, whose task it was to deal speculatively with revealed truths, needed no historical skills or training for the adequate performance of [the] task [of interpretation]. Dogma, not history, provided him with the material necessary for the pursuit of his craft; and a stern magisterium was there to see that he reached the correct conclusions."[53]

Even though Pius XII's encyclical *Humani Generis* (1950)[54] tempers the polemical excesses of *Pascendi*, it essentially reiterates the earlier writing's condemnation of theological creativity. Taking as its opponents the promulgators of the French reform movement "nouvelle théologie," *Humani Generis* raised the specter of modernism to confront the growing chorus of voices for theological and ecclesial renewal that had begun to gather strength in the years following the Second World War.[55] Any doubt that the disdain expressed early in the letter for the evils of "evolution," "immanentism," and "historicism"[56] extends to the theological appropriation of these ideas is quickly dispelled by the text's eventual denial of theological authorship. The encyclical recognizes only the value of "positive" theology, the attempt "to show how a doctrine defined by the Church is contained in the sources of revelation," not in a general way but, quoting Pius IX, " 'in that sense in which it has been defined by the

53. Ibid., 20.

54. The translation of *Humani Generis* employed here appears in *The Papal Encyclicals* 1939–1958, 175–84; *Acta Apostolicae Sedis* [hereinafter abbreviated *AAS*] 42 (1950): 561–78. References to the encyclical's numbered paragraphs are cited instead of page numbers.

55. For a discussion of the "nouvelle théologie," see Roger Aubert, *La Théologie catholique au milieu du XXe siècle* (Paris: Casterman, 1954), 84f. Also Mark Schoof, *A Survey of Catholic Theology 1800–1970*, trans. N. D. Smith (New York: Paulist Newman Press, 1970), 201–9.

56. *Humani Generis*, 5–7.

Church.' "[57] This directive implicitly denies the theologian's right to exercise the talent of creative authorship, conceiving of the theologian's role instead as the iterative promulgation of the magisterium's teaching. The letter maintains that "our Divine Redeemer has given [the deposit of faith] for authentic interpretation not to each of the faithful, not even to theologians, but only to the Teaching Authority of the Church."[58] Like *Pascendi*, *Humani Generis* conflates theological authorship and the specifically heroic conceptualization of this ability, concluding that theological creativity of any sort inevitably portrays the magisterium as a stumbling block along the way of the theological quest: "Unfortunately, these advocates of [theological] novelty easily pass from despising scholastic theology to the neglect of, and even contempt for, the Teaching Authority of the Church itself, which gives such authoritative approval to scholastic theology. This Teaching Authority is represented by them as a hindrance to progress and an obstacle in the way of science."[59]

These critical judgments show how little change there was in the magisterium's regard for the romantic paradigm and its notion of theological authorship in the forty-three years separating the encyclicals of Pius X and Pius XII. Both letters regard the modern paradigm as a pretender to legitimate ecclesial authority for two interrelated reasons. First, the modern paradigm affirms the authority of individual theological insight for discerning and reformulating the meaning of the ecclesial tradition, now understood developmentally. Second, it is judged inherently to extend this individual authority to heroic proportions, seeing the theologian as a creative genius subjectively responsible to God, ecclesial society, and the self but necessarily at odds with institutional authority. Both encyclicals offer the magisterium's defensive position in a perceived conflict for teaching authority in the church, a conflict disjunctively conceived as a struggle between theological creativity and faithfulness to the traditional teaching office of the magisterium.

This understanding of the theological vocation as uncritical service to the magisterium at the cost of individual authority was virtually ignored in the documents of the Second Vatican Council. In his opening address to the council on October 11, 1962, John XXIII

57. Ibid., 21.
58. Ibid.
59. Ibid., 18.

set a new tone for relations between the magisterium and theologians that provided at least implicit authorization of the romantic paradigm of theological responsibility. "Our duty," he stated, "is not only to guard this precious treasure [of the faith], as if we were concerned only with antiquity, but to dedicate ourselves with an earnest will and without fear to that work which our era demands of us."[60] Theology must not seek merely the terminological updating of traditional teaching but must investigate the significance of faith in changing historical circumstances. In the words of the opening address, the "substance of the ancient doctrine of the deposit of faith is one thing, and the way in which it is presented is another."[61] *The Pastoral Constitution on the Church in the Modern World (Gaudium et Spes)* repeats this sentiment almost verbatim,[62] offering the clarification that "while adhering to the methods and requirements proper to theology, theologians are invited to seek continually for more suitable ways of communicating doctrine to the men of their times."[63]

These words constitute the magisterium's first formal acknowledgment of a division of labor, shared with theologians, in the teaching responsibilities of the church, an acknowledgment that assumes that the theological enterprise is a creative pursuit whose resources lie at least partially in the abilities of its practitioners. *Gaudium et Spes* refers to the context necessary for the exercise of this creativity by recognizing the demand for new theological investigations generated by recent developments in science, history, and philosophy and by calling for "a lawful freedom of inquiry and of thought" among all the faithful, a freedom "to express their minds humbly and courageously about those matters in which they enjoy competence."[64] If we take note of the fact that *Gaudium et Spes* was prepared in draft by a commission advised by council *periti* such as Yves Congar, Henri deLubac, and Jean Danielou, exponents of the "nouvelle théologie" of the 1940s against which the proscriptive statements of *Humani Generis* were directed, there can be little doubt that these words were

60. *The Documents of Vatican II*, ed. W. M. Abbott, S.J. (New York: America Press, 1966), 715.
61. Ibid.
62. "For the deposit of faith or revealed truths are one thing; the manner in which they are formulated without violence to their meaning and significance is another." *Gaudium et Spes*, 62; *The Documents of Vatican II*, 268–69.
63. *Gaudium et Spes*, 62; *The Documents of Vatican II*, 268.
64. *Gaudium et Spes*, 62; *The Documents of Vatican II*, 270.

written in purposeful consideration of the issue of theological responsibility.[65]

The council's ground-breaking recognition of the legitimate role of theological creativity was related to two conciliar positions that pressed beyond the heritage of Trent and Vatican I: its positive regard for historical development, especially the development of doctrine,[66] and its willingness to consider the magisterium's infallibility in the broader context of its relationship to the *sensus fidei* of the entire church.[67] As demonstrated in our examination of its nineteenth-century origins, the romantic paradigm understood the theologian to be primarily responsible to the developing experience of the entire ecclesial community. In this experience, the paradigm assumes, lie the significant and enduring moments in the development of tradition that theological talent must discern and articulate if the doctrinal present is to be bound meaningfully to the past and promoted into the future. By embracing a more historical view of tradition unfolding in the whole church, now understood as the "People of God" and as invested with the spirit of truth, Vatican II implicitly adopted a romantic understanding of tradition and ecclesiology that could be served only by an equally romantic understanding of theological responsibility.

Although the idealistic spirit of theological *aggiornamento* was realistically tempered in the years soon after the council, it continued to thrive. Vatican pronouncements on theological responsibility during this period document the magisterium's gradual acceptance of the notion of theological authorship. If only from a historical perspective, it is remarkable that the magisterium's acceptance of the romantic conception of authorship took place within a single pontificate. At the close of the council, Paul VI thought of theology as "delegated" to the magisterium in the manner expected by *Humani Generis*.[68] His rejection of what he finds most reprehensible in the

65. *The Documents of Vatican II*, 269–70, n. 203.

66. *Dei Verbum*, 8; *The Documents of Vatican II*, 116.

67. *Lumen Gentium*, 12; *The Documents of Vatican II*, 29–30. For a discussion of the theological implications of the notion of the *sensus fidei*, see Wolfgang Beinert, "Bedeutung und Begrundung des Glaubenssinnes (Sensus Fidei) als dogmatischen Erkenntniskriteriums," *Catholica* 25 (1971): 271–303; Luigi Sartori, "What Is the Criterion for the *Sensus Fidelium*?" in *Who Has Say in the Church?* (*Concilium*, 148), ed. J. Moltmann and H. Küng (New York: Seabury Press, 1981), 56–59.

68. See Max Seckler, "Die Theologie als kirchliche Wissenschaft nach Pius XII. und Paul VI.," *Theologische Quartalschrift* 149 (1969): 220f.

romantic paradigm, a heroic understanding of authorship, is expressed in his address to the International Congress on the Theology of Vatican II, *Libentissimo sane animo* (October 1, 1966):

> [T]here is a growing tendency right now to belittle or deny the relationship of theology to the Church's magisterium. When we try to analyze the mentality and outlook of educated men of our day, we find it has this distinctive cast: they put excessive reliance on their own capabilities; they are of the opinion that authority in any form must be rejected; and they are convinced that a person can manage to acquire all types of knowledge on his own initiative and shape his life accordingly.
>
> Regrettably, this liberty—or rather, license—is sometimes extended, to a greater or lesser degree, to knowledge of the faith and to the field of theology. According to this view, no external or transcendent guiding norm is to be accepted. It is as if the whole realm of truth could be circumscribed within the bounds of human reason, or even created by it; or as if nothing could be established so absolutely and so definitively that it does not allow for further progress or subsequent refutation; or as if a system would be of even more value if it corresponded more fully to subjective instincts and emotions. Hence an authoritative magisterium is rejected, or at best, its function is restricted to vigilance against errors.[69]

Convinced that the exercise of theological authorship could not avoid the snares of heroic excess, Paul VI tended to reject the integrity of theological creativity in the earliest period of his pontificate. In this respect his initial views on the role of the theologian in the church differed little from those formed by the hierarchy in the heat of the modernist crisis.

Within a short time, however, Paul VI departed from the automatic identification of theological creativity and heroic disdain for the magisterium made by his preconciliar predecessors and began to articulate in occasional writings and speeches the heritage of the council on this issue. This is particularly evident in his address to the inaugural session of the International Theological Commission, the founding of which at the recommendation of the 1967 Synod of Bishops is perhaps the best institutional evidence of the magisterium's recognition of the legitimacy of theological authorship. Rather than

69. *The Pope Speaks* 11 (1966): 350; *AAS* 58 (1966): 890.

simply reaffirming the importance of theological responsibility to the magisterium, the address, *Gratia Domini nostri* (October 6, 1969), solidifies the division of labor in teaching authority sanctioned by Vatican II. Speaking to the theologians, Paul VI expresses his intention "to recognize the laws and exigencies that are part and parcel of your studies . . . , to respect the freedom of expression rightfully belonging to theological science, and the need for research inherent to its progress."[70] Describing the nature of theological responsibility as a synthesis of freedom and fidelity, the address calls on theologians to be "faithful to the object of your studies, the faith, even as you are confident about the possibility of carrying on these studies in accord with their own principles and your personal talents."[71]

This later position of Paul VI has remained the view of the magisterium on its relationship to theological reflection and thus on the nature of theological responsibility.[72] According to it, theologians enjoy the creative freedom of authorship and therefore possess teaching authority in the church. This authority, however, does not stand on equal footing with that of the magisterium.[73] Creativity and insight are affirmed as necessary ingredients of the theological enterprise, though these talents are not understood to be free from normative measure. They flourish meaningfully within the context of faithfulness to the magisterium, which the theologian serves, though not

70. *The Pope Speaks* 14 (1969): 202; *AAS* 61 (1969): 715.

71. *The Pope Speaks* 14 (1969): 202; *AAS* 61 (1969): 715. Cf. "Quinque iam anni" (December 8, 1970), *The Pope Speaks* 15 (1971): 330; *AAS* 63 (1971): 103. See also Juan Alfaro, "Theology and the Magisterium," in *Problems and Perspectives of Fundamental Theology*, ed. R. Latourelle and G. O'Collins (New York: Paulist Press, 1982), 354.

72. Max Seckler does not recognize this shift in the thought of Paul VI on the issue of theological responsibility. Defining the modern conception of theology in terms of its scientific status rather than in terms of the integrity of authorship, Seckler sees the appearance of a "new style" of magisterial regard for postconciliar theology in the addresses of John Paul II to academic audiences at Cologne Cathedral (November 15, 1980; *AAS* 73 [1981]: 49–58) and St. Konrad in Alttötting (November 18, 1980; *AAS* 73 [1981]: 49–58). See "Kirchliches Lehramt und theologische Wissenschaft: Geschichtliche Aspeckte, Probleme und Lösungselemente," in *Die Theologie und das Lehramt* (Quaestiones Disputatae, 91), ed. W. Kern (Freiburg: Herder, 1982), 54.

73. This specific assumption of the Catholic reception of the romantic paradigm militates, though only formally, against Avery Dulles's proposal to recognize two magisteria in the church: one hierarchical, the other theological. Speaking in these terms might give the impression that the magisteria are equal in ecclesial authority. "Two Magisteria: An Interim Reflection," in *Proceedings of the Catholic Theological Society of America*, ed. L. Salm, 35 (1980): 155–69.

at the expense of private judgment, which, when professionally discharged, possesses relative authority.[74]

One finds an even more direct assertion of theological authority in the "Theses on the Relationship between the Ecclesiastical Magisterium and Theology" (1975), produced and approved by the International Theological Commission[75] undoubtedly with the support of the Congregation for the Doctrine of the Faith.[76] The theses make reference to the shared teaching authority of the church, which "should be put into practice in a co-responsible, cooperative, and collegial association of the members of the magisterium and of individual theologians."[77] The text continues by noting that theologians "derive their specifically theological authority from their scientific qualifications," at the same time stating the concern that these abilities "cannot be separated from the proper character of this discipline as the science of faith."[78] Most striking in the theses is the affirmation of the romantic paradigm's connection between theological talent and development. It is incumbent on the magisterium, the fourth thesis states, to "preserve the personal and indispensable responsibility of individual theologians, without which the science of faith would make no progress."[79]

This same sentiment was expressed by John Paul II in an address to an assembly of Spanish theologians at the Pontifical University of Salamanca on November 1, 1982. Calling on theologians to achieve renewal "as creative as it is faithful," the pope presented the challenge of theological creativity in a manner that recalls the very context for the exercise of authorship originally proposed by Schleiermacher and Drey: "The theologian cannot limit himself to preserving the doctrinal treasure inherited from the past; rather he must seek an understanding and an expression of the faith which make possible its

74. Jon Nilson, "The Rights and Responsibilities of Theologians: A Theological Perspective," in *Cooperation between Theologians and the Ecclesiastical Magisterium*, ed. L. J. O'Donovan, S.J. (Washington, D.C.: Catholic Univ. of America, 1982), 62–75.

75. A translation of the text, along with a commentary by its authors, Otto Semmelroth, S.J., and Karl Lehmann, appears in *Readings in Moral Theology No. 3*, 151–70.

76. See Francis A. Sullivan, S.J., *Magisterium: Teaching Authority in the Catholic Church* (New York: Paulist Press, 1983), 174.

77. "Theses on the Relationship between the Ecclesiastical Magisterium and Theology," in *Readings in Moral Theology No. 3*, 154.

78. Ibid., 156.

79. Ibid., 154.

acceptance in the manner of thinking and speaking in our time. The criterion which ought to guide theological reflection is the search for a renewed understanding of the Christian message in the dialectic of continuity in renewal and vice versa."[80] In a homily delivered on October 23, 1981, John Paul II observed that theological discernment and construction, the exercises of authorship, are essential to the proper development of doctrine which takes shape in history as ecclesial tradition: "The task of a mature theology is, finally, that of reading the present in light of Tradition, of which the Church is the depository. Tradition is life. In it the riches of the Christian mystery are expressed, gradually manifesting, in contact with the changing events of history, the virtualities implicit in the perennial values of revelation."[81]

This brief sketch prompts an observation that can give further direction to the present project. The acceptance of the romantic paradigm of theological responsibility in the Roman Catholic tradition is quite recent. Its duration has been short in comparison with the eight hundred years that its predecessor, the classical paradigm, has flourished as the accepted model for Catholic theological reflection. Perhaps, then, it is to be expected that the redefinition of ancient assumptions would lead to the ambivalent and sometimes hostile relations between theologians and the magisterium that have been characteristic of the period since the Second Vatican Council. Faced with this situation, theologians need to suggest ways in which the value of theological authorship can be conveyed to the church, especially to the magisterium, which continues to be suspicious of its exercise and nostalgic for the days when theologians conceived of their work as mimesis. We now turn to this task.

CREATIVE FIDELITY AS A
THEOLOGICAL *HABITUS*

If one views the history of the romantic paradigm of theological responsibility in the Catholic tradition as a gradual struggle for its acceptance, then the Second Vatican Council was a watershed in the new paradigm's tumultuous history. The paradigm's outright rejection in the encyclicals of Pius X and Pius XII gave way to its qualified

80. "Como en mi," *The Pope Speaks* 28 (1983): 119–20; *AAS* 75 (1983): 260–61.

81. "Con queste," *The Pope Speaks* 27 (1982): 102.

acceptance as Vatican II emphasized the themes of the historicity of faith and its development in tradition, thereby paving the way for the recognition, expressed in the addresses of Paul VI and John Paul II, of the special talents of theological discernment and construction in the life of the church. Yet, somewhat surprisingly, the actual acceptance of theological authorship as a valid conceptualization of the theological task has not led to happy relations between theologians and the magisterium since the pontificate of Paul VI. On the contrary, these relations have been fraught with tensions that have centered on the very issue of authorship and the status of theologians as author-itative interpreters of and teachers in the tradition. How might we account for this anomaly?

One often-heard and one-sided answer is that the magisterium's actions in calling to task theologians such as Hans Küng, Edward Schillebeeckx, Charles Curran, Leonardo Boff, and Matthew Fox were simply misguided. Accused in this view of an uncompromising authoritarianism, the magisterium is portrayed as set in its reactionary ways and unwilling to allow the insights of theological creativity to modify its understanding of the church in the world in any fashion. Were we to draw on the categories posed in this study, we could express this accusation by attributing the magisterium's actions toward these theologians, as different as they were, to its lingering commitment to the classical paradigm and its expectation that the-ologians legitimately practice their craft mimetically and not imag-inatively. This position would account for recent, and what in all likelihood will be ongoing, theological disputes by laying blame on the magisterial teaching office of the church alone, a point of view that is often attractive to the theological community. Such an expla-nation, however, is unnuanced and takes into account neither the fact of magisterial approval of the notion of theological authorship nor the complex history of struggle within which that recognition was achieved and by which it continues to be influenced.

A more balanced explanation for the strained relations between the magisterium and theologians would attribute the magisterium's ambivalence about theological authorship to the paradigm's original and occasionally recurring tendency to conceive of the theological vocation along the romantic lines of a heroic quest for truthful in-novation. The magisterium has consistently and correctly, I believe, rejected this particular dimension of the romantic conceptualization of authorship from the time of *Pascendi* to the present, though at some cost to productive relations between the magisterium and the-ologians. As the romantic paradigm ascribes to individual talent the responsibility of ecclesial discernment, the magisterium fears the dis-tancing of its own ecclesial office from the church at large or, worse, the theological conceptualization of its own authority as being out of touch or even at odds with the *sensus fidei*. As the romantic par-adigm ascribes to theological discernment the vocational power to promote the tradition, the magisterium fears that its legitimate efforts to judge innovation in light of the time-honored tradition of the past will be portrayed by the theologian as an obstacle to doctrinal de-velopment.

But these legitimate concerns unfortunately have often led the magisterium to identify the power of theological discernment and construction with the heroic embellishment of authorship, a perver-sion, I would say, of an authentic understanding of the role of this talent within the church. The magisterium remains wary of a talent potentially, but not at all necessarily, in the service of individual aggrandizement. The result of the magisterium's consistent identi-fication of theological authorship with its specifically heroic concep-tualization is twofold: the magisterium's tendency to stifle a valuable resource of ecclesial vitality and its tendency to regard even the le-gitimate exercise of authorship, which includes responsible criticism of magisterial teaching, as a narcissistic symptom of a heroic mentality bent on conflict with the church. This confusion could be circum-vented by understanding the talent of theological authorship as a development within the traditional conception of the theological prac-titioner's proper subjective disposition.

From the time of the High Middle Ages through the seventeenth century, classical theology in the Catholic and Protestant traditions deemed the theologian's subjectivity a topic worthy of consideration. Thomistic, nominalist, and Protestant orthodox theologies reflected on the vocational call to theology by delineating the characteristics of a measured theological temperament. This subjective bearing was known as the theological *habitus*, a disposition of receptivity to the assistance of God's grace which aided the theologian in cultivating the right representation of God's word and will in scripture and tradition. Within the classical paradigm, the *habitus* was conceived as a theologian's inclination of faithfulness to the traditional sources of revelation and, in the case of Catholicism, to the authority of the church. Whether conceived as naturally acquired to some degree or as supernaturally infused, the *habitus* was portrayed as an intellectual power enabling the perfection of the act of faith to the extraordinary reaches of theological wisdom itself and as a disposition of ecclesial loyalty that guided the theologian's prudent exposition of the truth of revelation.[82]

If Schleiermacher and Drey are cited as illustrations of the idea of theological authorship in its first appearance, then there seems at first glance to be little room in their understandings of the theological vocation for the conception of a theological *habitus*. Although they delineate the task of authorship in slightly different ways, both understand its creativity as essential to the doctrinal construction of ecclesial tradition. For Schleiermacher, acts of ecclesial description issue from the talent of theological divination, which fathoms the present state of historical faith in order to single out those vital, heterodox, and potentially lasting determinations of contemporary belief, which, informed by the orthodoxy of the past, point the tradition toward the future course of its authentic development. For Drey, a truly scientific theology is equally mindful of its role in the development of doctrine. Acts of theological understanding constantly reconstruct the truth of the fixed dogmatic tradition so that a living orthodoxy might emerge from its encounter with the faith of the contemporary moment. In both cases the theological imagination builds a relationship between the received wisdom of the ecclesial past and the developing truth of the ecclesial present.

With these views Schleiermacher and Drey proposed new understandings of what theology is, of the way it functions in the life of the church, and of the role played by the theologian's subjectivity in relation to traditional authority. Since they allowed the theologian's personal agency a more active role than the traditional understanding did, we might judge precipitously that the romantic theologians replaced this older understanding with the conception of authorship. Although it may be tempting to follow Edward Farley in distinguishing classical from modern theology by the latter's unfortunate loss of the former's idea of theology as habitual wisdom,[83] we might

82. See Yves M.-J. Congar, *A History of Theology*, trans. H. Guthrie, S.J. (Garden City, N.Y.: Doubleday & Co., 1968), 131–32, 260–68. Cf. Edward Farley, *Theologia: The Fragmentation and Unity of Theological Education* (Philadelphia: Fortress Press, 1983), 46–47, n. 12, n. 15.
83. Farley, *Theologia*, 42–44.

do better to think of the modern notion of theological authorship as a modification of the traditional conception of the *habitus* to the new circumstances in which theology found itself at the dawn of the modern age.

Schleiermacher and Drey, like all who legitimately advocate the modern notion of theological authorship, insisted on the theologian's faithfulness to tradition and conceived of theology as an expression of the faith of the church. In consonance with the classical conception of the *habitus*, they maintained that the theologian's proper disposition was one of commitment to God's revelation, regardless of how their particular confessional loyalties led them to conceive of its manifestation. But their times, and ours, clamored for a recognition of the possibilities of historical change, the role of contemporary experience in the narrative of truth, and the need to interpret such development in ways that were unprejudicial to the integrity of theology as a discipline. This situation demanded that the theologian regard creativity not only as a quality of the theological task rightly executed but also as a subjective ability of the theologian committed to the authority of a tradition both established and developing. The result was an understanding of the *habitus* grounded in the classical understanding of the theological disposition as traditional commitment but extended to include the creative and critical engagement of authorship. This conceptualization of the *habitus* as creative fidelity entails a view of theological responsibility to God, to the traditional sources of God's revelation, and to the historical medium in which they are appropriated by the believing church.[84]

Put in a slightly different fashion, but again considering the modern formulation of an ancient description of personal ability, we might say that the magisterium's ambivalence toward theological authorship stems from the modern assumption that theological teaching authority issues from an ecclesial charism, that of the discernment of the tradition's movement and the theological construction of its

84. Joseph DiNoia has recently proposed that the traditional conception of the theologian's *habitus* can shed light on contemporary reflections on the nature of theological thinking: J. A. DiNoia, O.P., "Authority, Public Dissent and the Nature of Theological Thinking," *The Thomist* 52 (1988): 185–207. DiNoia is concerned, however, with the *habitus* as a way of accounting for the theologian's fidelity to the authority of "God himself in his self-descriptions and in his dispensations in our regard" (191), and not with the *habitus* as a means for explaining how fidelity and creativity stand in tension in the theological enterprise.

development.[85] As Karl Rahner has observed, a characteristic of ecclesiology under what has here been called the classical paradigm is
a tendency to institutionalize the charismatic factor in the church by
locating its spiritual vitality in its hierarchical offices alone. The ecclesiology of Vatican II required that "over and above these official
charismata there must also be non-institutional charismata," which
"official functionaries of the Church must not merely tolerate . . .
but actually examine . . . and cultivate."[86]

From a historical perspective, this situation is understandably an
awkward one. Claims for the charism, or in secular terms talent, of
theological authorship are only as old as the romantic paradigm,
which has been recognized by the magisterium for only the past
twenty-five years. In a relatively short time teaching authority in the
church has been extended beyond the hierarchical offices in which it
has traditionally resided. This need not be a cause of concern for the
magisterium if the proper boundaries of teaching authority in the
church are clearly defined. Although both the magisterium and theologians share teaching authority in the church, that authority is
defined by the different tasks of their ministries. The teaching authority of the magisterium is defined primarily by the responsibility
of proclamation, the teaching authority of theologians primarily by
the responsibility of research and study.[87] Both are in service to the
truth of the gospel and the living witness to it in tradition, and, as
such, both share the charism of ecclesial discernment.

85. Max Seckler has suggested a much more elaborate paradigmatic division
of theological history based not on the emergence of authorial creativity but on
various sorts of relationship between the ecclesiastical teaching office and theological
science. The fourth of the seven paradigms Seckler proposes centers on "the idea
of a witness to the truth that is both charismatic and theological, which stands in
opposition to all administration and attestation of the truth through offices and
institutions" ("Kirchliches Lehramt und theologische Wissenschaft: Geschichtliche
Aspeckte, Probleme und Lösungselemente," in *Die Theologie und das Lehramt*, 38).
Seckler identifies this approach, however, with the reform movements of the late
Middle Ages and the Reformation and sees this theological charism as popular witness
and proclamation rather than as the individual talent of theological discernment.
86. Karl Rahner, "Observations on the Factor of the Charismatic in the Church,"
in *Theological Investigations XII*, trans. D. Bourke (New York: Seabury Press, 1974),
86–87.
87. Helmut Pfeiffer, "Theologie und Lehramt: Fundamental-theologische Über-
legungen zur Rolle und Funktion der theologischen Forschung und Lehre in der
Kirche," *Trierer Theologische Zeitschrift* 90 (1981): 213f.

If the manner in which the early romantic theologians expressed the power of authorship—as virtuosity or genius—seems inappropriate and perhaps even arrogant today, then we would do well to recall the challenge posed to them by the circumstances of history and culture. Like their romantic contemporaries, Schleiermacher and Drey made extraordinary claims for the power of the creative imagination in order to account for the place of a modern sense of individuality amid remarkable changes in historical, political, and cultural realities. From the standpoint of intellectual history, their descriptions of theological authorship can be situated near the end of a development extending throughout the late eighteenth century and in the course of which increasingly stronger claims were made for the integrity and power of the imagination. Nevertheless, Schleiermacher and Drey broke with many of their contemporaries by pursuing a moderate course within the romantic tradition. Their appeal to the language and intellectual categories of their time did not lead them to herald the prophetic value of the individual at the expense of tradition but to insist upon the workings of theological authorship as talent faithful to the church. Their insistence that the contributions of authorship be measured by the tradition the theologian serves remains the legitimate heritage of the romantic paradigm for their successors to the present day, a heritage that is best expressed in the conception of authorship as the *habitus* of creative fidelity.

Within this heritage there remain legitimate concerns about the persistence of a heroic conceptualization of the theologian for understanding the dynamics of the originality paradox in an ecclesial setting, a seemingly unavoidable consequence of even the most moderate expressions of the romantic temperament. Yet even if theological creativity has occasionally erred on the side of heroic excess, it would be a mistake of greater magnitude to assume that the talent of authorship is ecclesially anomic in principle. This realization on the part of the magisterium would do much to enhance the cooperative workings of ecclesial authority in our time and in the future.

The avoidance of unfruitful relations between the magisterium and theologians, however, cannot simply be the responsibility of the magisterium. Members of the theological community must be aware of the ever-present temptation to extend the charism of theological authorship to heroic proportions and thus to negate its authority. Although the romantic paradigm ideally understands the theologian to be responsible to the experience of the church, the creative and scholarly demands of an academic career easily lead to circumstances in which the theologian understands the object of his or her vocational responsibility to be the professional community in which he or she usually flourishes, the academy. This situation encourages the theologian to conceive responsibility primarily as faithfulness to the critical principles of the academy as embodied in the individual's scholarly work rather than as faithfulness to the developing tradition of the church. Such a heroic understanding of the role of theological talent accords undue authority to the individual theologian and has no legitimate role in a tradition that ranks the sacramental reality of the church as a whole higher than the charismatic gifts of its individual members.

Perhaps the occasional antagonism between the magisterium and theologians cited as a source of concern in the *Final Report* of the 1985 Extraordinary Synod in Rome has been rendered more intelligible by the paradigmatic analysis of theological responsibility offered here. This subject could, of course, be considered from many perspectives. The present analysis of shifting paradigms has attempted to draw attention to the important issue of theological creativity and its responsible exercise in the church as a way of understanding the Catholic tradition's often uneasy encounter with modernity. Although the notion of theological authorship has been a source of ambivalence for the church, this ambivalence can be attributed more to unexamined beliefs and stereotypical opinions about theological authorship than to theologians' abuse of their talent.

Conceiving of this talent as the *habitus* of creative fidelity, as a genuine development in the classical notion of the theological *habitus*, could do much to remedy this situation. As any development suggests abiding consistency in the midst of change, the same can be said of the development of the conception of the theological *habitus*. The steadfast commitment to ecclesial authority that characterized the traditional conception of the *habitus* was raised to a new level of meaning as it was brought into relationship with the modern appreciation for the contributions of individual talent to any creative endeavor, including theology. In such an understanding, the *habitus* of creative fidelity is an ecclesial charism that assists the church in its self-understanding and guides the tradition in its development. Cooperation between the magisterium and the theological community in the service of the gospel and tradition can best be achieved if theologians responsibly exercise their charism of authorship and the magisterium assesses this charism without prejudice.

Chapter Four

Deconstruction, Postliberalism, and the Romantic Paradigm

*O*NE WAY to define the modern character of the theology of the past two centuries is in terms of its practitioners' shared assumption that theology is a creative endeavor and that its creativity derives from the personal insights and abilities of its practitioners. The use of the term *modern* as a label of opprobrium for theology under the romantic paradigm anxiously expresses the challenge posed to more classical understandings of theology by its new disciplinary assumptions, including the assumption of theological authorship. The classical paradigm of theological responsibility sees the theological task as the mimetic representation of the tradition of scriptural and ecclesial authorities and tends to judge theological innovation as a departure from the unchanging deposit of orthodoxy, however it is defined. The romantic paradigm understands theological responsibility in relation to the historicity of revelation's meaning in the developing faith of the church. In this view the theologian functions as an individual author whose personal sensitivity to the workings of truth in the ecclesial community, expressive talent, and intuitive ability to apprehend future directions for the ongoing development of the tradition all constitute indispensable qualifications for the authentic exercise of the theological vocation.

As the romantic paradigm emerged in the work of Schleiermacher and Drey, imagination and talent were regarded for the first time in the history of theology as necessary sources for the substance of theological reflection. Although the classical paradigm denied the legitimacy of individual theological authorship and so remained on guard against any hint of theological innovation, the new understanding conceived of the theologian as an author whose creativity was at the very core of the theologian's vocational charge. This key assumption of the new paradigm may have had its beginnings in the thought world of early nineteenth-century Romanticism, but it has since transcended the narrower perspective of the romantics and taken hold among the disciplinary canons of modern theologians, regardless of their particular agendas, conclusions, or styles. Our special interest in theological authorship centers on the ambivalence this assumption continues to generate in ecclesial authority disputes and, as described in the next chapter, in discussions of theological method.

The originators of the new paradigm appealed to the then-current notion of the romantic hero as a model for their conception of the theologian's authorial contribution to the tradition's doctrinal development. Like the romantic hero, the theologian was conceived as an artist who mediated between the natural and the supernatural worlds by means of an ability to fathom their historical intersection, in this case, in the present life of the church. This talent presented the theologian with an ideal with respect to which vocational identity was formed. Like the romantic hero engaged in an ongoing imaginative quest realized in artistic production, the theological author encountered vocational responsibility to the church in the elusive goals of articulating the vitality of its present faith, identifying its relationship to the faith of the orthodox past, and charting its possible directions into the future.

The heroic understanding of the theologian enabled theology to be conceived as a creative endeavor and allowed theology to stand among other modern disciplines that recognized the practitioner's imaginative agency as a dimension of their method. But it also set the terms for an inescapably ambivalent relationship between the theologian's imaginative ability and the expectation that theological reflection be faithful to the established creeds of the past. This ambivalence has been especially accentuated in the Roman Catholic tradition. The assumption that the theologian is an author, and so possesses qualified teaching authority in the church, has received gradual recognition on the part of the magisterium itself since the pontificate of Paul VI. The magisterium continues to be fearful, however, that the modern theological author all too often exercises creativity in the style of the romantic hero, in a context of *Sturm und Drang* in which the individual's imaginative innovations necessarily clash with the supposedly sedentary concerns of the tradition and its institutions.

This heroic imagery happened to be the way in which the early romantics expressed their understanding of theological creativity as they appealed to the metaphors for imaginative agency available in their time and culture. Yet theologians were not solely responsible for propagating the imagery of heroism. As we have seen, the most exaggerated heroic understanding of the theological author was an invention of the magisterium in the course of the modernist crisis, an expression of largely unfounded concerns about the consequences of theological creativity for its own authority. Although theologians continue to abide by disciplinary assumptions that are, broadly speaking, romantic, the heroic understanding of authorship is by now an antiquated means for expressing the exercise of theological talent. Yet the rhetorical history of the notion of authorship continues to influence the ways in which the theologian's talent is perceived. For the theologian the heroic rhetoric often suggested by the very notion of authorship presents the temptation to elevate individual vision at the expense of the ecclesial community, to see dissent as the ordinary posture of the theologian, and to speak ostensibly on behalf of a church that in reality the theologian no longer serves. For the magisterium the heroic cast to the notion of authorship presents the temptation to judge any exercise of authorship, no matter how faithful or true, as the expression of a solitary voice necessarily contemptuous of tradition.

In spite of the ambivalence with which the exercise of theological authorship continues to be regarded in the Catholic tradition, I believe that its many contributions to the quality of theological reflection in the modern period have enhanced ecclesial tradition both theoretically and practically and that in the balance of ecclesial vitality the achievements of theological authorship far outweigh the confusion caused in the church by misunderstanding or occasionally misusing this talent. This observation will be examined further by considering the romantic paradigm's current suitability within the Catholic tradition.

TESTING THE LIMITS OF MODERN AUTHORSHIP

Although the romantic paradigm has gradually found acceptance within the Catholic tradition, this historical occurrence is no reason in principle to hold to its assumptions if others appear that are more effective in elucidating the truth of scripture and tradition. The past, as Kuhn has taught, is no guarantee for the present or future acceptability of disciplinary assumptions of any sort. The analysis of the paradigm shift from classical to romantic assumptions in theology may suggest that change comes slowly and often with great resistance in a traditionally-minded discipline that takes God and God's revelation as its object. But in the post-Enlightenment age only uncritical allegiance or historical myopia could lead one to judge a particular disciplinary paradigm as sacrosanct. The romantic paradigm of theological responsibility, no less than its classical predecessor, needs to be evaluated with a keen sense of the transience of all forms of human knowing.

If relations between the magisterium and theologians continue to be troubled, then perhaps the fault lies not as much with the principals in the ecclesial dialogue as it does with the terms in which the dialogue itself is framed. If discourse between liberal and conservative theologians is burdened by caricature and mutual suspicion (in spite of the fact that their paradigmatic assumptions are fundamentally the same), then perhaps this signals that a new paradigm already is breaking out of the old and preparing to replace it. Has the romantic paradigm of theological responsibility run its historical course? Have its disciplinary assumptions become tired, much as the passionate ideals of the early romantics yielded to the disappointment expressed in the languished brooding of the late romantic heroes of Byron and Balzac? The romantic paradigm one day surely will be superseded as cultural circumstances different enough from our own require the formulation of new assumptions for the discipline of theology. The task in this chapter, however, is not to engage in speculation about the shape of theology in a hypothetical future but to question whether recent challenges to the romantic paradigm constitute more viable theological approaches for the Catholic tradition. Two types of challenge to the romantic paradigm have emerged in our own time, one from outside, the other from inside the paradigm's boundaries.

In principle, a challenge to the romantic paradigm from outside its boundaries would pose an alternative to its assumptions. A position like this would not merely seek to modify or adjust aspects of the romantic paradigm that it judged to be in need of reform but would hold to tenets, whether old or new, fundamentally at odds with those described in this study as modern. Two such alternatives, departures from the assumptions of the romantic paradigm, currently exist. The first is the classical paradigm of theological responsibility, which, in relation to its romantic successor, can be described as premodern. Chapter 3 considered the extent to which the assumptions of the premodern paradigm have survived, and even been empowered, in the post-Enlightenment period. Since the emergence of the romantic paradigm, however, its premodern predecessor has been an anachronistic approach that lacks disciplinary integrity. To hold and to practice the disciplinary assumptions of the classical paradigm in our own time would entail the repudiation of the historicocritical method and the rejection of the most basic academic standards for theological reflection. For these reasons the method of the classical paradigm now stands in the history of theology as a thing of the past. The classical paradigm can continue to provide instruction and enlightenment to modern disciplinary practice but not as a viable alternative to the romantic paradigm.

The other challenge to the romantic paradigm from outside its boundaries is a new arrival in the history of ideas, one that claims the position of contentious successor to romantic values and expectations. In recent years voices from the quarters of several disciplines have called into question the fundamental assumptions of modern sensibility. Insisting that the romantic vision has been fractured in the devastating experience of the twentieth century, these voices diagnose our own era as postmodern, an assessment whose negativity reflects its judgment on the coherence and meaningfulness of nineteenth- and twentieth-century Western culture. From reactionary to revolutionary, hopeful to despondent, constructive to nihilistic, the possible responses to this diagnosis are so diverse that a precise definition of the postmodern is all but impossible.[1] Certainly the best known and most influential expression of the postmodern critique has been advanced through the literary theory of deconstruction. This approach to the reading of texts, perhaps the most radical form

1. For discussions of the various ways in which postmodernism can be portrayed, culturally as well as intellectually, see Jean-François Lyotard, *The Postmodern Condition: A Report on Knowledge*, trans. G. Bennington and B. Massumi (Minneapolis: Univ. of Minnesota Press, 1984); Jürgen Habermas, "Modernity versus Post-Modernity," *New German Critique* 22 (1981): 3–22; Fredric Jameson, "Postmodernism, Or the Cultural Logic of Late Capitalism," *New Left Review* 146 (1984): 53–92.

of postmodernism, has special import here because of its attention to the question of literary authority. In many respects deconstructive theory takes as its point of departure an attack on the very notion of authorship, an attack that, if at all successful, has immediate implications for the modern understanding of the theological practitioner. Deconstructive analysis already has been appropriated theologically in a fair number of works, but the most provocative effort so far has been Mark Taylor's attempt to delineate the features of a deconstructive theology in his book *Erring: A Postmodern A/theology*.[2] We will explore the consequences for traditional theology of opting for the deconstructive alternative to the romantic paradigm.

A second type of challenge to the romantic paradigm has come from within its own boundaries. In principle, such an approach does not depart from the assumptions of the romantic paradigm, as would its premodern and postmodern alternatives, but would question the paradigmatic assumptions to which it remains committed in order to expose their limitations and offer correctives. This sort of challenge stems from a dissatisfaction with the romantic paradigm and is motivated by a suspicion of the way theological practitioners have understood and enacted its assumptions. Not surprisingly, the assumption of theological authorship would be a prime candidate for such suspicion because it occupies an important place among the romantic paradigm's defining traits. The most notable challenge to the romantic paradigm from within is found in the lifework of Karl Barth. But a more focused challenge, one in the Barthian line of dissatisfaction with romantic sensibilities and critical of their methodological positioning of authorship, can be found in the recent work of George Lindbeck. Lindbeck's portrayal of theology in terms of a cultural-linguistic "rule" theory in his book *The Nature of Doctrine: Religion and Theology in a Postliberal Age*[3] is a very cogent attempt to modify

2. Mark C. Taylor, *Erring: A Postmodern A/theology* (Chicago: Univ. of Chicago Press, 1984). For a discussion of Taylor's book, see the symposium on *Erring* in *Journal of the American Academy of Religion* 54 (1986): Thomas J. J. Altizer, "The Triumph of the Theology of the Word," 525–29; Alphonso Lingis, "The Self in Itself," 529–34; Joseph Prabhu, "Blessing the Bathwater," 534–43; Edith Wyschogrod, "Crossover Dreams," 543–47; Mark C. Taylor, "Masking: Domino Effect," 547–55.

3. George A. Lindbeck, *The Nature of Doctrine: Religion and Theology in a Postliberal Age* (Philadelphia: Westminster Press, 1984). For a discussion of Lindbeck's book, see the symposium on *The Nature of Doctrine* in *The Thomist* 49 (1985): William C. Placher, "Revisionist and Postliberal Theologies and the Public Character of Theology," 392–416; Colman E. O'Neill, O. P., "The Rule Theory of Doctrine and Propositional Truth," 417–42; James J. Buckley, "Doctrine in the Diaspora," 443–59; David Tracy, "Lindbeck's New Program for Theology: A Reflection," 460–72.

the romantic paradigm systematically from within its boundaries. It will be examined here as a possible resource for treating the issue of authorship in Catholic theological method.

As different as they are, Taylor's and Lindbeck's projects self-consciously criticize romantic assumptions regarding the theologian's creative and constructive authorship. Each represents a *via negativa* through romantic assumptions—Lindbeck's path leading to the boundaries of the paradigm but never traversing them, Taylor's course cutting quickly through the same boundaries and winding beyond them. Exploring their respective concerns about theological authorship will enhance our understanding of the contours of the romantic paradigm. Taylor's and Lindbeck's attention to this issue is especially helpful in evaluating the romantic paradigm's present status as a disciplinary matrix for Catholic theology.

DECONSTRUCTION AND THE EFFACEMENT OF THE AUTHOR

Unlike its classical predecessor, the romantic paradigm positioned the foundations of theology not in an ahistorical understanding of scripture and the tradition of authorities but in the historical encounter between scripture, tradition, and ecclesial faith. This decidedly historical understanding of disciplinary foundations required the special contributions of theological authorship to mediate between established authority and contemporary experience as they met in the believing community's ongoing appropriation of the meaning of divine revelation. Taylor and Lindbeck both make the romantic conception of theological authority the object of their critical regard, though it is only in Taylor's deconstructive a/theology that this criticism has devastation as its goal.

The opening word of the title of Mark Taylor's *Erring: A Postmodern A/theology* is a parody of the general idea of historical purposiveness that is the specific heritage of the romantic concept of human temporality. For Taylor "erring" describes the aimless wandering through texts, culture, and life itself that is the only honest recourse for one who has deconstructed romantic presuppositions in the face of the death of God and the concomitant death of history as the sphere of divine self-revelation.[4] The death of God is, of course,

4. There are many studies on deconstruction, but particularly able is Jonathan Culler, *On Deconstruction: Theory and Criticism after Structuralism* (Ithaca, N.Y.: Cornell Univ. Press, 1982). For a brief introduction, see Mark C. Taylor, "Introduction: System . . . Structure . . . Difference . . . Other," in *Deconstruction in Context: Literature and Philosophy*, ed. M. C. Taylor (Chicago: Univ. of Chicago Press, 1986), 1–34.

a recurring modern theme that in itself does not define the deconstructionist's position. Taylor argues that the shift from a modern to a postmodern perspective takes place as one recognizes the groundlessness of modern culture's celebration of the death of God as the birth of the self, empowered now by the personal and social energies previously needed to sustain traditional religious belief. Postmodern culture accepts the death of God as the death of the authorial self.[5]

Taylor maintains that in addition to being a "relatively 'recent invention,' " the Western notion of the self is an explicitly theological conception whose existence flourishes in an epoch that "extends roughly from Augustine's *Confessions* to Hegel's *Phenomenology of Spirit*."[6] Taylor regards this age of onto-theological speculation as one in which divinity and intellection are inextricably related, as an age characterized by an inexorable tendency to see human subjectivity as reflective of, and eventually identical with, the consciousness of God. From the perspective of cultural history, this identification was explicitly affirmed in the romantic tradition's exaltation of the self as the foundation of truth through its powers of creativity and meaningful construction. Following in the steps of deconstructionists such as Gilles Deleuze, Paul De Man, Julia Kristeva, and especially Jacques Derrida, Taylor sees his task as the disassembling of the romantic notion of the creative imagination, a task that is required as long as there is cultural life in the notion of an authorial self that reflects and even embodies the creative powers of the divine. For a deconstructionist like Taylor, who defines his critical target as the tradition of theological construction, the death of God inescapably entails the death of the self and so of the self who, under the romantic paradigm, is conceived as a theological author.[7]

5. Other postmodern attempts to undermine the authorial self can be found in the social criticism of Michel Foucault and the literary criticism of Roland Barthes. See, for example, Michel Foucault, "What Is an Author?" in *Language, Counter-Memory, Practice: Selected Essays and Interviews*, trans. D. F. Bouchard and S. Simon (Ithaca, N.Y.: Cornell Univ. Press, 1977), 113–38; Roland Barthes, "The Death of the Author," in *Image-Music-Text*, tran. S. Heath (New York: Hill and Wang, 1977), 142–48.

6. Taylor, *Erring*, 35.

7. Taylor's interest in the notions of authorship and authority is reflected in his earlier work, especially *Kierkegaard's Pseudonymous Authorship: A Study of Time and the Self* (Princeton, N.J.: Princeton Univ. Press, 1975); *Deconstructing Theology* (Chico, Calif.: Scholars Press, 1982); "Text as Victim," in *Deconstruction and Theology* (New York: Crossroad, 1982), 58–78. See also his more recent books *Altarity* (Chicago: Univ. of Chicago Press, 1987) and *Tears* (Albany: SUNY Press, 1990).

More specifically, then, Taylor's image of "erring" is a parody of the modern theological notion of doctrinal development. While the romantic paradigm defines theological responsibility with regard to a developing appreciation of divine revelation in the history of ecclesial experience, Taylor's postmodern perspective finds history to be directionless, unreservedly accepting its "endless drift of meaning."[8] While the romantic paradigm understands the theological author to possess special authorial talent in service to the church, Taylor's a/theology denies the possibility of such a foundational notion of creativity by proclaiming the death of the author and of authorial truth claims grounded in subjectivity, whether collective (as in the case of the church) or individual (as in the case of theological imagination). For Taylor meaning is not defined by the "presence" of truth in history but by the "absence" that characterizes the network of differentiation that culture is. This last point merits further discussion and can be illustrated by Jacques Derrida's deconstructive analysis of the activity of writing—the form of graphic representation most common to culture in general and to theological culture in particular.

Deconstruction calls into question the very notion of truth as reference that has characterized the Platonic heritage of Western intellectual culture. Such a metaphysical understanding of reality presupposes a separation between the signifier and the signified, the former serving as a graphic conveyor of the latter's meaning. Underlying this notion of signification as reference is what Derrida calls the "transcendental signified,"[9] a belief in a comprehensive truth that unites and defines the entire system of meaning. In Derrida's view this essentially theological presupposition prejudices the very way in which meaning is imaged, both mentally and graphically. Such a perspective cannot but assume that the world of significative construction is derivative, exteriorly portraying an inner world of subjective presence that shares more immediately in the consummate presence of the transcendental object of signification. Deconstruction is an effort to undermine the "logocentrism" of traditional Western metaphysics by denying the priority or privileged position it grants to the subjective, and finally divine, realm of truth. This denial entails

8. Taylor, *Erring*, 175.
9. Jacques Derrida, *Of Grammatology*, trans. G. C. Spivak (Baltimore: Johns Hopkins Univ. Press, 1976), 20, 23. Cf. Jacques Derrida, *Positions*, trans. A. Bass (Chicago: Univ. of Chicago Press, 1981), 19f.

the identification of the signifier and the signified, which in turn subverts the Western assumption that truth is encountered through a process of dialectical reasoning founded on some at least implicitly theological notion of a transcendental ground of meaning.

For Derrida meaning does not possess foundations but is characterized by an indeterminable network of differences. The "absence" within any supposed system of meaning—the unspoken, the implied, the contrary—constantly proliferates its incompleteness, defying the completed construction of an actual truth in the recognition of the utter potential of differentiated signification.[10] In this view meaning is never characterized by completeness or "closure," abiding expectations of traditional theories of representation which flourish in what Derrida calls the age of the book. Meaning is a never-ending process that Derrida describes as an intertextual "play"[11] of writings.

From the standpoint of the metaphysics of presence and consciousness, writing is a threat to meaning. Graphic representation creates the possibility of misrepresentation as the written signifier is necessarily distanced from what the tradition of logocentrism assumes to be the locus of truth in thought, or even in speech. Deconstructive theory accepts, and actually celebrates, the supplementary character of writing; indeed it does so to such a degree that it adheres to the hermeneutical principle that writing is not the supplement of an original meaning, however imperfectly imaged in a system of signs. Writing, Derrida insists, is a sheer dissemination of meaning that ever gives rise to further writing and that to writing again. This expanding network of textuality defies all efforts of authority to halt or direct its proliferation; it is directionless and so for the deconstructionists happily full of possibilities precisely because it is not responsible to an originary truth, whether it is the transcendent creativity of the divine author or the immanent creativity of a human author.[12]

10. The very notion of *différance* functions in Derrida's project as a criticism of foundationalism and its assumption that there are determinable conditions that establish the possibility of a text's meaning. For Derrida "the 'causality' of *différance* is authorless, and indeed ultimately without authority" (Irene E. Harvey, *Derrida and the Economy of "Différance"* [Bloomington: Indiana Univ. Press, 1986], 188).

11. "One could call *play* the absence of the transcendental signified as limitlessness of play, that is to say as the destruction of onto-theology and the metaphysics of presence" (Derrida, *Of Grammatology*, 50).

12. For a discussion of writing as the absolute freedom of speech, see Jacques Derrida, *Writing and Difference*, trans. A. Bass (Chicago: Univ. of Chicago Press, 1978), 12f. Cf. Richard Rorty, "Philosophy as a Kind of Writing: An Essay on Derrida," *New Literary History* 10 (1978): 141–60.

Following Derrida, Taylor's regard for the Western notion of the self as a theological conception is not only a historical but also a thematic observation that addresses the issue of authorship and authority. According to the classical presuppositions of the Western tradition, the authorial self reflects the divine author; the creative productions of authorial selves imitate the divine creativity. "Quite clearly," Taylor asserts, "God is not just any author, nor is His book just any book. God is the Author of authors who dictates the Book of books. For this reason, God is the Author to whom all authors finally defer, and His Book is the Book to which all books ultimately refer."[13]

Taylor's deconstructive a/theology maintains that authorship—whether divine or human—inevitably entails a deferral of the author's presence (that is, his or her intention, meaning, responsibility, and so forth) to a literary production, which, in the absence of its creator, no longer maintains authorial propriety. The very activity of writing as an effort to supplement a given meaning compromises the authority of that original meaning and, *a fortiori*, the authority of the supplement. This is true even if the literary enterprise is understood as mimetic reproduction, for "the mimetic book is actually duplicitous." It "*doubles* and hence *supplements* the original Book."[14]

The application of this insight to theological writing under what I have called the classical paradigm exposes, Taylor argues, the process by which the classical notion of theological authority undermines itself:

> Apparently servile writing actually inverts the relation of slave to Master, author to Author, book to Book, and secondary to primary. From a mimetic perspective, the Word of the Master is believed to be complete. Since the purpose of the author is to rewrite the work of the Author, the aim of books is [to] repeat the Book. . . . If, however, the primal book can be supplemented by a secondary work, the original source cannot be complete. The strange "logic" embodied in this supplement (book) suggests that the ostensible origin (Book) is not really original at all. . . . Instead of representing something that is temporally and ontologically prior, the Book seems to be the product of a creative author and not the work of the Creator/Author.[15]

13. Taylor, *Erring*, 81.
14. Ibid., 83.
15. Ibid.

This authorial inversion resulted in a "shift from mimesis to poiesis," the very rise of romantic consciousness and its assumption that the "negation of the transcendent author manifests itself in the affirmation of the creative author."[16]

As significant as this transition seems for the liberation of individual voice, the romantic conception of authorship, Taylor notes, remains essentially theological. It assumes that the author's constructive efforts are creative acts that reveal his or her intended meaning. As such, the human author functions in the role of the classically divine; immanent creativity eclipses transcendent creativity as imaginative signification eclipses its metaphysical counterpart.

Deconstructive theory sees this romantic conception of authorship as the last stronghold of the onto-theological tradition and its attachment to the illusory completeness of the book. Modern consciousness sees the author as the source of genius expressively concretized in representation that is not merely imitative but ever faithful to the historical development of truth. In counterpoint, postmodern, deconstructive criticism proclaims the death of the author as an inescapable consequence of the death of God. For Taylor the very notion of a purposive, temporal development, whether in secular or doctrinal history, merely shifts premodern authoritative assumptions into a historical setting still committed to the metaphysics of presence, logocentrism, and the separation of the signifier and the signified. The historical consciousness of Romanticism, in turn, is only a single step away from the recognition of the deconstructive erasure of the human author and of the author's traditional desire to speak a finally authoritative word. Claims on behalf of historical development are actually a partial recognition of the supplementarity of writing and hence a reluctant admission of the fictional status of the author. From the perspective of such a deconstructive analysis, romantic construction is exposed as writing, purposeful development as intertextual play, and doctrinal development as a temporal wandering without real pattern or authoritative direction.

Even though Taylor's deconstructive a/theological perspective is thoroughly at odds with the assumptions of classical and modern Catholic theology, in some respects his work is instructive and perhaps, though not in its own terms, capable of theological appropriation. Taylor's analysis of traditional authority highlights the extent

16. Ibid., 83, 84.

to which this power and its conceptualization has shifted to adjust to different historical circumstances. It illuminates the pluralistic conceptions of authority in the theological tradition. It highlights the family resemblance between classical and romantic understandings of authority that enable both to be described as traditional. In spite of their differences on the matter of individual authorship, the premodern and modern paradigms insist that scripture and tradition are normative for the ecclesial community and for the theologies it produces to enhance an understanding of God's revelation. From its critical posture beyond the romantic paradigm, Taylor's a/theological evaluation of this conception of normativeness sheds light on the breadth of the spectrum of acceptable notions of traditional theological authority, a spectrum extending through premodern and modern paradigmatic assumptions, though clearly not those of radical postmodernism.

Especially helpful is Taylor's calling attention to the connection between the notions of authority and authorship and so to the close association between authority and literary production. In its criticism of a theological tradition that has always advanced its authoritative teaching through literary production, *Erring* serves as a reminder of a persistent desire in Western thought to identify human with divine authority in a particular expression of completed or "closed" truth. Taylor's analysis shows how little it matters whether this temptation manifests itself in the classical paradigm's inability to entertain the possibility of an innovative doctrinal "supplement" to past authorities or in the romantic paradigm's heroic temptation to silence the past by sacralizing the contemporary pronouncements of the individual theological author. Each form of authoritarianism exhibits the desire of authorship, whether collective or individual, to speak a final word to which no other can be added and so to distort the process of language and literary production of which deconstructive theory is so aware.

But it is Taylor's insistence on literary process at the expense of authoritative foundations that defines his work as an attack on the premises of Christian theology and makes his postmodern alternative to the romantic paradigm an unacceptable one. Clearly Christian theology encounters its contradiction in deconstruction's radical affirmation of the death of God. The deconstructive a/theology that Taylor sketches in *Erring* is finally a philosophical position that ventures beyond formal criticism and enunciates a stance hostile to the fundamental authoritative claims of any traditional theology, whether premodern or modern.[17] While deconstruction may make us more aware of the many uses and abuses of theological authority, its critical posture cannot be adopted substantively by a confessional tradition that proclaims the death of God as a salvational event at the core of human meaning and not as a cultural event heralding the aimless play of history.

More specifically, Catholic theology finds its broad commitment to various degrees of inspired authorship destroyed in Taylor's insightful linkage between the cultural deaths of the divine and human authors. In its assertion that human meaning in tradition evaporates upon the cultural death of God, Taylor's a/theology is equally an "a/anthropology." It can only repudiate the religious justification for the claims on behalf of human dignity, responsibility, and authority that Catholic theology numbers among the assumptions of its confessionally informed doctrine of human nature. This deconstructive judgment on the inseparable relationship between the divine and the human denies the possibility of revelation and its meaningful interpretation and so undercuts the very conceptions of authorship on which premodern and modern Catholic theologies are based. In this regard the modern conception of the theologian's imaginative authorship suffers no less than the classical notion of God as the sole author of scripture and tradition. Taylor's philosophical position on the proliferating effects of the death of God could only be rejected by a tradition whose theological authority is grounded in the divine authorship of scripture, in the collective authorship of the tradition of authorities, including the magisterium, and in the individual authorship of the theological imagination.

17. Walter Lowe has noticed the degree to which Taylor goes beyond the use of deconstruction as a hermeneutical strategy and articulates a philosophical position that, to some degree at least, claims authority: "Now Taylor tries to give us something of this sort [the deconstructive analysis of hidden subtexts] by his close attention to wordplay, to pun, free association, and etymology. But his predominant concern, it would seem, is to find in deconstruction not simply an open-ended *strategy* for engaging particular texts, but a set of convictions about the way things are. No amount of talk about free play and wandering can alter the fact that deconstruction has in some sense become a 'position' whose principle [*sic*] tenets are to be made manifest" ("A Deconstructionist Manifesto: Mark C. Taylor's *Erring*," *Journal of Religion* 66 [1986]: 328). This substantive dimension of Taylor's work is irreconcilable with the mainstays of Roman Catholic theology.

POSTLIBERALISM AND THE CONSTRAINT
OF THE AUTHOR

George Lindbeck's *The Nature of Doctrine* is a provocative attempt to rethink classical and especially modern understandings of religious truth and their articulation in the language of doctrine and theology. To the degree that his book offers a critique of the romantic paradigm of theological responsibility it might be understood in broad terms as postmodern in its perspective. Lindbeck himself accepts this description of his project.[18] He would, however, care to distinguish his own position from postmodernism in general, his frequent use of the self-designation "postliberal" serving as a constant reminder of his unwillingness to stand in the same camp as those proclaiming the end of traditional meaning.[19] Although Lindbeck would be unhappy with any material comparison between his theological project and Taylor's, both works share an antipathy toward the romantic conception of authorship in general and theological authorship in particular. Lindbeck's treatment of this theme will illustrate both his commitment to the modern assumption of theological authorship and his desire to constrain what he believes to be its tendency to sacrifice theological content for the sake of cultural relevance.

Above all, Lindbeck's project is motivated by ecumenical concerns. Premodern and modern understandings of doctrine, he believes, have not provided categories that facilitate rapprochement in interdenominational dialogue. In a classical perspective, doctrines are seen as "informative propositions or truth claims about objective realities."[20] This "propositionalist" understanding attributes authority

18. Lindbeck, *The Nature of Doctrine*, 135, n. 1. William Werpehowski points out the sense in which the postliberal approach can also be described as postmodern: "A properly 'postliberal' or 'postmodern' theology forsakes [the liberal or modern] pattern of easy accommodation to contemporary human experience in part because that pattern, ironically, runs the risk of irrelevance" ("Ad Hoc Apologetics," *Journal of Religion* 66 [1986]: 282).

19. Other proponents of the postliberal approach, broadly understood, include Hans W. Frei, *The Eclipse of Biblical Narrative: A Study in Eighteenth and Nineteenth Century Hermeneutics* (New Haven: Yale Univ. Press, 1974); *The Identity of Jesus Christ: The Hermeneutical Bases of Dogmatic Theology* (Philadelphia: Fortress Press, 1975); Stanley Hauerwas, *A Community of Character: Toward a Constructive Christian Ethic* (Notre Dame, Ind.: Univ. of Notre Dame Press, 1981); Charles M. Wood, *The Formation of Christian Understanding* (Philadelphia: Westminster Press, 1981); Ronald F. Thiemann, *Revelation and Theology: The Gospel as Narrated Promise* (Notre Dame, Ind.: Univ. of Notre Dame Press, 1985).

20. Lindbeck, *The Nature of Doctrine*, 16.

to doctrines to the degree that they correspond to the religious truths they represent. Romantic or modern approaches to the expression of faith regard doctrines as "noninformative and nondiscursive symbols of inner feelings, attitudes, or existential orientations."[21] This "experiential-expressivist" understanding attributes authority to doctrines to the degree that they articulate the living experience of the church or, to specify more exactly in light of our broader consideration of the romantic paradigm, to the degree that they articulate the living experience of the church as discerned by one of its theologically talented members.[22]

Each of these approaches is unsatisfactory for the purposes of ecumenical dialogue and rapprochement because neither can seriously entertain "the possibility of doctrinal reconciliation without capitulation."[23] Propositionalism finds it difficult to account for the variabilities of time and culture at work in the development of doctrine. Its loyalty to a correspondence theory of truth, and thus to the principle of contradiction, militates against the reconciliation of religious truth claims that are conceptually or expressively dissimilar. Experiential-expressivism does not locate the authority of doctrine in the adequacy of its representation but in the hidden dimension of the believer's subjectivity, to which, it is assumed, the language of doctrine conforms. Doctrinal reconciliation becomes superfluous within this model because its understanding of language as utterly variable symbolism vitiates the normative power of doctrine, according authority instead to a nebulous experience believed to be common to all. Lindbeck proposes a functional understanding of doctrine that enables "the intertwining of variability and invariability in matters of faith."[24] To that end he suggests that doctrines be understood neither as cognitivist truth claims nor as symbolism communicating the religious imagination but as "communally authoritative rules of discourse, attitude, and action."[25]

21. Ibid.
22. Lindbeck notes a third theory of doctrine, illustrated in the work of Rahner and Lonergan, which adopts the perspectives of both cognitivism and experiential-expressivism. He dismisses this view, however, as an unhappy hybrid, which, even at its best, must "resort to complicated intellectual gymnastics and to that extent [is] unpersuasive" (*The Nature of Doctrine*, 17). The single paragraph that quickly dismisses such "[t]heories of the third type" is the closest Lindbeck comes in his book to discussing the most typically Roman Catholic approach to theology under the romantic paradigm.
23. Lindbeck, *The Nature of Doctrine*, 16.
24. Ibid., 17.
25. Ibid., 18.

According to Lindbeck, religions can be understood to function analogously to languages and cultures—that is, broad systems of meaning that, though malleable in various times and places, are defined and directed by the intrasystematic rules that structure their vision of reality. A religion, from this perspective, is understood primarily as its public rather than as its private dimension; more particularly, as the normative rules that indispensably though fluidly convey a tradition's meaningful assumptions, beliefs, actions, and hopes. As a system of meaning, a culture lives by an assemblage of rules that provide its stability and structural coherence. Whether these rules are the grammar of a language, the axioms of geometry, acceptable expressions of grief, or the greeting customs of a culture, they fix a pattern within which life can be lived from day to day and from generation to generation. Yet the pattern is not so rigid as to be impervious to change and the demands of particular circumstances. Lindbeck proposes that a religious tradition's doctrine functions as such a collection of rules. To the degree that the Christian tradition's teaching defines the boundaries for its meaningful belief and action, doctrines, Lindbeck argues, are better understood "as expressing second-order guidelines for Christian discourse rather than first-order affirmations about the inner being of God or of Jesus Christ" or of any other matter of faith.[26] Doctrines, in this view, primarily are neither propositional representations of ontological realities nor symbolic expressions of the religious consciousness. They structure, both positively and negatively, the meaningful framework within which the commitment of faith can be affirmed and practiced.

The ecumenical advantage Lindbeck finds in a regulative approach to doctrine is its ability to entertain the possibility of doctrinal reconciliation without capitulation. It is able to avoid the exclusivity that propositionalism insists governs the adjudication of differing doctrinal claims, while maintaining the possibility of intrasystematic objectivity. Its regulative stance is able to avoid the danger of relativism that accompanies experiential-expressivism, while recognizing historical variability in the tradition's application of rules and the pluralistic contexts in which they are coherently applied.

Lindbeck's fascinating book has been so widely read, appreciated, and criticized that it would not be worthwhile to delineate its argument further here or to assess in any general way its strengths and

26. Ibid., 94.

weaknesses. I would like instead to focus on a dimension of *The Nature of Doctrine* that is implied but not specifically developed: the conception of theological authorship that attends the cultural-linguistic rule theory of doctrine. As noted, Lindbeck's project proceeds from a desire to foster ecumenical dialogue by reconciling the concerns of classical and romantic theologies. His rule theory of doctrine attempts to secure the classical commitment to traditional stability while at the same time acknowledging the romantic insistence upon addressing the ever-changing contingencies of history. "A postliberal," Lindbeck states, "might propose to overcome this polarization between tradition and innovation by a distinction between abiding doctrinal grammar and variable theological vocabulary."[27] Although reconciliation is Lindbeck's avowed interest, it is important to realize that the assumptions of classical and romantic or liberal theology receive very different critical scrutiny at his hands.

Lindbeck is fully aware of the challenge posed to a cognitivist or propositionalist theory of truth by post-Kantian epistemological assumptions and so of the difficulties faced by such a theory of truth in the modern age. He appreciates, though, the stability that the propositionalist theory of truth was able to provide to classical theology, and at several points in his discussion he takes pains to point out that a cultural-linguistic understanding of contextualized meaning is not inconsistent with the older theory of truth.[28] Experiential-expressivism does not receive such an accommodating evaluation. Although he admits that this model has governed the impressive work of modern thinkers such as M. Eliade, T. Campbell, and J. S. Dunne, Lindbeck believes that the theological employment of experiential-expressivism has encouraged the false view that religious traditions are "optional aids in individual self-realization rather than . . . bearers of normative realities to be interiorized."[29] Experiential-expressivism leads to a perception of religious truth as a completely relativized and marketable commodity,[30] a perception that encourages the vapid and contentless Christianity of modern liberal culture. Among the reasons for Lindbeck's pejorative regard for the theological heritage of modernity is his dissatisfaction with the way he

27. Ibid., 113.
28. Ibid., 63–69, 80.
29. Ibid., 23.
30. Ibid., 22.

believes theological authorship is frequently conceived and practiced in the liberal approach.

In the final chapter of *The Nature of Doctrine*, "Toward a Post-liberal Theology," Lindbeck sketches the tasks of theology from a cultural-linguistic point of view and in so doing delineates a view of theological authorship that intends to avoid what he believes to be the pitfalls of its preponderant use in the liberal theological tradition. Lindbeck does not address the issue of authorship directly. Rather his understanding of the sort of authority possessed by the theological practitioner is suggested amid his proposals for a postliberal appropriation of the concerns of Western Christian theology: the concern for faithfulness in systematic or dogmatic theology, practical theology's concern for applicability, and foundational theology's concern for intelligibility.

The concern for faithfulness brings us face to face with the issue of theological responsibility. Unlike classical theology, which expects theological faithfulness to the propositional truth of scripture and the tradition of authorities, or liberal theology, which expects faithfulness to the developing meaning of God's revelation in history, a postliberal theology would judge faithfulness as intratextuality. In this understanding the responsibility of the theologian is determined by the scriptural texts that his or her tradition regards as normative and that the theologian must describe. The authoritative basis for theological reflection in this view is located neither in the experience of the church at large nor in the talent of theologians but in those texts—Lindbeck has in mind the biblical canon and the pronouncements of the early councils—that articulate the meaningful context within which Christian life flourishes. The theologian is responsible for clarifying the rules that govern this intratextual world of meaning and for showing how these rules speak to the contemporary situation of religiocultural life.

This process of interpretation, however, is not one in which text and experience are set in a fine correlative balance. According to Lindbeck, "it is the religion instantiated in Scripture which defines being, truth, goodness, and beauty, and the nonscriptural exemplifications of these realities need to be transformed into figures (or types or antitypes) of the scriptural ones. Intratextual theology redescribes reality within the scriptural framework rather than translating Scripture into extrascriptural categories. It is the text, so to speak, which absorbs the world, rather than the world the text."[31]

31. Ibid., 118.

Theology in this understanding is description, though not in the sense of a phenomenology grounded in general human experience. In Lindbeck's view theology involves the description of scripture or (though perhaps as reflexively) the retelling of the gospel tale. The scriptural text is accorded such a priority in Lindbeck's understanding of faithfulness that the theological enterprise is conceptualized in somewhat reiterative terms. In the strictest sense, theology here possesses no method. It follows no theory invoked to elucidate the contemporary meaning of the gospel. Theology in this model follows only the directive that it extend the biblical vision and that it do so not by translating its message into extrabiblical and easily consumable categories but by faithfully preserving the integrity of scripture in the context of cultural circumstances foreign and even hostile to its values.

Lindbeck does not see the task of theology as redundant or devoid of creativity. He insists that there is "no more demanding exercise of the inventive and imaginative powers than to explore how a language, culture, or religion may be employed to give meaning to new domains of thought, reality, and action," a view that leads to the apologetical claim that "[t]heological description can be a highly constructive enterprise."[32] In spite of these observations, Lindbeck remains suspicious of the subjective underpinnings of romantic theological construction, of the idea that theological talent as a matter of course can be expected to be both creative and faithful. Judged postliberally, the theological imagination does not deserve the ready confidence placed in its abilities in the romantic paradigm.

Although Lindbeck recognizes the role of authorship in theologizing, he tries to define an understanding of its activity that embraces both premodern and modern conceptions of authority. With the classical paradigm, Lindbeck emphasizes the responsibility of the theologian to an authoritative tradition (in his terms, a tradition of doctrinal rules). Lindbeck has no desire, however, to point theology back to precritical assumptions. Like all who assume the validity of the romantic paradigm of theological responsibility, Lindbeck recognizes the need for the reinterpretive power of authorship in the history of faith. He insists, however, that the exercise of individual authorship requires the theologian to defer almost entirely to the

32. Ibid., 115.

authority of the scriptural tradition in order to avoid a creative extension of the *regula fidei* in which novelty is erroneously judged to be the measure of imaginative power. Fearing the liberal willingness to trade away the substance of the tradition to gain an ephemeral relevance, Lindbeck insists that true authorial creativity issues in the theologian's measured efforts to describe the present historical moment in scriptural categories. He affirms the role of the theological author but assumes that the author's individual insights are legitimately and even fruitfully constrained by the tradition to which he or she belongs. In order to make Lindbeck's implicit views on theological authorship more explicit, we need to consider his treatment of the other concerns of the theological task: applicability and intelligibility.

Applicability is the particular concern of practical theology, a concern that Lindbeck sees realized in what he calls a theological appropriation of futurology. Even though the rules for theological reflection issue from scripture, the actual work of theological interpretation involves the application of these rules to the present and indirectly to the human future latent within it. A particular theological interpretation is viable not solely because of faithfulness. It must also relate the scriptural rules to the present and imminently future circumstances of faith. As one would expect from Lindbeck's understanding of theological faithfulness, this hermeneutical endeavor is defined in opposition to romantic versions of revisionistic interpretation:

> In brief, a theological proposal is adjudged both faithful and applicable to the degree that it appears practical in terms of an eschatologically and empirically defensible scenario of what is to come. . . . In the construction of such scenarios, the crucial difference between liberals and postliberals is in the way they correlate their visions of the future and of present situations. Liberals start with experience, with an account of the present, and then adjust their vision of the kingdom of God accordingly, while postliberals are in principle committed to doing the reverse.[33]

While making allowances for the inevitable stereotyping that attends polemically defined positions, we should note that Lindbeck's

33. Ibid., 125–26.

view on authentic theological prognostication reflects his understanding of intratextual faithfulness. He assumes that the authorial work of practical theology is rightly determined by biblical eschatology and its vision of a future in which the promise of the gospel is fulfilled. By the same token, he is clearly uncomfortable with the romantic paradigm's more typical notion of applicability, which, he thinks, places too much confidence in the theologian's ability to discern the present moment of historical faith and to guide its development into the future. "Theological forms," Lindbeck states, "of [predictive applicability] are more like contemporary futurology than biblical prophecy. Unlike prophecy, futurology does not depend on first-order inspiration or intuition, but is a second-order enterprise that draws on the full range of empirical studies in an effort to discover 'the signs of the times.' "[34] Faithfulness to the scriptural narrative, and not to the inventiveness of the theological imagination, accounts for good theology. In Lindbeck's judgment individual theological talent counts for little when measured against the objective authority of the scriptural tradition or even against objectifiable assessments of the human condition garnered from the ad hoc application of social-scientific or humanistic methodologies.

As has already been noted, it would be incorrect to think that Lindbeck fails to recognize individual talent as a dimension of the theological enterprise. But he understands individual talent not as the power of divination and guidance but as skill in depicting the present circumstances of faith within the categories of the biblical narrative. Such skill is the basis of the intelligibility that any theology expects. It is a facility for theological description, the assumed faithfulness of which in the postliberal model mitigates the power granted to individual talent in the romantic notion of theological authorship. Such skill, which is better depicted as stolid craftsmanship than as creative talent, serves no theory. It is practiced in an ad hoc fashion as the theologian searches for ways in which the biblical message might interpret culture. Indeed, in Lindbeck's schema, this skill functions in the stead of the conception of foundations—whether classically metaphysical or romantically imaginative—in traditional formulations of the theological enterprise. Chapter 5 will note that Lindbeck's appeal for a nonfoundational theology articulates a stance on theological method that seeks the same constraint of the romantic

34. Ibid., 125.

author that he commends in his discussion of theological faithfulness, applicability, and intelligibility.

IMPLICATIONS FOR THE CATHOLIC TRADITION

To what extent do the deconstructive and postliberal views on authorship provide resources for modifying the romantic paradigm of theological responsibility, particularly as the paradigm is practiced in a religious tradition that holds that teaching authority is shared, albeit unequally, by the magisterium and theologians? To be sure, the romantic paradigm has had a relatively short and ambivalent history in the Catholic tradition. Although magisterial pronouncements since the pontificate of Paul VI indicate an acceptance of the romantic notion of theological authorship, and so of the teaching authority of theologians, suspicions—sometimes founded and sometimes not—about the model's possible extension of individual authority to heroic proportions have often led to poor relations between the magisterium and the theological community. Do the postmodern assessments of the power of theological authorship suggest a way to move beyond the romantic paradigm to a conception of theological responsibility that will avoid these confrontational dynamics?

Taylor's postmodern celebration of the death of the author can be formally valuable for its insights into the historicity of meaning, especially meaning that traditionally has been supported by various conceptions of authorship, human as well as divine. But in all material respects, Taylor's deconstructive a/theology does not present a viable alternative to the romantic paradigm because its assumptions about God, tradition, and the self are irreconcilable with those of the Catholic tradition. Indeed, if *Erring* expresses a postmodern anthropology that voices the experience of contemporary men and women, then its pages delineate a challenge to magisterial authority in comparison with which concerns about the misuse of a romantic exercise of authorship simply pale. Further, in comparison to the deconstructive effacement of the author, the romantic commitment to the imaginative self, creatively enlivened through its sensitivity to God's presence in the world, appears to confirm the Catholic tradition's anthropology, specifically as defined in the Tridentine *Decretum de Justificatione* (1547). As Trent refuses to speak even of a "theological" loss of self in God's justification of the individual, affirming instead

159

the integrity of the human will in the encounter with grace,[35] so too the romantic paradigm's anthropological assumptions disallow a notion of the theologian as irresponsibly effaced in scripture, tradition, or the indeterminacies of culture, affirming instead the creative power of authorship in responsible dialogue with the authority of scripture and tradition.

Lindbeck's suspicions of the pretensions of romantic authorship lead him to define a very different postmodern stance from Taylor's, the resemblance between them traceable largely to their shared dissatisfaction with the modern paradigm. Unlike Taylor, Lindbeck does not deny the author as an illusory remnant of the age of the book. Indeed, his postliberal response to romantic theology is a conservative manifesto calling for a return to the Book and the doctrinal rules governing the belief and action for which it calls. Lindbeck holds to the Christian belief that the Book is divinely authored, and it is with regard to its authority that he believes the tradition of doctrinal rules to be sanctioned. These theological assumptions lie behind Lindbeck's strong and legitimate reservations about the power of the theological author. While fully embracing the modern recognition of historicity and the variability it implies for speaking the language of faith in the present, Lindbeck regards narrative intratextuality, and not authorial talent, as the medium of historicity. He fears that the romantic notion of theological authorship illegitimately accords the theologian the power to make, rather than apply, the rules of the doctrinal tradition. The exercise of such power all too easily leads to the usurpation of the tradition's authority, which lies primarily in its scriptural teachings and only secondarily in the applicative skill of the faithful theologian modestly and rightly constrained by the tradition's limits on his or her creativity.

In judging whether this postliberal understanding of theological authorship would serve the Catholic tradition better than its romantic counterpart, we would do well to note Lindbeck's view of the historical situation theology faces presently and the temptation that situation poses to the theologian's creative aspirations. Lindbeck's postliberal stance seems resigned to an inevitable and strong conflict between Christianity and culture into the foreseeable future. He assumes that his theological program could never be widely adopted

35. *Enchiridion Symbolorum Definitionum et Declarationum de Rebus Fidei et Morum*, ed. H. Denzinger-A. Schönmetzer, S.J. (Freiburg: Herder, 1965), 370–71, 372 (pars. 1525, 1526, 1531).

in the context of modern, bourgeois culture, so antithetical to that culture's "psycho-social" assumptions is the understanding of the Christian vision he commends. Indeed, Lindbeck anticipates a Christian future in which communities of faith will consist of small enclaves of the committed, who define their religious self-identity not only positively with regard to the regulative tradition but also negatively with regard to the values of modern culture.[36] Lindbeck decries the romantic exercise of theological authorship as a nearly irresistible temptation to confuse creativity with novelty and faithfulness to the tradition with a never-ending search for a fleeting relevance destructive of Christian identity.

Even assuming the correctness of Lindbeck's diagnosis and prognosis—and I think there is plenty of evidence to support his vision—one might question the adequacy of his remedy. Lindbeck sees the crisis of Christian faith in the modern world as nothing less than the threat of its extinction. His notion of constrained authorship addresses that threat through the theologian's efforts to describe the meaning of the biblical text not for the culture at large but for the community of faith and in so doing to instruct the community in authentic speaking and acting. One might say that Lindbeck's alternative to the "modern" theologian very much resembles the ancient Christian catechist living in a pagan world. Such a portrait does much to explain Lindbeck's attempt in *The Nature of Doctrine* to articulate a nonfoundational prolegomenon to any future theology.[37] Foundational theologies seek theoretical grounding in a nonscriptural anthropology, epistemology, or method because they assume the need to engage culture in and through theological reflection and find the possibility of rapprochement in an appropriate secular theory. For Lindbeck the possibility of such rapprochement has evaporated. Maintaining the distinctiveness of the tradition is the far greater challenge facing theologians, especially since its loss to a significant degree can be attributed to the common canons of practice for theological talent in the modern period.

Although I agree with Lindbeck's assessment of the vapidity of cultural Christianity and sympathize with his concerns about the

36. Lindbeck, *The Nature of Doctrine*, 127.
37. For a discussion of the ecclesiological implications of this prolegomenon, see George A. Lindbeck, "The Story-Shaped Church: Critical Exegesis and Theological Interpretation," in *Scriptural Authority and Narrative Tradition*, ed. G. Green (Philadelphia: Fortress Press, 1987), 161–78.

romantic dissolution of meaningful authority, I do not think that his postliberal version of theological authorship would suit the Catholic tradition better than the dialogical models of authorship that have been prevalent since the beginnings of the romantic paradigm. In order to respect the broad strokes of Lindbeck's program, one needs to contextualize his criticism of the romantic paradigm. While it may be legitimate to argue, as Lindbeck does, that the exercise of the romantic conception of theological authorship has led to a modern crisis in authority within the Protestant tradition, one might ask if the results of the appropriation of the romantic paradigm in the Catholic tradition have been as deleterious. Indeed, one might question whether, in spite of the occasional tension between the magisterium and theologians, the Roman Catholic adoption of the paradigm has not redounded to the benefit of the tradition. On a fundamental level, an affirmative answer to this question attends a simple recognition of the authority of the Second Vatican Council.

There are many good reasons to prefer Lindbeck's postliberal modification of the romantic paradigm, not least among them its steadfast commitment to the position that the theologian's vocational challenge is to be as good as the tradition. It should not be overlooked, however, that Lindbeck's theological program does not assume a tradition in which institutional authority plays an important role. If Lindbeck's notion of theological authorship were to be appropriated in a Catholic context, then the regulated intratextual world to which the theologian would owe faithfulness would include the biblical canon, the magisterial pronouncements of the tradition, and the continuing dicta of the magisterium as authoritative interpretations of these texts. Were the theologian understood not as an imaginative contributor to the tradition whose work was subject to the assessment of the magisterium but as a describer of the magisterially interpreted tradition, the notion of theological responsibility at work would be thoroughly classical and its accompanying assumptions about authorship quite akin to the theological positivism expected by Pius XII in his encyclical *Humani Generis* (1950). Recent magisterial pronouncements attesting to the creative dimension of the theological task suggest the unacceptability of such a view. The objective structures of authority in the Roman Catholic tradition provide a framework for an ecclesial dialogue that fully respects the participation of the concerns of contemporary culture and the theologian's ability to judge their ecclesial implications. The church's identity is ever re-formed through such a conversation, which needs the voices of its past and present, its institutional and charismatic dimensions, and its two, albeit unequal, teaching authorities—the magisterium and the-ologians.

Finally, in a real sense the Catholic tradition's understanding of rapprochement between church and world, especially as articulated in *Lumen Gentium* and *Gaudium et Spes*, presupposes the exercise of romantic theological authorship. The imaginative foundations op-erative in constructive authorship are, much like the metaphysical foundations of the classical paradigm, an affirmation of the church's need to translate its message to the world and so to engage the world through its redemptive claims. This commitment to cultural en-gagement is seen especially in the romantic paradigm's alignment of authorial creativity and the prophetic dimension of the theological vocation. The theologian's discernment, construction, and direction of the tradition, rightly conducted, are motivated both by the faith that his or her insights are worthy of the tradition and the hope that culture, always in need and yet always good, will find the continuing relevance of the tradition worthy of acceptance.

In light of these assessments of the available alternatives to the modern notion of theological authorship, I would reiterate the current value of the romantic paradigm for the Catholic tradition and con-clude that the conflicts regarding ecclesial teaching authority occa-sionally attending its practice ought not to be attributed to the par-adigm's irreconcilability with traditional Catholic assumptions.

Part Three

Method, Mediation, and the Authorial Imagination

Chapter Five

Confessional Commitments and Foundational Theology

*B*Y *DEFINING* a theological agenda at the margins of the romantic paradigm, George Lindbeck steps back from the modern assumptions he largely shares and fixes a vantage point from which he is able to perceive and give account of their limitations. His program for a postliberal theology resembles political, liberation, and feminist theologies in its critical regard for the tradition within which it reflects and in the need it sees for a hermeneutics of suspicion as a dimension of its undertaking. Unlike these other romantic approaches to the theological task, though, postliberalism focuses its suspicion particularly on the individual theologian's authorial voice. Unlike political, liberation, and feminist theologies, postliberalism does not cast a suspicious eye on the authoritative past, judging the past instead to possess the Christian integrity so lacking in contemporary ecclesial life and theological reflection. The heroic proclivity of romantic authorship is the antagonist in *The Nature of Doctrine*'s implicit narrative of ecclesial and theological corruption in the modern period.

This programmatic vigilance toward the responsible exercise of theological talent distinguishes the postliberal approach as a significant development in the history of modern theology. This judgment may seem disproportionate to the relatively small amount of time that has passed since the appearance of Hans Frei's *Eclipse of Biblical Narrative* (1974), the work that provided a matrix for the small but growing family of theologians that can be described as postliberal. But if the roots of this family tree are recognized as stretching through the soil of Barthian theology, the postliberal approach is by now firmly implanted in the modern tradition and is a formidable, if somewhat dissatisfied, representative of the broad configuration of theological assumptions that constitute the romantic paradigm.

In this chapter the postliberal program will again focus the discussion. Having shown its ability to delineate the boundaries of the romantic paradigm, it will now prove helpful in defining the boundaries of modern Catholic theology. As valuable as Lindbeck's correctives to the romantic paradigm may be in a general sense, their implementation as such in a Catholic setting would present significant ecclesiological difficulties. First, the constrained authorship commended by Lindbeck would tend to foster an understanding of theological responsibility very much like the neoscholastic positivism officially sanctioned in Pius XII's encyclical *Humani Generis* (1950). In this view ecclesial authority would be identified exclusively with the pronouncements of the magisterium, which in turn would all but eclipse the creativity and authority of the theological author. Such a sublation of theological authorship would rest on a conception of ecclesial authority inconsistent with the spirit of the Second Vatican Council, herald a new integralism, and bring modern Catholic theology very close to classical paradigmatic assumptions. Second, Lindbeck's postliberal theology does not subscribe to Vatican II's understanding of the relationship between church and world and so does not actively seek the rapprochement between theology and culture that that relationship implies.

Although chapter 4 hinted at the anthropological issues at stake in the conversation between postliberalism and the Catholic tradition, those issues remained peripheral to the ecclesiological focus there. In this chapter, confessional anthropology will be highlighted as a way of understanding the possible stances one might take on the nature of theological authorship and will do so by addressing the topic of theological method. It is no doubt jejune to observe that an ecclesiology of rapprochement—or any ecclesiology for that matter—is rooted in anthropological assumptions, ignorance of which will impede a richer understanding of the *ecclesia* that a theological treatment intends to portray. It should be as jejune to observe the same of theological method, but such is often not the case. Perhaps a lingering residue of what Gadamer has called the Enlightenment's "prejudice against prejudice," manifesting itself in the expectation that the theoretical concerns of method above all should be value-free, accounts for this inconsistency.

Anthropological assumptions, however, inevitably attend all theological *loci*, and distinctively Catholic assumptions will have confessional implications even for the often tacit *locus* of theological method.

By saying this I do not mean to suggest that there is a particular, thematic anthropology that is essentially Catholic, as though some specific understanding of human nature—whether Platonic, Aristotelian, existentialist, or some other—has the confessional sanction of the Catholic tradition. Broadly speaking, though, the Catholic tradition professes an anthropology that it believes to be revealed in scripture, defined in council, and explanatory of human life before God. Lindbeck's postliberal program can be instructive to Catholic theology in a number of ways, not least in its cautious regard for the modern exercise of theological authorship. But a disparity between the anthropological assumptions of Lindbeck's theology and the confessional anthropology of the Catholic tradition suggests, at the very least, that Catholic theologians need to choose how Lindbeck's postliberal approach can be employed consistently in their work. An analysis of this disparity will help to define the spectrum of acceptable approaches to theological method in the Catholic tradition and to locate the theological practitioner within that spectrum.

The chapter will proceed to this end by evaluating Lindbeck's claim that good theology should be nonfoundational in its approach. This prescription for salutary theologizing accepts the consensus among contemporary pragmatic philosophers that "foundationalist" thinking and argumentation are logically indefensible. This philosophical conclusion, Lindbeck argues, exposes the inadequacies of the foundational character of theological thinking and argumentation in the modern period. Although Lindbeck does not offer his criticism of foundational theology as an explicit judgment on the integrity of modern Catholic theology, much of modern Catholic theology in fact has understood itself as "fundamental" or "foundational" in its approach.[1] Understanding the implications of Lindbeck's critique for Catholic theology, then, is important. To this end, an attempt will be made to determine how Lindbeck uses the metaphor of "foundations" in his criticism of modern theology and how his use of this metaphor reflects theological assumptions about human nature and the vocational responsibility of the theologian.

1. For a historical examination of this theological approach, see Monika K. Hellwig, "Foundations for Theology: A Historical Sketch," in *Faithful Witness: Foundations of Theology for Today's Church*, ed. L. O'Donovan and T. H. Sanks (New York: Crossroad, 1989), 1–13.

The analysis will advance in three steps. First, the philosophical critique of foundationalism will be examined by considering the work of Richard Rorty and Jeffrey Stout as illustrative of this position. Second, Lindbeck's postliberal argument on behalf of nonfoundational theology will be considered. Third, a distinctively Catholic understanding of authorship and its relationship to foundational approaches to theological method will be sketched. If successful, these reflections will venture a theological anthropology of theological talent in the Catholic tradition and by doing so take a few, first steps toward remedying the consistent inattention to assumptions about the practitioner in discussions of theological method.

THE PHILOSOPHICAL CRITIQUE
OF FOUNDATIONALISM

In recent years Richard Rorty's *Philosophy and the Mirror of Nature* (1979) has been an important focus of discussion about possible directions philosophy might take in moving beyond the intellectual heritage of both empiricism and idealism. Rorty judges this heritage to be bankrupt, unable to provide insightful directions for present philosophical inquiry or even to pose the proper questions for the orientation of its discipline. His book is an attempt to diagnose the cause of that bankruptcy and to suggest ways in which the economy of philosophy might be revitalized. Rorty attributes the poverty of present-day philosophy to the way in which the problems of its discipline have been conceived since the beginning of the modern period. Epistemology is the culprit in Rorty's account, specifically the manner in which epistemological theory since Descartes has defined its task as the grounding of the larger edifice of philosophical inquiry. Rorty's purpose is "to undermine the reader's confidence in 'the mind' as something about which one should have a 'philosophical' view, in 'knowledge' as something about which there ought to be a 'theory' and which has 'foundations,' and in 'philosophy' as it has been conceived since Kant."[2]

Philosophical issues, Rorty argues, have all too long been determined by the cast of foundationalism, an epistemological assumption more or less traditional in character that can now be recognized as a conceptual error concerning the nature of knowledge.

2. Richard Rorty, *Philosophy and the Mirror of Nature* (Princeton, N.J.: Princeton Univ. Press, 1979), 7.

Foundationalism, the very label a term of opprobrium, identifies a view that holds that knowledge must have a basis, a "foundation," if its larger conceptual and judgmental network is to possess coherence. In Rorty's understanding, the idea of "foundations of knowledge" insists that there are "truths which are certain because of their causes rather than because of the arguments given for them."[3] This understanding of epistemology as an account of the causal basis of knowledge is in some ways as old as the Greek philosophical tradition. It can be traced to the specifically Platonic view that the mind is compelled or "caused" to hold something as known because of the power of the object of knowledge over it. The result of this compulsion is a noetic experience so certain, shared, and founded that the very act of questioning its necessity and epistemic primacy becomes absurd. "For Plato," Rorty notes, "that point was reached by escaping from the senses and opening up the faculty of reason—the Eye of the Soul—to the World of Being."[4] But in the history of philosophy, Plato's flight from sensibility was only one possible and ancient course to the same foundationalist commitment of the moderns.

The title of Rorty's book refers to the prevalent, though often tacit, metaphor that underlies epistemological discussions in the modern period. The Cartesian separation of mind and body isolated the mind as a discrete object of philosophical concern. In Rorty's provocative phrasing, this "invention of the mind" led to successive attempts to posit various of its qualities or abilities as natural, though nonetheless extraordinary, "foundations" for the structure of human knowledge. The mind increasingly came to be conceived by moderns as human nature's "glassy essence," a peculiar property of the intellect capable of mirroring an otherwise ungraspable truth and of doing so with the same necessity characteristic of Platonic thought. In such an epistemological framework, the justification of noetic claims or judgments through argumentation is a meaningful enterprise only if offered as a supplement to a causal explanation of the very possibility of knowledge. The subjective dimensions of mental life were invoked in the modern period to give account of epistemic causality, to explain how the mind could mirror truth and ground noetic unity.

In weaving his narrative of the "tyranny of epistemology," Rorty aims to expose the capriciousness of the various strategies to establish

3. Ibid., 157.
4. Ibid., 159.

noetic foundations. Descartes settled on the foundations of knowledge by sifting through the more ambiguous representatives of mental life until he arrived at clear and distinct ideas, themselves indubitable and self-evident. What was self-evident to Decartes, however, was not to Locke, who insisted that another experience, the determining power of sense impressions, presented compelling and utterly common grounds on which all of our knowledge rests. Lockean empiricism established "foundationalist epistemology . . . as the paradigm of philosophy"[5] and of all the examples of foundationalism best illustrates the relationship between mind and nature expressed in the title of Rorty's book. Rorty's portrayal of the mind as a mirror of nature less aptly applies to Kant, for the Copernican revolution heralded for epistemology in the *Critique of Pure Reason* maintains that it is nature that mirrors the mind. But Kant's idealist counterpoint to Humean empiricism continues to hold in an even more sophisticated manner than his philosophical predecessors that the mind's "glassy essence" causally explains the possibility of knowledge by lending foundational coherence to the otherwise confused manifold of sensibility. When one recalls that the foundations of knowledge are supposed to be certain and obvious, the very pluralism in the foundationalist quest stands as a self-critique of its venture.

The mutual deconstruction of foundationalist positions in the history of philosophy, however, is a secondary line of attack in Rorty's assault upon foundationalism. His principal argument against there being foundations for knowledge calls attention to the metaphorical undercurrents of epistemological theorizing and the ways in which these have prejudiced the conceptualization of how knowing occurs. Rorty contends that modern philosophy's consistent depiction of the mind as a mirror reflecting a stable truth led to the imaging of the noetic moment as a visual "confrontation" with this veridical reflection. This ocular metaphor encouraged the supposition that knowledge possesses a basis as immediate and as certain as a visual representation in an experience of optical perception. Such imagery did much to secure a largely unquestioned allegiance to the foundationalist project, leaving to those engaged in it only the task of determining exactly wherein that immediacy and certainty lay. This imagery, Rorty insists, is as illusory as the foundationalist assumption it intends to convey.

5. Ibid., 59.

Rorty's critique intends to pave the way for a conception of the philosophical enterprise freed from the vain search for foundations. He commends a pragmatic and behaviorist approach to philosophy that forsakes the inevitably confrontationalist character of epistemological programs in favor of what he describes as a more "edifying" approach to philosophical inquiry.[6] "Hermeneutics," Rorty claims, ". . . is what we get when we are no longer epistemological."[7] Hermeneutics, described here as "an expression of hope that the cultural space left by the demise of epistemology will not be filled,"[8] sees conversation and not discovery as the proper model for philosophical discourse and inquiry. While the foundationalist approach of "confrontation" attempts to constrain conversation by manifesting the supposedly final truth of representation to the mind's eye, a pragmatically conducted hermeneutics recognizes the inability of finally determining the truth of anything and instead regards understanding as an ongoing process accomplished through meaningful dialogue. Indeed, Rorty envisages the future of his discipline as one in which the desire for systematic problem solving will make way for a conception of philosophy as a reactive enterprise, as a discipline ever vigilant to the pretensions of epistemological theorizing and the search for foundations, as well as eager to expose such pretensions as the residue of an outdated and useless conceptualization of the philosophical task.

Although Rorty's critique of foundationalism has been one of the best known and most influential in recent years, its originality lies largely in its attention to the rhetoric of foundationalist assumptions and to the ways in which that rhetoric has perpetuated the foundationalist fallacy. Rorty's actual conclusions about the errors of foundationalism differ little from the principal criticisms of foundationalism that have been offered by a host of philosophers in the course of the past century.

Marking the spirit of Cartesianism as his antagonist in an 1868 essay, Charles Sanders Peirce concluded that "[w]e have no power of Intuition," that "every cognition is determined logically by previous cognitions," and that, because there is "no power of thinking

6. Ibid., 357f.
7. Ibid., 325.
8. Ibid., 315.

without signs," no logical reason exists for positing some foundational point of departure for this intellectual process.[9] In much the same fashion Ludwig Wittgenstein observed in his later work that philosophy "may in no way interfere with the actual use of language; it can only describe it . . . [and] it cannot give it any foundation either."[10] Wilfrid Sellars has pointed to the proclivity in acts of human knowing, even those constituted empirically and noninferentially, to accept what Sellars calls the "Myth of the Given," the "idea that there are inner episodes, whether thoughts or so-called 'immediate experiences,' to which each of us has privileged access," and "that knowledge of these episodes furnishes *premises* on which empirical knowledge rests as on a foundation."[11] For Sellars this myth does not preserve a benign or higher truth but perpetuates a logical fallacy that distorts our expectations about what knowledge is and how it functions. Sellars agrees with the Harvard philosopher Willard Van Orman Quine that "empirical knowledge, like its sophisticated extension, science, is rational, not because it has a *foundation* but because it is a self-correcting enterprise which can put *any* claim in jeopardy, though not *all* at once."[12] In his *Beyond Objectivism and Relativism* (1983), Richard Bernstein has presented an eloquent rejoinder to what he describes as the "Cartesian anxiety" that pervades modern philosophy's elusive and, in his judgment, foolhardy search for foundations. Bernstein rejects that anxiety's assumption that the only alternative to the objectivist standpoint of foundationalism is "relativism, skepticism, historicism, and nihilism."[13] He argues against

9. Charles Sanders Peirce, "Some Consequences of Four Incapacities (1868)," in *Collected Papers of Charles Sanders Peirce*, vol. 5, ed. C. Hartshorne and P. Weiss (Cambridge, Mass.: Harvard Univ. Press, 1960), 158. Cf. in the same volume, "Questions Concerning Certain Faculties Claimed for Man (1868)," 135–55.

10. Ludwig Wittgenstein, *Philosophical Investigations*, 3d ed., trans. G. E. M. Anscombe (New York: Macmillan, 1968), 49.

11. Wilfrid Sellars, *Science, Perception and Reality* (New York: Humanities Press, 1963), 140.

12. Ibid., 170. Cf. Willard Van Orman Quine, *From a Logical Point of View* (New York: Harper & Row, 1963), 41: "Our statements about the external world face the tribunal of sense experience not individually but only as a corporate body."

13. Richard J. Bernstein, *Beyond Objectivism and Relativism: Science, Hermeneutics, and Praxis* (Philadelphia: Univ. of Pennsylvania Press, 1983), 2–3. For further discussion of the philosophical problem of foundationalism, see Ernest Sousa, "The Raft and the Pyramid: Coherence versus Foundations in the Theory of Knowledge," *Midwest Studies in Philosophy* 5 (1980): 3–25; "The Foundations of Foundationalism," *Nous* 14 (1980): 547–64; William C. Placher, *Unapologetic Theology: A Christian Voice in a Pluralistic Conversation* (Louisville, Ky.: Westminster/John Knox Press, 1989), 24–38.

the widespread attachment to the Cartesian dichotomy by enlisting Gadamer, Habermas, Rorty, and Arendt as conversation partners to illustrate how philosophy might be conceived as a dialogical activity responsive to the call for praxis in human communities.

This consistent and largely united attack on foundationalism has been so effective that a consensus has been reached in the scholarly community that at least any naive or "strong" form of foundationalism is philosophically untenable. Pragmatism, analytic philosophy, and the philosophy of science have successfully exposed the sorts of foundationalism espoused by the likes of Descartes, Kant, and the empiricists as unwitting expressions of a rationalist variety of dogmatism, which, ironically, cannot pass the test of close rational analysis. In fact the antifoundationalist critique has been so compelling that one rightly wonders what, if anything, continues to be at issue in this philosophical discussion. In his study *The Flight from Authority* (1981), Jeffrey Stout has shown that what continues to be at issue in the debate about foundationalism can be traced to the different ways in which its participants are committed to the heritage of modern Western philosophy.

Nearly all philosophers have recognized the force of the arguments against foundationalism. But some philosophers, Stout notes, have been unwilling to forsake *any* form of foundationalism, fearing, no doubt, the relativism they believe would ensue if the antifoundationalist position were embraced completely. William Alston, for example, has admitted that a self-certain—what he calls iterative[14]— foundationalism is beyond the power of reason. Yet Alston seeks to define a more minimalist or "weak" foundationalism—a position that avoids the pitfalls of dogmatism while espousing the foundationalist claim that there are beliefs justifying other beliefs that themselves require no justification.

Alston, Stout observes, is willing to relinquish what have now been exposed as the naive expectations of a foundationalist stance. He does not require that foundationalist beliefs be infallible, indubitable, incorrigible, self-justified, radically independent of other beliefs, immediately demonstrable, immediately given, or self-certain.[15]

14. William P. Alston, "Two Types of Foundationalism," *Journal of Philosophy* 73 (1976): 171.

15. Jeffrey Stout, *The Flight from Authority: Religion, Morality, and the Quest for Autonomy* (Notre Dame, Ind.: Univ. of Notre Dame Press, 1981), 28–29.

Rather, Alston advocates a minimal foundationalism that "requires only one thing of its foundationalist beliefs—namely, that they be immediately justified."[16] Beliefs that are justified mediately possess what Alston calls "warrant-increasing properties,"[17] which gain strength by a process of mutual validation within a network of beliefs. Immediately justified beliefs, however, are not justified by appeal to "any other justified belief."[18] Or as Stout puts it, Alston seeks a grounding for knowledge in a belief "warranted by virtue of some property or set of properties *other than relations to other beliefs*,"[19] hence a belief that is at least minimally foundationalist in character.

Whether such a minimal foundationalist belief actually exists is a question decidedly secondary on Alston's list of priorities. Above all he is interested in establishing the logical possibility of a form of foundationalism capable of eluding the attack that has devastated the traditional notion of privileged belief.[20] Stout notes that in Alston's proposal minimal foundations need not be firm or fixed. In fact Alston concedes that what is counted as a minimal foundation in the present might very well be abandoned in the future if criticism or revision shows it to be untenable. Such foundations would be minimalistic indeed and, Stout sardonically suggests, perhaps "minimally interesting at best."[21] All of Alston's argumentative efforts seem intent on rigging a theoretical safety net for a noetic high-wire act that seems to come off quite well every time without one. Or as Stout coyly observes, a minimalist foundational belief "is immediately justified just in case what justifies it does not include other justified beliefs."[22]

Stout recognizes that Alston's effort to establish the logical possibility of some even weak form of foundationalism is an attempt to

16. Stout, *The Flight from Authority*, 29.
17. Alston, "Two Types of Foundationalism," 170.
18. William P. Alston, "Has Foundationalism Been Refuted?" *Philosophical Studies* 29 (1976): 289.
19. Stout, *The Flight from Authority*, 31.
20. "Although I am convinced that simple foundationalism is the most defensible form of foundationalism, especially if it also divests itself of other gratuitous claims for foundations, such as infallibility and incorrigibility, I do not claim that it can actually be made to work. Though it escapes the main antecedent objection, it still faces all the difficulties involved in finding enough immediately justified beliefs to ground all our mediately justified beliefs. And on this rock I suspect it will founder" (Alston, "Two Types of Foundationalism," 185).
21. Stout, *The Flight from Authority*, 36.
22. Ibid., 29.

confront the logical problem of an infinite justificatory regress. If one of the tasks of philosophy involves the justification of beliefs, none of which are foundational, then the process of justification could only be conducted mediately within the network of mutually dependent beliefs. The foundationalist fears this prospect, judging that the process of justification would then be either an infinite regress (which could never be completed) or an utterly circular begging of the question (which defies the very idea of justification).[23] But this concern, Stout points out, this anxiety in the face of relativism, overestimates the consequences of the antifoundationalist critique for the philosophical task of justifying beliefs. "Let us assume for the moment," Stout proposes, "that the 'regress' argument is conclusive. What does it force us to conclude? Only, I take it, that if justification must stop somewhere, we should expect to be able to find in any epistemic context 'some stock of well-entrenched beliefs which set the bounds within which current enquiry proceeds.' So far as I know, no antifoundationalist has ever denied this."[24]

In order to find in minimal foundationalism what he seeks, Stout presses, Alston must embrace some of the dogmatic qualities of traditional foundationalism that have been discredited by the antifoundationalist critique and from which he correctly has distanced his position. "If the point [of Alston's argument]," Stout notes, "is to *establish* . . . stronger foundations in the face of skeptical objection, then immediate demonstrability seems necessary. If the point is to reconstruct knowledge from the foundations, without presupposing the validity of epistemic principles, then iterative [or self-certain] foundationalism seems needed."[25] Yet Alston concedes the untenability of immediate demonstrability and identifies himself as a critic of iterative or self-certain foundationalism. To what end, then, his defense of even a minimal foundationalist position?

The real answer to this question cannot be found in Alston's argument alone but, Stout contends, in the commitment Alston makes to the traditional heritage of modern philosophy. Indeed, Alston's logical weavings illustrate both his fidelity to the spirit of

23. Alston, "Has Foundationalism Been Refuted?" 300–302. Cf. Alston, "Two Types of Foundationalism," 171f.

24. Stout, *The Flight from Authority*, 33.

25. Ibid. In spite of his rhetorical tone, Stout is not speculating about Alston's goals but addressing the philosophical advantages that Alston himself attempts to glean from the foundationalist project. See Alston, "Two Types of Foundationalism," 179–82.

Cartesianism and the extent to which that faith has been shaken by the ascendancy of pragmatism. Alston, Stout observes, understands himself as a true son of Descartes, placing Descartes in the position of authoritative precursor. But the arguments of more recent philosophy have exposed the naïveté of the Cartesian claims about the constitution of knowing and have done so to such a degree that even a faithful son like Alston can invoke the authority of the intellectual parent only "by so reading the precursor's work as to retain its terms but to mean them in another sense."[26] Alston is eager to retain the traditional vocabulary of foundationalism, although it is a vocabulary "now emptied of content."[27] In fact, Stout concludes, "the disagreement between contemporary foundationalists and their antifoundationalist targets is largely verbal"[28] and only now a matter of sifting through their confused verbiage to discover an intellectual armistice declared in the absence of anything substantive about which to fight. For Stout this peace is a victory for the antifoundationalists and heralds the passing of the Cartesian age. However well-intentioned Alston's efforts, they neither promulgate the traditional Cartesian project nor establish an understanding of philosophical justification distinguishable in any meaningful sense from the mediate approaches espoused by his alleged antifoundationalist opponents.

Characterizing the logical repartee of the foundationalist debate as an authority dispute in the tradition of modern philosophy is revealing. What otherwise might be judged to be an arcane disagreement about the logical possibility of traditional inductive theorizing appears to be much more when Stout places it in the context of the philosophical tradition and the loyalties and disloyalties that that tradition has engendered. The adoption of a historical perspective does not necessarily entail Stout's conclusion that Alston's "minimal foundationalism" only echoes the death knell of Cartesianism. From a foundationalist perspective the wide acceptance won by the antifoundationalist position among philosophers could as easily be portrayed as the unfortunate ascendancy of those who have made the "linguistic turn" and pointed philosophy in relativistic directions, whether they are historicist, pragmatist, or analytical. But this is only to make the obvious point here that the explanatory possibilities of

26. Stout, *The Flight from Authority,* 35.
27. Ibid., 36.
28. Ibid., 89.

historical context, particularly one understood as a tradition, are extremely diverse and are always informed by one's sense for the meaning of history.

Taking a cue from Stout's attention to the importance of tradition for understanding even the most theoretical of debates, the next section considers how the postliberal appropriation of the antifoundationalist position might better be understood if placed in the history of theology and in the context of the confessional commitments that inform that history.

NONFOUNDATIONALISM AND POSTLIBERALISM

In *The Nature of Doctrine* Lindbeck introduces the antifoundationalist critique in two distinguishable yet related ways. The early chapters of the book invoke the antifoundationalist position implicitly rather than explicitly and focus on how a foundationalist bias has skewed the very conceptualization of religion and theology since the Enlightenment. The last chapter of the book explicitly criticizes the workings of theology as a foundational discipline, one whose intelligibility is dependent on the credibility of an extrabiblical assumption or theory. Here Lindbeck makes direct appeal to the issues and concerns raised in the foundationalist debate as he addresses their implications for theological method. Let us consider each approach in turn.

A sort of foundationalism is at work, Lindbeck believes, in the very suppositions that the modern world holds about the nature of religious experience and in the way such experience informs the liberal understanding of the theological task. In a manner analogous to the philosophical criticism of privileged access to the noetic grounds of knowledge, Lindbeck criticizes the assumption that theology is grounded in a religious experience that exists, as it were, prior to and independently of linguistic structures. "It is conceptually confused," he asserts, "to talk of symbolizations (and therefore of experiences) that are purely private."[29] But all too often modern theology fosters just that confusion by making the erroneous notion of privileged access its first principle. Theology in this common, though for Lindbeck skewed, conceptualization is a second-order activity

---

29. George A. Lindbeck, *The Nature of Doctrine: Religion and Theology in a Postliberal Age* (Philadelphia: Westminster Press, 1984), 38.

that brings inner experience to expression and in so doing relates its truth to the wider scope of human experience and action. Within this experiential-expressive orientation, theology is constructed upon subjective foundations whose unthematized, private, and ahistorical qualities are seen as providing stability for its reflective edifice, an edifice weathered by the elements of Enlightenment and post-Enlightenment criticism.

The result, Lindbeck judges, is just the opposite. The liberal undertaking does not provide a firm and reliable grounding for theology. On the contrary, it commits theology to a never-ending process of translation in which the nebulous character of its private foundations provides little, if any, normative direction to theological construction and in which ecclesial doctrine is utterly accommodated to the changing circumstances of time and place. Postliberal theology sees at least a dimension of its critical mission in exposing the liberal conceptualization of religion and theology as one built on shifting sands rather than upon a sure and stable foundation. A theology construed in grammatical or cultural-linguistic terms is the postliberal remedy for this ecclesial malady.

The antifoundationalist critique is invoked more directly in Lindbeck's discussion of how a postliberal theology properly goes about its business. In the typically liberal understanding, foundational or apologetical theology must seek to articulate a common epistemological basis in order to establish the possibility of conversation between theology and secular culture. Only through such a common theory, the foundationalist maintains, will theology have a means of keeping its own insights current and of making them intelligible to the extra-ecclesial world. Bespeaking the foundational position, but only for the sake of argument, Lindbeck notes that

> [t]he great strength of theological liberalism . . . lies in its commitment to making religion experientially intelligible to the cultured and the uncultured among both its despisers and its appreciators. It is in order to clarify the gospel in a world where it has become opaque that liberals typically choose the categories in which to expound their systematic theologies; and it is by their success in communicating to the modern mind that they assess the faithfulness of their endeavors. This same concern accounts for the liberal commitment to the foundational enterprise of uncovering universal principles or structures—if not

metaphysical, then existential, phenomenological, or hermeneutical. If there are no such universals, then how can one make the faith credible, not only to those outside the church but to the half-believers within it and, not least, to theologians?[30]

To this last stated rhetorical plea Lindbeck answers that "[p]ostliberals are bound to be skeptical . . . about apologetics and foundations."[31] An aprioristic approach to the task of theology all too easily serves interests that identify intelligibility with relevance. Doctrinal integrity quickly evaporates in the foundational propensity to translate the gospel through a universal medium or theory. "Resistance to translation," Lindbeck points out, "does not wholly exclude apologetics, but this must be of an ad hoc and nonfoundational variety rather than standing at the center of theology."[32] Only at the cost of its self-identity does theology try to become all things to all people.

Whether it is described as cultural-linguistic, postliberal, or antifoundationalist, Lindbeck's program intends to counter the detrimental effects of theological foundationalism by offering an alternative to the liberal tradition's repeated efforts to ground theology in some dimension of human experience. For the postliberal, the theologian's task is to apply the grammar, the rules, of the tradition to discrete cultural circumstances in an ad hoc fashion so that the broader world of human meaning can be shaped by the scripture's authoritative narrative. It is the coherence of tradition, rather than the credibility of theory, that guides the theological enterprise. Lindbeck recognizes that such an antifoundationalist stance can easily be accused of fideism or, in philosophical parlance, irrationalism.[33] But such charges betray the prejudice of the foundational perspective— that intelligible relations between the ecclesial and the secular can be established only through an epistemology that facilitates meaningful, theological translation. For Lindbeck, however, one need not account for such intelligibility through universal presuppositions at all. From a nonfoundational perspective, theological intelligibility "comes from [the theologian's ad hoc] skill, not theory, and credibility comes from good performance, not adherence to independently formulated criteria."[34]

30. Ibid., 129.
31. Ibid.
32. Ibid.
33. Ibid., 130.
34. Ibid., 131.

Lindbeck's first type of antifoundationalist critique proceeds from what is presented chronologically in his book as the second. In other words, Lindbeck's attempt to reconceive theology cultural-linguistically is a function of what he considers the actual tasks of a postliberal theology to be. Theology is better understood as a grammar because such a model enables a nonfoundational understanding of its intelligibility, faithfulness, and applicability, an understanding that Lindbeck supports for at least two reasons. First, a nonfoundational theology respects the cogent arguments made by pragmatic philosophers against the viability of privileged access. The conclusions of philosophers like Rorty and Stout have shown that meaning in general cannot be justified foundationally, and theological meaning is in no way exempt from this antifoundationalist critique. Second, a nonfoundational approach to theology provides a suitable response to what in Lindbeck's judgment is problematic about modern, liberal theology.

This last point will be the focus of the remainder of this section and will involve the more precarious task of articulating the negative and often tacit judgments that lead a thinker to advocate a particular intellectual program. This attention to the negative side of Lindbeck's proposal is justified to some degree by that proposal's very nature. Clearly a methodological agenda described as "nonfoundational" cannot account for its program only in positive terms because it is a statement of what such a program is not as much as of what it is. Investigating this negative dimension of postliberalism in terms of the issue of authorship can be especially illuminating.

Like philosophers who identify themselves as antifoundationalists, Lindbeck chooses language over experience as a medium for meaning. Unlike his philosophical counterparts, Lindbeck does not attack Cartesianism as such, though we might say that he offers his theological program as a strategy to counter the widespread commitment to a theological version of Cartesianism that he believes to be the common fare of experiential-expressivists. This concern about the priority of the subjective in many forms of modern theology is evinced in Lindbeck's conception of constrained authorship. A nonfoundational understanding of theological authorship does not deny the contributions of authorial talent to the theological enterprise. But such an understanding insists that the contributions of authorial talent be minimal and applied ad hoc, its maximalist or heroic tendencies ever constrained by the doctrinal grammar of the ecclesial tradition.

If this reading of Lindbeck is defensible, then it may prove interesting to understand his reservations about foundational theologies in the same terms.

Foundational theologies, Lindbeck thinks, incorrectly ground the theological enterprise in some dimension of human subjectivity—whether it is the immediacy of religious experience or a rationally constructed theory enabling the liberal translation of the gospel message into secular categories. But its experiential grounding as such cannot account for a theology gone astray. After all, an aggrandized authorial talent relies on the foundationalist approach in constructing particular theological positions, and the accordance of priority to such theological power is what causes Lindbeck concern. Recalling Rorty's attention to the rhetorical use to which an image like "foundations" must invariably be put, I would propose that the image of "foundations" in Lindbeck's theological program seems to function as a metaphor for the personal talent on which the exercise of romantic authorship rests. If such an interpretation is tenable, then the actual "foundation" that Lindbeck's nonfoundationalist position attempts to undermine is what he judges to be that talent's recurring tendency to construe the grammar of Christian tradition falsely, to construct theological positions that reflect the mind of a heroic author much more than the faith of the ages. Just as experience is given priority over its expression in the liberal approach, a particular dimension of that same human experience—theological talent—is given priority over the skills that Lindbeck sees as the real embodiment of proper theological activity. In this regard Lindbeck's antifoundationalism can be seen as a theological strategy to guard against what he sees as a "foundationalist" exercise of authorial talent.

As Stout's historical placing of Alston's rarified arguments proved enlightening, so might a similar placing of Lindbeck's proposals. Any attempt to understand postliberalism in historical terms, however, runs the risk of accepting only the post-Enlightenment context that Lindbeck poses as the framework for his discussion. It may be more illuminating to situate Lindbeck's antifoundationalism and the view of theological authorship it suggests within the confessional setting configured by the most basic Reformation doctrines.

The antifoundationalist argument of *The Nature of Doctrine* may appear on the surface as the use of relatively recent philosophical conclusions to further the ends of a new theological proposal. But one need not look much beneath the surface of Lindbeck's argument to consider whether his confessional commitment to the Lutheran tradition makes its antifoundationalist perspective theologically attractive. Of itself, antifoundationalism is a philosophical stance reached through sophisticated arguments against the integrity of naively inductive logic. From the perspective of classical Lutheran doctrine, however, it supports a confessional judgment regarding the inability of the innate power of reason to know God or to foster an understanding of things spiritual. The words of the *Formula of Concord* (1577) represent this position well:

> Although man's reason or natural intellect still has a dim spark of the knowledge that there is a God, as well as of the teaching of the law (Rom. 1:19-21, 28, 32), nevertheless, it is so ignorant, blind, and perverse that when even the most gifted and the most educated people on earth read or hear the Gospel of the Son of God and the promise of eternal salvation, they cannot by their own powers perceive this, comprehend it, understand it, or believe and accept it as the truth. On the contrary, the more zealously and diligently they want to comprehend these spiritual things with their reason, the less they understand or believe. . . .
>
> Thus Scripture denies to the intellect, heart and will of the natural man every capacity, aptitude, skill, and ability to think anything good or right in spiritual matters, to understand them, to begin them, to will them, to undertake them, to do them, to accomplish or to cooperate in them as of himself.[35]

In the entire history of philosophy, one would be hard pressed to find a position better suited than antifoundationalism to corroborate this religious understanding of the power of human reason *coram Deo*. As different as the Lutheran criticism of theological speculation and the antifoundationalist criticism of Cartesianism may be, each from its theological or philosophical point of view decries the constructive power that is all too quickly accorded to human reasoning. Each stands, theologically or philosophically, against the assumption that reason can fashion a truthful complex of knowledge based on the inherent abilities of the mind. Both render harsh judgments on reason's creative capacity to function apart from traditions or communities of meaning, whether ecclesial or philosophical. If we broaden the critical attention to reason shared by sixteenth-century Protestantism and modern antifoundationalists to include a

---

35. "Formula of Concord (1577)," in *The Book of Concord*, ed. T. G. Tappert (Philadelphia: Fortress Press, 1959), 521–22.

more romantic description of human ability as the power of imagination, then the relationships among classical Protestant belief, antifoundational criticism, and Lindbeck's suspicion of theological authorship become clear. In this respect we might see Lindbeck's antifoundationalism as an effective means for preserving the very confessional grammar that his theological program is concerned to safeguard.

The antifoundationalist positions advocated by philosophers like Peirce, Wittgenstein, Rorty, and Stout establish their claims through logical argumentation that exposes the untenability of foundationalist assumptions. Logical argumentation, however, never establishes a religious position. The *Formula of Concord*'s confessional judgment regarding theological reasoning is neither a discursive conclusion nor, primarily at least, a stance on theological method. Above all it voices the seminal Protestant belief on the relationship between faith and works, a teaching classically articulated in Article 20 of the *Augsburg Confession* (1530): "We begin by teaching that our works cannot reconcile us with God or obtain grace for us, for this happens only through faith, that is, when we believe that our sins are forgiven for Christ's sake, who alone is the mediator who reconciles the Father. Whoever imagines that he can accomplish this by works, or that he can merit grace, despises Christ and seeks his own way to God, contrary to the Gospel."[36] As the reformers never tired of reiterating against the charge of antinomianism, the affirmation of the doctrine of *sola fide* does not obviate the importance of good works. The primacy of faith, though, means that works neither justify nor in any way enhance the grace that establishes their goodness. "It is also taught among us," the *Augsburg Confession* continues, "that good works should and must be done, not that we are to rely on them to earn grace but that we may do God's will and glorify him."[37]

One cannot account for Lindbeck's prescription for a nonfoundational theology simply by reference to the sixteenth-century creeds cited above. These creeds do not explain, in some reductive manner, Lindbeck's understanding of constrained authorship. Nor is it suggested that Lindbeck would espouse the sixteenth-century conceptualizations and expressions of human nature and its relationship to God. It is interesting, however, to note the degree to which Lindbeck's

36. "The Augsburg Confession (1530)," in *The Book of Concord,* 42.
37. Ibid., 45.

nonfoundational understanding of constrained authorship reflects the doctrinal sensibilities of this classical Protestant position. The tasks of postliberal theology, like all human acts, are works subject to the same doctrinal rule on the relationship between faith and works expressed in the confessional statements cited above. In Lindbeck's postliberal theology, the works of the theological imagination are, if not totally depraved, at least suspected of depravity. Theological endeavor does not legitimately take place through any creative work of one's own but *sola gratia*, through the divinely authored text's predetermination—Lindbeck would say "regulation"—of the theological author's faithful works.[38] Lindbeck would not care to break with the romantic paradigm's insistence on the integrity of individual authorship and on the need for creativity in the act of theological interpretation. Although committed to the spirit of the classical Protestant teaching on works, he does not depart intellectually from the modern principle of creative authorship. But truly good theological works, the product of authorship, must be utterly expressive of the intratextual setting that defines the theologian's faithfulness. A postliberal theologian remains on guard against what he or she judges to be the natural tendency on the part of romantic authorship to understand creativity as a human work, the product of an unguided talent that subverts the mission of faithful reflection in the imaginative construction of a *theologia gloriae*.

If there is merit to this reading of Lindbeck, then he is led to propose a nonfoundational theology not only by the cogency of philosophical antifoundationalism but also by a consonance between his own confessional commitments and that philosophical position. Although the critique of foundationalism can serve as a propaedeutic to any number of philosophical positions (such as analytic philosophy, pragmatism, or hermeneutics), antifoundationalism as a critical stance advocates no particular philosophical viewpoint and so satisfies the classical Protestant expectation that reason make no speculative contribution to theological reflection. Most basically, though, the antifoundationalist position is an effective way to express the doctrinal anthropology of the Reformation in the setting of modernity.

Lindbeck objects to foundational theologies for reasons that can be described as a posteriori: he judges that experiential-expressive

---

38. Lindbeck himself uses this analogy with respect to the praxis of a religious community. See Lindbeck, *The Nature of Doctrine*, 128.

theologies from the time of Schleiermacher to the present have in fact forsaken traditional substance for cultural relevance. But there also seems to be a sort of a priori reason—or better put, a faith commitment—that leads Lindbeck to be suspicious of foundational theologies. Theological reflection, like all things human, is pridefully reluctant to recognize the inability of nature apart from God's grace. Foundational theologies, a fortiori, encourage a solipsistic exercise of authorship by their methodological commitment to the priority of human nature and its experience rather than to the traditional authority of the scriptural text. For Lindbeck an exercise of theological authorship not constrained by the cultural-linguistic approach will produce theological works that bespeak a fallen nature's anthropocentricity rather than God's promise of salvation revealed in scriptural tradition.

I do not offer this analogy between Lindbeck's understanding of constrained authorship and the doctrinal anthropology of the Reformation as a criticism. Indeed, I consider the confessional faithfulness of his position to be one of its strengths. Throughout *The Nature of Doctrine*, though, Lindbeck presents the postliberal program as one that can be put to the service of theology as such, irrespective of confessional differences. But would a nonfoundational theology be the only viable theology for a confessional tradition that did not share the anthropological presuppositions of the Reformation doctrine of *sola gratia*? This question puts at issue the viability of Lindbeck's postliberal program for theology done in the Roman Catholic tradition. The last section of this chapter attempts to justify the negative answer I would give to this question.

AUTHORSHIP AND CATHOLIC ANTHROPOLOGY

The Catholic tradition's normative anthropology is explicated in various confessional documents but nowhere more seminally or directly than in the Council of Trent's *Decree on Justification* (1546). Like the *Augsburg Confession* and the *Formula of Concord*, this conciliar document formulates a doctrinal understanding of the human person in terms of what is deemed the proper relationship between nature and grace, between human ability and the saving power of God. According to Trent, justification begins in the supernatural power of "God's prevenient grace through Jesus Christ," a call of God to the individual that is not merited and that expects a response. "The purpose of the call," in the words of the decree, "is that they who are turned away from God by sin may, awakened and assisted by God's grace, be disposed to turn to their own justification by freely assenting to and cooperating with that grace."[39]

The cooperation deemed necessary here is not the assertion of autonomous power on the part of the human being. Nor does the language of the decree suggest that the relationship between God and the person is coequal, as though commensurate powers are at work in the event of justification. The power of grace is both the beginning and end of salvation. Without God's grace, "the person could not move towards justice in God's sight," and grace remains the power of justification amid the cooperative efforts of the individual. Yet, the decree insists, the power of grace makes room for the contributions of human nature to the event of justification, however small these contributions may be. The consequence of this relationship between nature and grace is that "when God touches the human heart with the illumination of the Holy Spirit, the person who accepts that inspiration certainly does something [*neque homo ipse nihil omnino agat*] since the person could reject it."[40]

Prior to Trent the church's teaching on the relationship between nature and grace had not been given such precise definition as a matter of faith at an ecumenical council. Trent's *Decree on Justification* was formulated, in fact, as a polemical counterpoint to the Protestant doctrine of *sola gratia*. How, then, does the Catholic teaching on justification differ specifically from the Protestant? Both confessions expound their positions on justification by at least implicit appeal to the Genesis account of the creation of human nature in the "image and likeness of God" (Gen. 1:27) and the consequences of sin for that original relationship between God and humanity. By insisting that salvation begins with a call to the sinner and is brought to fulfillment at least partially through the cooperative efforts of the individual, the Catholic tradition highlights the importance of the free choice of the will in the event of justification. Although that power, an expression of the *imago Dei*, is enfeebled by the shared sin of humanity, it retains some measure of integrity even after the fall. This vestigial

39. *Enchiridion Symbolorum Definitionum et Declarationum de Rebus Fidei et Morum*, ed. H. Denzinger-A. Schönmetzer, S.J. (Freiburg: Herder, 1965), 370 (par. 1525).
40. Ibid.

integrity of human nature necessarily contributes something of its own to the conversion toward God to which the individual is beckoned and in which the individual is assisted by grace. The *Augsburg Confession* and the *Formula of Concord* portray this same relationship as one in which the power of divine grace is so determinative of the individual's relationship to God that no human effort can complement or cooperate with grace in any way. Thoroughly vitiated by the fall, human nature in the Protestant teaching shares not the slightest congruity with grace. The consequence of sin is the utter loss of the original dignity of the *imago Dei* within human nature. Human works may be salvationally ennobled in the sense that they give form to the grace of God, which, by possessing them, establishes their goodness. But fallen human nature is so utterly unworthy of the benefits of Christ that it cannot even acquiesce in its passive reception of the justification grace brings.[41]

As the doctrinal anthropology of the sixteenth-century Protestant creeds regulates the postliberal understanding of constrained theological authorship, the doctrinal anthropology of Trent suggests certain parameters for the right exercise of authorship in the Catholic tradition. But what view of authorship can be construed from the teaching of Trent? One that is broad, general, and decidedly minimalist, to be sure, but that is nevertheless significant for configuring a Catholic understanding of the theological practitioner and the confessional consistency of the method he or she practices.

At the very least, a Catholic anthropology of theological talent would situate the theologian's authorial works in the same context of dignity and responsibility affirmed of human acts in the *Decree on Justification*. Given Trent's specific attention to human works that play a part in the drama of salvation, there may be a reluctance to rank the work of theologizing, as reputable as it may be, among them.

---

41. I cannot offer this brief sketch of the differences between Protestant and Catholic understandings of justification without noting both the growing consensus between Roman Catholics and Lutherans on this doctrine and George Lindbeck's important contributions to this ecumenical dialogue. The text expressing this consensus, "Justification by Faith, by the Lutheran–Roman Catholic Dialogue Group in the United States," *Origins* 13 (October 6, 1983): 277–304, does not claim, however, that unanimity exists between Lutherans and Roman Catholics on the doctrine of justification but only that it is questionable "whether the remaining differences on this doctrine need be church-dividing" (279). My analysis in these pages raises the issue of whether Lindbeck's commendation of a nonfoundational approach for theology makes the doctrine of justification "theology-dividing" for the confessions.

But it is precisely the romantic paradigm's portrayal of theologizing as a human talent that supports the inclusion of authorship among those human acts that proceed from and yet cooperate with grace. This is not to say that good theologizing brings one to salvation. But it is to say that there is in the Catholic tradition a doctrinal basis for affirming the place of theological talent as a human enterprise that contributes something of its own integrity to the responsible delineation of God's revelation in history.

To the degree that theological authorship can be conceived as a charism it, like all human talents, is God-given and ever directed in its practice by grace. A Catholic understanding of talent, however, would not attribute its rightful exercise exclusively to the divine, as though talented action were only a manifestation of grace amid the humanly depraved and fallen. An account of theological authorship could claim consistency with Trent's anthropology only by insisting upon the necessary and unique cooperation of the theological author with grace and thus upon the role of authorial talent in theological endeavor. Although Trent's doctrine of justification does not explicitly endorse the integrity of theological talent, its affirmation of human dignity *coram Deo* supports the expectation of modern authorship that the individual theologian, in the words of the decree, "certainly does something" in the insightful construction of the doctrinal tradition. The act of theologizing, of course, cannot proceed from a human dignity exempt from human fallenness, and for this reason suspicion about how theological authorship might be exercised is always justifiable. But this judgment can be made only a posteriori, through the evaluation of discrete acts of authorship, and not a priori as is more characteristic of the postliberal approach. At the very least, a Catholic understanding of theological authorship need not share the suspicion in principle regarding its exercise that seems to be the agenda of postliberalism's notion of the constrained theological author.

A minimalist Catholic anthropology of authorship also has implications for theological method. If the issues of authorship, anthropology, and the metaphor of "foundations" are as related as has been suggested here, then there would seem to be not only an inconsistency between the confessional assumptions of the Catholic tradition and the postliberal understanding of authorship but also a consonance between the doctrinal anthropology of the Catholic tradition and the sort of foundational approach to theology that postliberalism judges to be methodologically aberrant. This would be true for the ecclesiological reasons explored in chapter 4. The Catholic understanding of the church's universality calls for an apologetical dialogue with the world that presupposes the contributions of a foundational theology.

But more in line with the argument presented here, Trent's affirmation of the dignity and responsibility of human experience before God permits, and perhaps even encourages, appeal to that experience as an important dimension of theological reflection. To the extent that the modern period is cognizant of the historicity of that experience, the constructive efforts on the part of Catholic authors of foundational theologies to find new ways to express the truth of faith and to convey its intelligibility by reference to secular, theoretical explanations of the meaning of human experience is confessionally warranted. In this respect the "foundations" that foundational theologies seek is a metaphor for the assumptions of a doctrinal anthropology, as it was for Lindbeck. In a Catholic setting, however, that anthropology presupposes that human experience—lapsed yet responsible, sinful yet able to cooperate with grace—can serve as a common ground on the basis of which the meaning of the gospel can ever be appreciated anew. This affirmation of human ability even amid the fallenness of nature need not be the explicit point of departure for any theology that calls itself Catholic. It is difficult to imagine, however, that any theology could be distinctively Catholic without making this doctrinal perspective central to its exposition of the relationship between God, self, and world. While this does not mean that a Catholic theology would need to adopt a foundational approach to method in order to be true to its confessional assumptions, it does suggest that the postliberal proscription against a foundational method for theology is not valid in a Catholic context.

Earlier discussion has shown that two principal arguments are raised against the adoption of such a foundational approach—one theological in its concerns, the other philosophical. If Catholic theological method may be, as it often is, foundational in its approach, then what of the postliberal charge that foundational theologies inherently compromise the authority of the scriptural narrative by seeking an extrascriptural basis for their interpretations of God's revelation? However this basis is defined—as an experience, a hermeneutical theory, an epistemology, or a metaphysics—its welcome admittance at the threshold of theological reflection is judged by postliberals to cause an unbiblical distraction to the authorial imagination that serves as its host. Moreover, if Catholic theological method may be, as it often is, foundational in its approach, then to what extent is it susceptible to the criticism of the most reputable philosophers of our time that foundationalism, as a theoretical description of the workings of reason, is untenable? We will consider each of these questions in turn.

The most developed theological argument against the viability of foundational theology has been offered by another advocate of the postliberal approach. In his book *Revelation and Theology: The Gospel as Narrated Promise*, Ronald Thiemann laments the subversion of the doctrine of revelation in the modern period as theologians have embraced some variety of foundationalism as a means of justifying the coherence of the theological enterprise. Modern theology's unwillingness to affirm the premodern assertion that knowledge of God is a gift of divine grace unfortunately has led to never-ending and utterly vain attempts to provide reasonable or, at the very least, experiential justifications for the possibility of such knowledge. Theologians have thus "taken on the additional task of showing how [their] language is warranted with reference to the reigning epistemology of the day," and "[m]odern doctrines of revelation have . . . become in part theoretical justifications for the Christian claim to knowledge of God."[42] Invoking the work of John Locke, Friedrich Schleiermacher, and Thomas Torrance as illustrations of the foundationalist procedure applied theologically, Thiemann concludes that such efforts are thoroughly capricious attempts to ground theology in some form of human intuition whose theoretical exposition is always found to be guilty before the logical court of antifoundationalist criticism. Any form of foundationalism, however applied, inevitably shows itself to be logically inconsistent and merely the elevation of bias to a privileged position in the network of reasoning.

Reason, however, matters less to Thiemann than faith when it comes to judging the deficiencies of foundationalist theologies. If a measure of any theology is its adherence to the most seminal of Christian beliefs, then, he claims, as a matter of principle, foundational theologies cannot accomplish what they set out to do. Any theology faithful to the Christian tradition must not depart from the

42. Ronald F. Thiemann, *Revelation and Theology: The Gospel as Narrated Promise* (Notre Dame, Ind.: Univ. of Notre Dame Press, 1985), 10.

distinctively Christian affirmation of the prevenience of God, "an indispensable background belief within the logic of Christian faith."[43] The priority of divine grace to all things human, whether knowledge of God, praxis, or theological reflection, is so central to Christian faith that forsaking the integrity of this belief amounts to theological deviancy. By trying to provide an epistemological justification for their very possibility, foundational theologies succumb precisely to this most basic of errors. Whereas the biblical witness consistently appeals to the prevenient grace of God in order to explain the self's reception of revelation and the salvation it heralds, the exposition of that witness in a foundational schema seeks a causal explanation for the possibility of knowledge of God within general human experience. The foundational approach thus "tends to subordinate the characteristic patterns of Christian speech to the patterns of the philosophical and apologetical argument."[44] Theology cannot abide such an inconsistency, Thiemann protests.

A nonfoundational, descriptive theology is the remedy that Thiemann prescribes for the disciplinary malady that he believes has spread so widely in the modern period. A descriptive theology eschews the search for foundations and "seeks its criteria of judgment within the first-order language of church practice."[45] The aim of such a theology is to expound the internal consistency of the gospel itself—to find, as it were, in the simple "logic" of the gospel a portrayal of God's relationship to humanity that obviates the need for the sufficient reasons of a foundationalist epistemology.[46] Thiemann maintains that a narrative approach to theological reflection is the best means to this end. The linguistic shape of scripture, he argues, is not accidental but expressive of the God who acts throughout its pages as the speaker of salvation. The promissory cast to scriptural language powerfully conveys the prevenience that Christians believe to be normative in the relationship between God and humanity, for the promise of scripture is that God *has* acted on behalf of humanity. Only a theology true to this narrated promise of scripture can be true as well to the content of its message. For Thiemann, foundational theologies can

43. Ibid., 78.
44. Ibid., 74.
45. Ibid., 75.
46. Thiemann presents a similar argument, though one directed specifically against the work of Gordon Kaufman, in Ronald F. Thiemann, "Revelation and Imaginative Construction," *Journal of Religion* 61 (1981): 242–63.

only undermine, while narrative theologies have the possibility of clarifying, the biblical proclamation of divine prevenience.

Like Lindbeck's *The Nature of Doctrine* I find *Revelation and Theology* to be a sophisticated and coherent proposal for correct theological procedure. The similarity between these works, however, is not limited to their high level of theological achievement. We should not overlook the extent to which Thiemann's theological program shares Lindbeck's subtext regarding the abuse of theological authorship in the liberal tradition. His indictment of modern theology's corruption of the doctrine of revelation can easily be read as a castigation of the romantic author's proclivity to value contemporary relevance above traditional normativeness. As intent as Lindbeck on regulating the imaginative excesses of the modern theological author, Thiemann highlights the way in which the promissory character of scriptural language conveys the self-identically Christian belief in the prevenience of God's grace to all things human. Theologians, he suggests, must be faithful to the biblical teaching on divine prevenience not only in the subject matter of their theologies but also in their vocational practice. Foundational approaches to theology ignore the implications of the doctrine of prevenience for authorial responsibility by grounding theological reflection nonscripturally in some dimension of human experience, and thus accord priority to the human over the divine. A nonfoundational, descriptive approach to theology accords priority to the divine gift that the scriptural text both proclaims and is, and places the imaginative capacities of the theologian under the governance of the Word.

Although Thiemann argues his concerns about theological responsibility cogently from the standpoint of his own confessional loyalties, we must be attentive to just how those loyalties lead him to define both methodological normativeness and methodological deviancy. All Christian theologians can agree that the doctrine of prevenience is an indispensable background belief to theological reflection and that the purport of this doctrine must permeate both theological content and the exercise of theological authorship. The doctrine of prevenience, however, is confessionally nuanced, a fact largely unacknowledged in the pages of *Revelation and Theology*. True to its tacit confessional commitments, Thiemann's theological proposal portrays the relationship between God and humanity in traditional Lutheran terms. The narrated promise of the gospel is at once made and enacted *sola gratia*, an understanding of the relationship between God and self, grace and works, that informs Thiemann's conception of the theologian's authorial responsibility as well. For Thiemann as for Lindbeck, a suspicion in principle about the "works" of the theological imagination requires that the theological author be constrained by the Gospel's narrative of grace. His commitment to this particular conception of prevenience and the understanding of theological authorship it entails leads him to regard foundational theologies as Pelagian or semi-Pelagian at best because they allow for some indispensable, and thus important, measure of authorial contribution to the process of theological construction.[47] In Thiemann's estimation the deviancy of foundational theologies derives from their naïveté, an unfounded innocence exhibited both in their quick willingness to find in human experience a reliable means of representing the purport of divine revelation and in their facile trust in the willingness of the theological imagination to champion the biblical message rather than the inventiveness of its own insights.

I readily concede that Thiemann is correct in his judgment that there is an inconsistency between foundational theologies and the doctrinal anthropology of classical Protestantism. Whether one judges foundational theologies to be inconsistent with the assumptions of modern Protestant theology as such depends on one's understanding of the doctrinal development undergone by the sixteenth-century confessions as they passed into the modern era. I will not defend here my opinion that modern Protestant theology can be foundational in its orientation. I would point out, however, that Thiemann's thorough criticism of foundational theologies is universally valid only if all Christian confessions espouse the sixteenth-century expression of the doctrinal anthropology of *sola gratia*. Clearly they do not. While maintaining that salvation begins with and is completed by the gift of divine grace, Trent's *Decree on Justification* affirms the cooperative role of human agency in the event of justification. The Catholic tradition maintains the prevenience of divine grace without compromise and yet claims that human agency plays some small but important role within the power of grace. Classical

47. In her study *God and Creation in Christian Theology*, Kathryn Tanner uses postliberal rule-theory to examine the doctrine of God's relationship to creatures. She is even more explicit than Thiemann in her judgment that modern theological discourse is inescapably Pelagian in its account of the relationship between God and human agency (*God and Creation in Christian Theology: Tyranny or Empowerment?* [Oxford: Basil Blackwell, 1988], 120–62).

Protestant tenets may judge this paradoxical claim to be semi-Pelagian at best. But this understanding of the relationship between nature and grace constitutes Catholicism's normative teaching on divine prevenience, in Thiemann's terms a background belief with which Catholic theology cannot dispense.

This background belief, I suggest, justifies foundational approaches to theology in the Catholic tradition, as well as the more constructive conception of theological authorship that they imply. Foundational theologies appeal to human experience as a common basis for an apologetical dialogue between faith and culture. But the very possibility of that appeal illustrates the degree to which Catholic theological method itself expresses the doctrinal anthropology of Trent. The Catholic tradition's belief that human experience, though fallen, retains some measure of its original dignity and integrity before God not only permits but also encourages the comparatively positive estimation of human experience that foundational theologies presuppose and on which they build. In a manner analogous to Trent's affirmation of human agency within the graced event of justification, the Catholic tradition may affirm the qualified authority of human experience as a resource for theological method, just as it may affirm the qualified authority of the experience of the theologian—including the theologian's talent—in specific, imaginative applications of that method.

But how does the foundational orientation of Catholic theology square with the contemporary philosophical consensus that foundationalism, as a theoretical description of the workings of reason, is untenable? The critique of foundationalism offered in the work of Peirce, Sellars, Rorty, and Stout, among others, has exposed a deficiency in traditional assumptions about what constitutes justified belief, particularly in the way that such assumptions have been invoked in order to support the viability of philosophical inquiry in the modern age. The antifoundationalist critique may be applied theologically, as it is in the work of Lindbeck and Thiemann. But we should not lose sight of the fact that theological versions of the antifoundationalist critique are more restrictive in scope than the philosophical versions of antifoundationalism that they appropriate. Functioning within the canons of theology, antifoundationalist theologians do not aim their criticism at the discipline of theology in ways that antifoundationalist philosophers certainly would were that discipline the object of their concern.

Philosophical versions of antifoundationalism advance *logical* analysis to reach the *philosophical* conclusion that no authoritative givenness regarding the nature, orientation, possibilities, or content of reasoning is immediately presented in or deducible from the operation of reasoning or its accompanying experiences. Christian theology, however, is a discipline whose reasoning proceeds from an authoritative givenness—the authoritative givenness of God's revelation of salvation through Jesus Christ, received in faith and appreciated in tradition. The task of theology is to interpret this authoritative givenness, to bring clarity to its ambiguities, to criticize its historical reception, and to invoke a sense of awe in the encounter with its mysteries. Whether Christian theological reasoning takes the form of description, speculation, or criticism, its reflection is rightly grounded in the authority of revelation and its reception in a particular confessional tradition.

Does this mean that theology as a discipline is guilty of the charge of foundationalism? As the preceding analysis has shown, answering this question is largely a matter of methodological semantics construed along academic and confessional lines. Postliberal theologians invoke the metaphor of "foundations" to describe the anthropological commitments exhibited in liberal theology's method and understanding of theological authorship. This theological version of antifoundationalism criticizes the authority accorded to human experience and ability in modern theology and defends the authority of classical Protestant beliefs. But if we invoke the philosophical definition of the metaphor of "foundations" as a belief justifying other beliefs that itself is incapable of being justified, then, in the judgment of antifoundationalist philosophers, the scriptural narrative functions every bit as much as a foundation in the postliberal theological program as human experience does in the foundational approaches to theology that the postliberals criticize. As a matter of semantic preference, Lindbeck and Thiemann employ the metaphor of "foundations" to refer to things of human rather than of divine origin, to human experience rather than to God's revelation, to nature rather than to grace. In effect their pejorative use of the term *foundations* connotes any dimension of the theological enterprise that threatens to usurp the authority of scriptural revelation. But presupposing as it does the given authority of revelation and its confessional understanding in history, all Christian theology is grounded in a belief incapable of rational justification beyond the circle of faith that itself provides justification for its more extensive network of beliefs. To the degree that postliberals, as all Christian theologians, accept the authoritative givenness of revelation for theological reflection, they would be, in the eyes of philosophers, no less subject to the philosophical critique of foundationalism than their liberal counterparts.[48]

If all theology rests on "foundations" in the broader use of that metaphor by philosophers who criticize foundationalism, then we must consider the implications of this criticism for theology as such, and not just for theologies that do not subscribe to the classical Protestant doctrine of divine prevenience. As long as theology remains theology and not the philosophy of religion, its disciplinary structure is shaken by philosophical versions of antifoundationalism as little or as much as theology's disciplinary structure has been shaken by philosophical criticism through the ages. To the extent that theology accepts the authoritative givenness of divine revelation as the basis for its reflection, its disciplinary coherence is measured primarily within the community of faith and not within the community of philosophical inquiry.

As a discipline, theology would be devastated by philosophical versions of the antifoundationalist critique only if it claimed an utterly commensurable relationship between theological reasoning and the revelational beliefs on which that reasoning is based. Philosophical antifoundationalism would prove fatal to theology's integrity only if the truth claims of revelation were subject to the same order of criticism as the reasonable arguments that proceed from the claims of revelation. Throughout theology's history, philosophers of different stripes have insisted on evaluating the claims of revelation in the same manner as the claims of reason, and to no one's surprise have concluded that theology is a pseudo-intellectual order based on indemonstrable premises. Philosophical antifoundationalism could easily join this critical assembly with the added advantage of a cogent argument ready to hand against the logical possibility of a justifying

---

48. Mark Wallace makes this same point by noting the ambiguity in the postliberal (he has Lindbeck specifically in mind) conception of "foundations": "What is even more problematic (and indeed ironic) about the Yale notion of foundationalism is that in its 'strong' version it does not apply to most of the theologians [who would be considered revisionist in approach], and, in its 'weak' version, while it does apply to these theologians, it also applies with equal force to those practitioners of postliberal theology who devised the label in the first place" ("The New Yale Theology," *Christian Scholar's Review* 17 [1987]: 163).

belief that itself cannot be justified. But theology as a discipline has never claimed the ability to plead its case from beginning to end before the court of logical reasoning. As a discipline whose provenance is within the church, theological reasoning continues to edify, enlighten, criticize, and clarify the truth of revelation for those in the community of faith for whom the rational unwarrantability of theology's foundation remains unproblematic.

This is not to say that the antifoundationalist critique does not touch theological reflection at all. But within the community of faith, the disciplinary integrity of theology has not crumbled in the face of philosophical antifoundationalism. Theologically, a variety of the critique of foundationalism could be invoked to argue within particular confessions against lines of theological reasoning that are inconsistent with their background beliefs.[49] Employed in this manner, antifoundationalist criticism could be helpful in exposing pretenders to the confessional premises that a particular ecclesial tradition identifies as its own. Lindbeck's and Thiemann's use of antifoundationalist criticism follows this very legitimate course to the degree that their proposals are offered as correctives to the theological reasoning characteristic of the liberal Protestant tradition.

Postliberalism, however, ventures beyond this modest use of antifoundationalist criticism in its reciprocal claims that a foundational theology of any sort compromises the Christian message and that good theology is nonfoundational in orientation. In defending these views, postliberalism employs the metaphor of foundations to describe a theological anthropology of cooperation, particularly the support that such an anthropology provides for a more constructive approach to the exercise of theological authorship. By claiming that authentic theology is nonfoundational in its approach, postliberalism fails to recognize the way confessional premises have shaped its adoption of the antifoundationalist critique and so does not acknowledge the limitations of its theological program.

Catholic theology, like all theology, can benefit from the antifoundationalist critique. The work of the philosophers discussed in

49. A theological use of the critique of foundationalism could possibly be invoked to argue interconfessionally against lines of theological reasoning inconsistent with background beliefs shared by all Christian confessions. Whether there are such beliefs that transcend confessional perspective and nuance is, however, debatable. If there are, one would think that their replacement by spurious foundational beliefs would be immediately obvious and so render criticism superfluous.

this chapter demonstrates the proclivity of all reasoning, and so of Catholic theological reasoning, toward naive credulity in accepting the authority of some singular and spurious foundation for its activity. As Francis Schüssler Fiorenza has argued convincingly, theology can be foundational in its approach without being foundationalist.[50] Whether that inauthentic foundation is the pretensions of heroic authorship, the ready answers of Denziger theology, or a fundamentalistic appeal to the authority of the magisterium, its inadequacies are more readily exposed and its spurious character more sharply defined with the aid of antifoundationalist criticism. The confessional commitments of Catholicism, however, demand that its theological reasoning proceed from its belief in the dignity of the human person before God, an authoritative doctrine that has implications not only for a general theological anthropology reflecting that belief but also for the significance of such an anthropology for the responsibility of theological authorship. Its regard for the place of human dignity in the economy of salvation commits the Catholic tradition to a recognition of the creative contributions of the theological imagination. In this respect Catholic theology can be "foundational" in the very sense that disquiets Lindbeck and Thiemann.

50. In his book *Foundational Theology: Jesus and the Church* (New York: Crossroad, 1986), Francis Schüssler Fiorenza proposes a foundational theology that "avoids the pitfalls of foundationalism" (xvii). The means to this end are to be found, he suggests, in a "reconstructive hermeneutic" that appeals neither to tradition nor experience alone as authoritative for theological interpretation but to the inseparable encounter between them, illuminated by the realization that all experience is hermeneutical and mediated culturally and historically. Theology falls prey to the foundationalist error, Fiorenza argues, when one pole of the correlation between faith and culture is accorded primacy. Only in their "reflective equilibrium" do these correlative poles avoid the foundationalism to which theology is prone.

Fiorenza's efforts to distinguish a nonfoundationalist orientation for theology is distinctly Catholic in its perspective. Postliberal theology's commitment to narrative interpretation would have difficulty with his premise that the method of correlation can be fine-tuned to avoid the problem of foundationalism (303). For postliberals the method of correlation itself represents the problem of foundationalism for theology. Fiorenza's belief in the viability of the method of correlation reflects his view that the "appeal to experience [as a prudential and reflective judgment] is . . . not foundational; nor can it be" (298).

Chapter Six

A Hermeneutics of Theological Authorship

*I*N HIS BOOK *Ecclesial Reflection,* Edward Farley suggests that the theologian's work can be conceived as an act of portraiture in which the colors of Christian belief are applied ever anew to the lengthy canvas of tradition. Theological portraiture is an "archaeological hermeneutic," an interpretation of living faith excavated from the rich meaning embedded in the symbols and mythos of Christian tradition.[1] Farley's metaphor of portraiture can be helpful for understanding not only the process of theological construction but also the vocational identity of the theological author. Indeed, much in this book might well be considered an example of portraiture that takes the author as its subject. This last chapter needs to touch up that portrait by considering the responsibility of the theological author in relation to the perduring problem of the theologian's creative fidelity in the Catholic tradition.

Certainly the best-known account of authorship in contemporary theology is David Tracy's vocational sketch of the theologian in his important book *The Analogical Imagination.* In order to clarify both the theologian's tasks and the communal settings in which they are accomplished, Tracy offers portraits of authorship that consider the social as well as the theological dimensions of the author's work. The former describes the several audiences the theologian addresses, while the latter delineates the methodological approaches that define the theologian's

---

1. Edward Farley, *Ecclesial Reflection: An Anatomy of Theological Method* (Philadelphia: Fortress Press, 1982), 214.

respective concerns. These portraits are mutually related. Theology, Tracy proposes, comprises three subdisciplines, each related principally to a particular audience or "public." Fundamental theologies, which "provide arguments that all reasonable persons . . . can recognize as reasonable," are related "primarily to the public represented but not exhausted by the academy." Systematic theologies, which concern "the re-presentation, the reinterpretation . . . of the particular religious tradition to which the theologian belongs," are related "primarily to the public represented but not exhausted in the church." Practical theologies, which are concerned "with the ethical stance of responsible commitment to and sometimes even involvement in a situation of praxis," are related "primarily to the public of society."[2]

Tracy's vocational portrait is an excellent example of the sort of attention that needs to be paid to the issue of theological authorship, if not as a theme in itself then at least as a matter of consideration in reflections on the nature and method of theology. Unlike so many theologians who treat the issue of authorship indirectly at best, or who virtually ignore its assumptions even as they take shape in their work, Tracy carefully articulates the vocational responsibility of the theologian by discussing what he or she does, and to whom and how she or he speaks. As exemplary and influential as it is, however, Tracy's portrait is too methodologically oriented to serve our purposes here. It considers authorship by schematizing the subdisciplines of the theological task but not by assessing the possibilities and limitations of theological talent as such. It considers the issue of theological responsibility by identifying the respective audiences that particular theological subdisciplines address but not by examining the crisis of individual imagination and traditional authority that has been the focus here.

To be sure, Tracy's vocational portrait cannot be blamed for serving his needs but not ours. Its principal concern is to offer an apologia for the organization of his three-volume treatment of the theological subdisciplines begun in *Blessed Rage for Order*,[3] continued in *The Analogical Imagination*, and to be completed in a work on practical theology yet to appear. The portrait of the theologian offered here cannot be presented in the context of such an extended and impressive project as

2. David Tracy, *The Analogical Imagination: Christian Theology and the Culture of Pluralism* (New York: Crossroad, 1981), 56–57.
3. David Tracy, *Blessed Rage for Order: The New Pluralism in Theology* (New York: Winston-Seabury Press, 1975).

Tracy's. My aim, like Tracy's, is to highlight the issue of vocational responsibility by considering how and in what contexts theological talent is exercised. I will do so, however, by continuing to develop what might be described as a hermeneutics of theological authorship.

Thus far, this study has attempted to achieve that goal by retrieving the value of traditional notions of ecclesial and human responsibility for understanding the modern paradigmatic assumption of theological talent. The possibilities of appreciating authorial talent as a theological *habitus*, as an ecclesial charism, or as an expression of Trent's doctrine of justification have been proposed in earlier chapters. Another possibility, though one I will not pursue here, might take the form of configuring the responsibility of theological authorship according to conceptions of authorial talent suggested by disciplines other than theology. Such an approach would be especially appropriate because the idea of the theological author has always been accompanied by romantic images that have carried strong and often negative resonances for a traditionally minded discipline like theology. Whether they stem from the worlds of philosophy, literature, the arts, or politics—new metaphors, images, and analogies could do much to clarify the proper exercise of theological talent, especially by countering and correcting the heroic image of the theological author that has been prevalent since the emergence of the romantic paradigm.[4] In this chapter, however, I will turn to the discipline of theology itself and explore an image implicit in its modern history that could prove helpful in formulating a Catholic understanding of theological talent: the image of the theologian as a mediator engaged in the imaginative task of mediating the sources of theology.

4. In his dissertation Bradford E. Hinze provides an example of this approach in his use of Gramsci's idea of the "organic intellectual" as a model for a community-based conception of theological authority ("Doctrinal Criticism, Reform, and Development in the Work of Friedrich Schleiermacher and Johann Sebastian Drey" [Ph.D. diss., Univ. of Chicago, 1989], 212f.). Cf. Cornel West, *Prophesy Deliverance! An Afro-American Revolutionary Christianity* (Philadelphia: Westminster Press, 1982), 118f.

Another resource for a hermeneutics of authorship might lie in the literary theory of Mikhail Bakhtin. Bakhtin's interesting distinction between the sort of characters produced by the genre of the epic and the sort of characters produced by the genre of the modern novel could do much to illuminate the expectations inherent in classical and romantic conceptions of the theological author. See M. M. Bakhtin, "Epic and Novel: Toward a Methodology for the Study of the Novel," in *The Dialogic Imagination: Four Essays*, ed. M. Holquist, trans. C. Emerson and M. Holquist (Austin: Univ. of Texas Press, 1981), 3–40.

MEDIATING THE SOURCES
OF THEOLOGY

The notion that theology has "sources" is a relatively recent one in the history of theological thinking. From a historical perspective, the notion of sources (in the plural) of theology is a consequence of the Protestant reformers' judgment, expressed in the watchword *sola scriptura*, that theology has a single, appropriate source. This criticism of the Roman Catholic tradition, unlike the more subjectively oriented watchwords *sola fide* and *sola gratia*, had direct implications for theological method. The claim that scripture alone was the basis for knowledge of God distinguished implicitly between the Bible and ecclesial tradition as respectively legitimate and illegitimate sources of the theological enterprise. Even though the reformers appealed to the tradition of authorities in practice, they were unwilling in principle to regard tradition as anything but the product of human corruption.

In defense of this criticism, Trent, and the Vatican councils following it, defined the nature of theological authority by speaking, at least implicitly, of sources of divine revelation in both scripture and tradition and so accepted the terms set for the post-Reformation period by the reformers themselves. Only with Trent's defense of tradition as a legitimate source of theology and its consequent assumption of a plurality of theological sources does mediation become possible as a description of the theological task. This does not mean that pre-Tridentine theology did not draw on multiple sources for the presentation of its knowledge or that the pre-Tridentine theologian was not engaged in an act of mediation. The medieval Catholic understanding of the classical paradigm, however, encouraged the conceptualization of theology's sources as singular rather than plural. Although conceptually possible since the sixteenth century, the task of mediating the sources of theology did not became a self-conscious enterprise until the early nineteenth century, with the romantic theologians.

The romantics conceived theological mediation broadly as an interpretive act that brought meaning to the relationship between traditional faith and contemporary culture. Whether faith appealed for its authority to scripture and tradition or to scripture alone, the cultural pole of theological mediation added contemporary experience to the longer (Catholic) or shorter (Protestant) list of the sources of theology. As they addressed the issue of method systematically for the first time in the history of theology, contributors to the literary genre of theological encyclopedia increasingly attended to the historicity of faith, the development of doctrine, and the role of the theologian within method as the agent of the theological task.[5] Romantic theories of the self entered the more structured lines of the encyclopedia's organization to shape an understanding of the theologian as a creative mediator of the sources of theology and a paradigm for modern theology that highlighted the imaginative work of the theological author.

The most typical Catholic theologies of the modern period prior to Vatican II continued to abide by the premodern assumptions that scripture and tradition expressed an undifferentiated truth whose unity did not require mediation and that experience could not be counted as a source of the theological enterprise. The need for the contributions of a theological mediator, therefore, was not appreciated until the antagonistic atmosphere of the modernist controversy was dispelled by Vatican II's spirit of *aggiornamento*. Only in the aftermath of the council did the conceptualization of theology as the mediation of its sources in scripture, tradition, and experience gain widespread acceptance in the Catholic tradition. Not surprisingly, only in the aftermath of the council has the ecclesial responsibility of the theological mediator, moreover, become a matter of special concern in the Catholic Church.

Unfortunately, in the years since the Council the issue of theological responsibility has been raised most often in settings of confrontation between the magisterium and theologians. Nearly all such attention to the issue of theological responsibility has been polemical and ad hoc in character, lacking the thoroughness and cohesiveness that one expects of unprejudiced, systematic reflection. Where there has been systematic reflection on the theologian's responsibility, it has tended to conceive of the issue as one of ecclesial polity in which the proper conditions are sought for settling or preventing confrontations between theologians and the magisterium.[6] As helpful as this

5. Bernard Lonergan's observation on the relationship between modern cultural sensibility and method is worth recalling here: "When the classicist notion of theology prevails, theology is conceived as a permanent achievement, and then one discourses on its nature. When culture is conceived empirically, theology is known to be an ongoing process, and then one writes on its method" (*Method in Theology* [New York: Herder & Herder, 1972], xi).

6. See, for example, *Doctrinal Responsibilities: Approaches to Promoting Cooperation*

approach has been in fostering cooperation between theologians and the magisterium, it has tended to overlook the degree to which the more basic issue of theological talent is often a tacit matter of concern to both parties and thus a matter that merits attention in any discussion of the theologian's ecclesial responsibility. The church needs to examine the issue of theological responsibility taking into account the history of the modern assumption that theologians are authors and appreciating both the possibilities and limitations of theological creativity. The image of the theologian as an authorial mediator can be particularly helpful in both of these respects.

AUTHORIAL MEDIATION AND TRADITIONAL CONTINUITY

Expressed in the most general terms, the mediation of theology's sources involves an imaginative interpretation of the meaningful relations among scripture, tradition, and contemporary experience. Theological mediation is stilted by the assumption that these sources are independent entities in the life of the church, as though theological truth draws its authority from one or more of the sources but not from them all. Such an understanding of the sources of theology could not lead to their being fruitfully mediated at all because their interpretive relations would merely involve either the imposition of the authority of the orthodox past upon the present or the updating of the orthodox past to satisfy the authority of the present. This static approach to the sources of theology is, indeed, the most common version of theological foundationalism in the Catholic tradition. A particular act of mediating the sources of theology could hope for success only if it proceeded from the assumption that scripture, tradition, and experience all share in the authority of ecclesial life and only if that assumption were exhibited in the work of the theological mediator. But what of the act of the imagination that produces theological interpretation? To what extent can the talent of the theological author be ranked among the sources of theology and, by virtue of such a ranking, be judged authoritative? How is it possible to speak

---

and *Resolving Misunderstandings between Bishops and Theologians* (Washington, D.C.: National Conference of Catholic Bishops, 1989). See also Ladislas Örsy, S.J., *The Church: Learning and Teaching* (Wilmington, Del.: Michael Glazier, 1987); *Cooperation between Theologians and the Ecclesiastical Magisterium*, ed. L. J. O'Donovan, S.J. (Washington, D.C.: Catholic Univ. of America, 1982).

theologically about the authority of something as nebulous as the imagination?

Were one to rank the talent of the theological mediator within the three sources of theology, it would clearly fall under experience. Experience in this sense, however, would be particularly circumscribed, and not at all as generic as the experience of the church or of society. As the theologian's experience, authorial talent is inescapably individual and personal in character. This individuality is not only an expression of theological style but also, and more substantively, a context for the theologian's vision of ecclesial truth. The exercise of theological talent involves judgments that draw the theologian's individual experience into such intimate relationship with the communal realities of church and society that it is virtually indistinguishable from them. Indeed, theological talent is measured by its ability to speak in an intellectually defensible manner on behalf of these groups and the truth they have to tell about God, humanity, and the world. But there is no denying that theological talent, like any talent, is fundamentally an individual affair and that mediating the sources of theology, though responsible to the church, is an act of the personal imagination.

Much of the magisterium's suspicion of theological talent seems to stem from an abiding uneasiness about the way in which the more particular experiences within a universal church can be authoritative sources of theological reflection. This tension between the authority of individual and universal experience is not limited to relations between theologians and the magisterium but permeates the church's most elementary understanding of its catholicity. Even the ecclesiology commended by Vatican II, which made great strides in shaping a more communal and less institutional understanding of the church, provides an illustration of it.

The council's "Dogmatic Constitution on the Church" (*Lumen Gentium*) speaks of authoritative experience in the church as a "sense of faith" (*sensus fidei*)[7] shared by the entire people of God. One cannot properly speak of the sense of faith as the subjectivity of the individual believer. Although its truth may be appropriated individually, the sense of faith is universal ecclesial experience. It bears the authority of the church, an infallibility that derives from its universality and

7. *Lumen Gentium*, 12; *The Documents of Vatican II*, ed. W. M. Abbott, S.J. (New York: America Press, 1966), 29.

its certainty that the "body of the faithful as a whole . . . cannot err in matters of belief."[8] *Lumen Gentium* recognizes the contributions of individual experience to the church, especially as such experience takes shape in God-given talent. The Spirit of God, the document states, "distributes special graces among the faithful of every rank." These charismatic gifts, "whether they be the most outstanding or the more simple and widely diffused, are to be received with thanksgiving and consolation, for they are exceedingly suitable and useful for the needs of the Church."[9] Yet the charismatic gifts, though "suitable and useful" for the church's needs, are not described as authoritative. As God-given talents humanly exercised in service to the church, one might think that the charismatic gifts would possess an authority of their own, even if that authority could not lay claim to the infallible and universal authority of the *sensus fidei*. Yet *Lumen Gentium* does not speak of the charismatic gifts in this manner, observing instead that the "judgment of their genuineness and proper use belongs to those who preside over the Church, and to whose special competence it belongs, not indeed to extinguish the Spirit, but to test all things and hold fast to that which is good."[10]

This last provision for the magisterium's power of oversight in the exercise of personal talent is a prerogative consistent with the priority *Lumen Gentium* accords to the universal and infallible experience of the *sensus fidei* over the individual and fallible experience of charismatic gifts. The exercise of magisterial authority with sole reference to the normativeness of the *sensus fidei*, however, all too easily suggests that particular, fallible experiences in the church, especially at the most personal level, cannot be regarded as authoritative. Magisterial authority is no doubt rightly concerned with the integrity of the *sensus fidei* because this experience defines the catholicity of the church. At times, however, the magisterium's devotion to the most universal dimension of ecclesial experience leads it to suspect the worth of more local experiences in the church, whose relationship to the *sensus fidei* is not immediately obvious. Seen through such eyes, the catholicity of the church is a rather staid abstraction, and not a universality drawn from a remarkable array of individual experiences manifested ever anew in the church's historical life. To the degree that this suspicion is institutionalized, any

8. Ibid.
9. *Lumen Gentium*, 12; *The Documents of Vatican II*, 30.
10. Ibid.

action of the magisterium, no matter how founded, can convey the false impression that only from its visible conformity to the church's universal experience does individual experience derive its value, to say nothing of its authority.

One could cite many examples of the magisterium's discomfort with the authoritative claims of more particular experiences in the church: from its often tentative approach to the practical problem of the inculturation of the church's universal teaching and rites within non-Western, local customs and practices, to its ambivalence toward local theologies, especially theologies of liberation, to its most recent formulation of a universal catechism as a norm for regional catechetical instruction. The magisterium's regard for theological authorship, even in the short time it has recognized that talent, is a very clear example of this same ambivalence. The act of theological authorship is at once among the most individual experiences within the church and yet one with the potential to exert a profound and constructive influence upon the church's universal experience. That potential alone bespeaks the authority of theological authorship. Throughout this study, however, the authority of theological talent has not been attributed to its transformative power within the church but to its own integrity, whether imaged as a theological *habitus*, an ecclesial charism, or as an expression of the Catholic tradition's doctrinal anthropology. A greater sensitivity to the historical circumstances in which theological talent came to be regarded as a source of theology, and theologizing an imaginative act of mediation, could add to our appreciation of theological talent's authority.

As the modern period dawned in the West, cultural shifts in the understanding of what authority is and how it is exercised led to a new conceptualization of meaning as the constructive work of an author, broadly understood. The role of the author in the process of meaningful construction has been described in ways too various to detail here. The romantic understanding of authorship, however, took for granted that meaning was in some important (though not necessarily exhaustive) way the product of human creativity and so the expression of an authority largely (though not necessarily exclusively) human. As human subjectivity was increasingly invoked as a source of authority, moderns turned more and more to the faculty of the imagination to account for the intellectual engagement they believed contributed fundamentally to the remarkable changes unfolding in their world. Reason was not displaced by the imagination within the human faculties. But in the intellectual rhetoric of the nineteenth and twentieth centuries, its power was increasingly described as instrumental and, unlike the imagination, incapable of fathoming the full range of human experience. The power of sensitivity, of discerning the pluralism that came to mark the reality of the modern world, was but one of the imagination's authorial traits. For the romantics, the imagination was the seat of creativity. It was understood as a faculty capable of mixing staid concepts and rote judgments into surprising configurations that voiced the experience of individuals and groups and in this way contributed to the ongoing construction of meaning in history. In the intellectual rhetoric of the eighteenth and nineteenth centuries, the power of the imagination was often described as individualistic, its meaningful work as original, and its most authoritative exercise as the work of genius.

Even in the face of the postmodern critique, the twentieth century largely remains committed to the early romantic portrayal of the imagination as a "plastic" faculty, that dimension of human subjectivity prized for its capacity to achieve unanticipated insights by imparting new shape to the given, the expected, and the customary. The imagination continues to be valued for its fanciful quality, for the uniqueness of its perspective, and for the openness of all its interpretations to revision. These features of the authority of the imagination—especially in its most common caricature as egoistic or solipsistic—made its acceptance problematic for the discipline of theology. The notion of an imaginative author defied the classical understanding of the theologian as one engaged in the mimetic work of faithful representation and seemed to do so by audaciously pitting the authority of the theologian against the authority of God and God's revelation.

In the Catholic tradition the magisterium's custodianship of ecclesial truth heightened this opposition by presenting a living authorial voice, one bespeaking the perspective of established ecclesial tradition, as a counterpoint to the voice of the theological author. These voices need not be at odds in principle, and usually they are not. But to the degree that the magisterium steadfastly avoids the conceptualization of its own authority as the work of imagination, preferring to attribute the subjective authority of its pronouncements to neoscholastic reasoning and natural-law argumentation, appeal to imagination as the intellectual faculty that mediates the sources of theology will remain questionable, and the authority of theological authorship as talent in service to the church will remain difficult for the entire church to conceive.

CREATIVE AND FAITHFUL

The remedy to this situation is not to exclude imagination from experiential descriptions of the theological enterprise. By now the imagination has gained such a foothold in the rhetoric of creativity that banishing this faculty from explanations of theological talent would be only slightly less felicitous than avoiding descriptions of the theological task as creative at all. The challenge for the entire church is to find a way beyond the prejudicial attitude that glibly regards talk of a faithful imagination as a contradiction in terms. To the extent that imagining can be conceived as a personal act and yet one ecclesial in nature, bound to and measured by the authority of scripture, tradition, and experience, the work of the theological mediator can begin to be appreciated as both creative and faithful and the norm of theological authorship as that of creative fidelity. This desideratum should not be difficult to achieve where there is good faith and openness to understanding.

A first step toward establishing the legitimacy of the notion of a faithful imagination might involve addressing the prejudicial manner in which the imagination's relationship to faithfulness has been understood in the modern period. Our historical study of the emergence of the imagination as a faculty of creativity has shown that even the most exaggerated romantic claims on behalf of imaginative power did not fail to take account of the imagination's responsibility to communal structures and traditions. There is nothing in the general history of the imaginative faculty's rise to prominence to suggest that faithfulness to tradition is alien to its nature.

Neither can such a suggestion be found in the specifically theological version of this history. The earliest romantic theologians did indeed model their understanding of theological authorship on the notion of the creative hero. That image, however, served principally to explain the workings of imagination in the discipline of theology and the more complex responsibilities of theological talent to God and to the church. The theological adoption of the image of the hero in the earliest years of the romantic paradigm in no sense was motivated by a desire to repudiate traditional ecclesial authority, nor has such a motivation prevailed in the history of modern theology. In many respects the heroic variety of authorship that has been criticized throughout this study as a distortion of theological authorship is an expression more of the church's fears than of the actual use of theological talent. Understanding the extent to which this legitimate fear has produced a caricature of the role of imagination in theological reflection would do much to dispel the biases surrounding the notion of theological authorship and the possibility of its ecclesial faithfulness.

Another avenue that might be followed in advancing the conceptual legitimacy of a faithful imagination could involve an appeal to the creative power of the imagination to explain the exercise of all authority in the church, not just the authority of the theological mediator. This does not mean that any exercise of authority in the church is imaginative, any more than any exercise of theological authorship is. But the authority of the magisterium, when exercised authentically and for the good of the church, could be conceived as creative and imaginative and so in a manner consistent with the accomplished work of theological authorship. Expressing their respective authoritative activities in similar terms would remove the conceptual and rhetorical wedge that has been placed between the magisterium and the theological community. In addition to banishing a disjunctive understanding of the relationship between creativity and fidelity, this common way of framing the issue of creativity would have the advantage of posing the challenge of creative fidelity for both the theological community and the magisterium. It would remind both parties that, in spite of their different authoritative roles in the church, each is measured by an ecclesial standard defined by the tension between creativity and fidelity.

Speaking of the faithful imagination of both the magisterium and the theological mediator need not be as difficult as it first appears. For centuries the church's teaching office and the theological community have appealed to the same dimension of subjectivity— reason—to describe the means by which the truth of divine revelation is expounded. The Catholic tradition has simply been more comfortable with the idea of reason's capacity for ecclesial loyalty to faith. But the history of modern theology has shown that there is no reason in principle that the magisterium and theologians could not continue to describe the relationship between faith and human subjectivity by referring to the same natural experience, albeit the experience of the imagination. In principle the same loyalty to faith of the imagination, that has for so long been assumed of reason, can be expected of the imagination as long as one remains wary of the prejudicial caricatures of the imaginative faculty as self-serving and undisciplined. Since the authority of the magisterium and the authority of the theologian finally owe responsibility not to each other but to God, this consistency in the conceptualization and rhetoric of ecclesial authority is not only desirable but also necessary.

Theological endeavor could contribute to the viability of this conceptualization and discourse by proposing ways in which the human encounter with God can be accounted for by reference to the experience of the imagination. Pneumatology would be an especially fruitful area to explore along these lines. Such an approach might very well speculate in the manner of Augustine's *De Trinitate* about the analogical possibilities within the modern discourse of the imagination for conceiving the reality of the Holy Spirit and the place of the Spirit in the Godhead. But the devotion of theological reflection to the development of a pneumatology of the imagination would prove far more beneficial to an understanding of the role of theological authorship in the church.

Broadly conceived, a pneumatology focused in this way would need to explore the workings of the imagination as a means for appreciating and explaining the active presence of the Holy Spirit in human history. Whether addressing the collective imagination of humankind, the imagination's more limited creative experiences within human communities, or the most particular and personal experiences of insight, a pneumatology of the imagination could do much to heal the breach between imagination and authority in the modern Catholic tradition.[11]

A pneumatology of the imagination true to its task would sketch the often surprising, coincidental, and even mysterious ways that consciousness builds creative associations and the unanticipated ways these proliferate far beyond the experiential circumstances from which they first emerged. These very qualities of the imagination fuel the suspicion of theological authorship wherever it is found. But they may also prove to be an important theological resource, especially in the extent to which these qualities of the imagination can convey the often surprising, unpredictable, and mysterious ways in which the grace of God, God's very presence, is encountered in human

11. I owe this idea to a suggestion by my friend John R. Sachs, S.J.

experience.[12] In such a framework the imaginative insights of the theological author can legitimately be understood as the yield of divine grace and the theological author's intellectual inspiration as a charismatic gift of the Holy Spirit. Although the exercise of theological authorship may appear in certain cases to be ecclesially undisciplined, the church needs to be open to the possibility that the unpredictable and apparently undisciplined character of theological talent may have its basis in, and actually be an expression of, the creative freedom of God's grace.

Finally, appreciating the ways in which creativity actually functions in mediating the sources of theology would do much to increase awareness of what that creativity's faithfulness entails. Mediating the sources of theology is an interpretive act in which the theologian's imagination discerns and articulates the meaningful relations among scripture, tradition, and experience. In the Catholic tradition the authorial imagination has typically been exercised by discovering dimensions of general human experience that can lend support to the larger edifice of theological construction. These foundational structures facilitate the act of mediation by providing a theoretical basis for expounding the relations between the sources of theology. As expressions of Catholic theology's commitment to the doctrinal anthropology of Trent, these foundational structures celebrate the dignity of human experience, its responsibility to the call of Christ's salvation, and the universality to which a Catholic theological vision has traditionally aspired. Johann Sebastian Drey's appropriation of Schelling's historical idealism, Karl Rahner's attention to the transcendental subject's conditions of experience,[13] Hans Urs von Balthasar's analysis of the senses as forms of religious apprehension, David Tracy's turn to the revelatory power of the classic, and Francis Schüssler Fiorenza's emphasis on the inherently creative dimensions of a fully developed hermeneutics[14] are all examples of how the

12. Theological reflection along these lines has already been ventured by Hans Urs von Balthasar, particularly in his use of the analogy of artistic inspiration for appreciating the experience of grace and in his appeal to the concept of "attunement" to explain the consonance between the religious sensibilities and God (*Seeing the Form*, vol. 1 of *The Glory of the Lord: A Theological Aesthetics*, trans. E. Leiva-Merikakis [San Francisco: Ignatius Press, 1982], 220f., 245f.). Von Balthasar, however, does not make theological authorship the focus of these concerns.

13. For example, Karl Rahner, *Foundations of Christian Faith: An Introduction to the Idea of Christianity*, trans. W. V. Dych (New York: Seabury Press, 1978).

14. Francis Schüssler Fiorenza, *Foundational Theology: Jesus and the Church* (New York: Crossroad, 1986).

imagination might appeal to foundational structures to account for the theoretical unity of a theological vision.

THE STYLE OF CATHOLIC THEOLOGICAL REFLECTION

In the time since the Second Vatican Council, this more abstract exercise of theological authorship has been accepted as the typical style of Catholic theological reflection. Several reasons could be cited for this. The compatibility between a foundational approach to theology and the confessional anthropology of the Catholic tradition is one. In addition, the imaginative construction of foundational structures is consistent with the tradition's time-honored conception of theology as speculation. Furthermore, the devotion of theological talent to the construction of foundational structures reflects a sacramental understanding of the theological task. The Catholic tradition's insistence upon the commensurability of nature and grace supports the foundational confidence that human experience can serve as a means for appreciating and understanding the truth of God's revelation in scripture and tradition. Above all, a foundational approach to theology defines the work of authorship in relation to experience, whose generality and abstractness at least approximates the universal experience that the church has traditionally judged to be most, if not exclusively, authoritative. To some degree, then, a theology that is foundational in emphasis mitigates the personal character of theological authorship and lessens the occasions for conflict with the magisterium. This consonance between the perspective of the magisterium and foundational approaches to theology is problematic only if regarded as normative and definitive of theology that is truly catholic.

In this same postconciliar period, Catholic theologians have often taken the lead in developing more critical approaches to the theological task and have done so by exercising authorship in a less traditional way. Political and liberation theologies in the Catholic tradition—Latin American, feminist, Hispanic-American, and Asianist, to name a few—continue to conceive the task of theology as one of mediation. Johannes Baptist Metz's reliance on Marxist analysis,[15]

15. Johannes Baptist Metz, *Faith in History and Society: Toward a Practical Fundamental Theology*, trans. D. Smith (New York: Seabury Press, 1980); *The Emergent Church: The Future of Christianity in a Postbourgeois World*, trans. P. Mann (New York: Crossroad, 1981).

Gustavo Gutiérrez's appeal to the universal experience of liberation,[16] Elizabeth Schüssler Fiorenza's attention to feminist criticism,[17] and Helmut Peukert's use of Habermas's critical theory[18]—all illustrate how the foundational approach continues to be employed even when it serves a hermeneutics of suspicion and a theological emphasis on praxis. But critical approaches to theology are distinguished by their judging local, rather than universal, human experience to be a much more important source for theological reflection. In this respect the foundational structures of critical theologies are not formulated from an essentialist but from an existential perspective and draw their strength from the more particular experiences of the marginalized. Whether these more particular experiences take the form of poverty, injustice, oppression engendered by colonialism, or the awareness of false consciousness within the church, their authority is valued highly as expressions of what Pope John XXIII called the "signs of the times," and as often overlooked, ignored, or resisted manifestations of the *sensus fidei.*

Theological authorship plays no less a role in critical than in speculative theologies, and its exercise is no less imaginative. Its role, however, befits the critical stage on which it is enacted. It should not come as a surprise, then, that its performance has often been poorly received by those in the ecclesial audience attracted to the less contentious style of theological speculation. Critical theologies rely on the theologian's power of discernment to fathom and articulate the innumerable calls for justice among the human family and in the very church that claims to live by the gospel. Theological authorship in a critical style involves mediating the sources of theology by creative appeal to experience that challenges traditional perspectives on orthodoxy, commonplace understandings of charity, and the false but prevalent assumption that authority is the prerogative of the privileged. Mediating the sources of theology in such an approach includes the theologian's analysis of the extent to which the most

16. Gustavo Gutiérrez, *A Theology of Liberation: History, Politics, and Salvation,* trans. C. Inda and J. Eagleson (Maryknoll, N.Y.: Orbis Books, 1988).

17. Elisabeth Schüssler Fiorenza, *In Memory of Her: A Feminist Theological Reconstruction of Christian Origins* (New York: Crossroad, 1984).

18. Helmut Peukert, *Science, Action, and Fundamental Theology: Toward a Theology of Communicative Action,* trans. J. Bohman (Cambridge, Mass.: MIT Press, 1986). See also Paul Lakeland, *Theology and Critical Theory: The Discourse of the Church* (Nashville: Abingdon Press, 1990).

common and longstanding interpretations of scripture and tradition are called into question by the experience of the marginalized. In its critical role, theological authorship is often the clearest and most informed voice for the many forms of dissent in the church that transcend the boundaries of economic status, color, or gender.

Although empirical, ad hoc, and praxis-oriented, the critical exercise of authorship is nonetheless the most imaginative use of theological talent in the contemporary church. Critical authorship's ability to uncover scriptural meanings previously hidden and, iron-ically, utterly central to the spirit of the gospel, its capacity to hear the silences as well as the pronouncements of tradition, and its insight into the use and abuse of power in both the world and the church, all testify to the scope of its imagination and justify its creative au-thority. To the degree that a critical approach to theological authorship bespeaks the experience of ecclesial particularity, it runs the risk of being misunderstood as talent in the service of a solitary vision or professional license squandered on a few rather than devoted to all in the church.

As the optimistic agenda of romantic theology has been tempered by the realism of the postmodern world, the role of ecclesial critic has increasingly befallen the theological author. The acceptance of this role by theologians has rarely, if ever, been the realization of pretentious dreams of heroic self-aggrandizement but simply a matter of facing ecclesial and vocational responsibilities that are inescapable and, more often than not, burdensome. Perhaps those in the church who equate dissidence with latent heresy or creative criticism with ecclesial infidelity will never be inclined to consider the possibility that a critical use of theological imagination can be as faithful to the tradition as the most reverent and heartfelt recitation of the Nicene Creed. But the openness of the church to a world increasingly com-plex and pluralistic and to the otherwise unimaginable dimensions of its own possibilities for growth will depend on both the work of the critical theological author and the ability of the church to regard such an approach to authorship as the product of an imagination faithful to ecclesial tradition.[19]

Understanding the imaginative range of theological mediation— as both the construction of foundational theory and the critical dis-cernment of local experience—may help us to appreciate the ways

19. Nicholas Lash has argued that the constructive and critical uses of theological talent are mutually constitutive (*Theology on the Way to Emmaus* [London: SCM Press, 1986], 3–17).

in which theological talent can be exercised faithfully. This analysis, however, should not suggest that theological creativity is naturally inclined to ecclesial faithfulness and exempt from compromising that fidelity. Although this study has shown the extent to which theological authorship has been subject to conceptual misrepresentation, institutional suspicion, and the exaggerations of caricature, it would be naive to conclude that a talent pure and pristine dwells among members of the theological community beneath the layers of misunderstanding and distortion that have often characterized theological authorship under the romantic paradigm. Theological talent rightly exercised is an expression not simply of grace but also of nature. To the degree that theological authorship is a charismatic gift, the church must be prepared to understand its work as the work of the Spirit. But to the degree that theological talent stems from human nature, it remains both dignified and fallen, responsible yet utterly in need, mindful of the direction of grace yet ready pridefully to pursue its own ends. If the confessional anthropology of Trent authorizes theological talent and the value of its disciplined imaginings for the church, then it also judges that talent within the history of sin which chronicles all human endeavor.

In the modern period's crisis of imagination and authority, theologians in the Catholic tradition have often been placed in the position of defending the integrity of what they do. Indeed, this book presents an extended apology of exactly this sort. Catholic theologians would do well, though, to devote some of the critical energy of authorship to a consideration of the ways in which the modern understanding of subjectivity itself can compromise the fidelity of theological authorship, much in the same way as postliberal theology has performed this task for the Protestant tradition. This reflexive criticism could take many forms, some of which have already been suggested as strategies by members of the general theological community. Theological authorship's evaluation of its own assumptions might investigate the extent of its reliance on a naively romantic configuration of subjectivity and the degree to which such an ahistorical and aprioristic conception of self stands in opposition to its confessional anthropology.[20] Such an evaluation might explore the

20. Rebecca S. Chopp, *The Power to Speak: Feminism, Language, God* (New York: Crossroad, 1989), 115–24. Cf. William M. Shea, "The Subjectivity of the Theologian," *The Thomist* 45 (1981): 205–6.

possibility of directing a hermeneutics of suspicion at theological authorship itself and understanding the ongoing exercise of the author's subjectivity as a process under the critique of both church and culture, "on trial," as it were.[21] Such an evaluation might consider ways in which the right exercise of authorial imagination can be checked by the broader powers of imaginative discrimination that function authoritatively in the church.[22] Through probings like these, the modern understanding of the self that has formed the basis of the disciplinary assumption of theological authorship would be put to the test of both postmodern sensibilities and traditional understandings of ecclesial authority.

Whether the modern view of self articulated in the notion of theological authorship can continue as a cultural assumption of the postmodern world is indeed questionable. But whether that modern understanding of self can be relinquished by Catholic presuppositions as the tradition faces the future is even more so. For this reason, the notion of theological authorship, itself a relatively new disciplinary assumption among theological practitioners, could very well be the heritage of the Catholic tradition for many years to come.

21. David Tracy points to the theological value of Julia Kristeva's understanding of subjectivity in a recent essay on method ("The Uneasy Alliance Reconceived: Catholic Theological Method, Modernity, and Postmodernity," *Theological Studies* 50 [1989]: 569).

22. David H. Kelsey, *The Uses of Scripture in Recent Theology* (Philadelphia: Fortress Press, 1975), 170–78. See also Garrett Green, *Imagining God: Theology and the Religious Imagination* (San Francisco: Harper & Row, 1987), 126–52.

Index of Names

Index of Subjects